THEORY AND METHOD IN
HIGHER EDUCATION RESEARCH

THEORY AND METHOD IN HIGHER EDUCATION RESEARCH

Series Editors: Jeroen Huisman and Malcolm Tight

Recent Volumes:

Volume 1:	Theory and Method in Higher Education Research. Edited by Jeroen Huisman and Malcolm Tight; 2015
Volume 2:	Theory and Method in Higher Education Research. Edited by Jeroen Huisman and Malcolm Tight; 2016
Volume 3:	Theory and Method in Higher Education Research. Edited by Jeroen Huisman and Malcolm Tight; 2017
Volume 4:	Theory and Method in Higher Education Research. Edited by Jeroen Huisman and Malcolm Tight; 2018
Volume 5:	Theory and Method in Higher Education Research. Edited by Jeroen Huisman and Malcolm Tight; 2019
Volume 6:	Theory and Method in Higher Education Research. Edited by Jeroen Huisman and Malcolm Tight; 2020
Volume 7:	Theory and Method in Higher Education Research. Edited by Jeroen Huisman and Malcolm Tight; 2021
Volume 8:	Theory and Method in Higher Education Research. Edited by Jeroen Huisman and Malcolm Tight; 2022
Volume 9:	Theory and Method in Higher Education Research. Edited by Jeroen Huisman and Malcolm Tight; 2023

THEORY AND METHOD IN HIGHER EDUCATION
RESEARCH   VOLUME 10

THEORY AND METHOD IN HIGHER EDUCATION RESEARCH

EDITED BY

JEROEN HUISMAN
Ghent University, Belgium

AND

MALCOLM TIGHT
Lancaster University, UK

United Kingdom – North America – Japan
India – Malaysia – China

Emerald Publishing Limited
Emerald Publishing, Floor 5, Northspring, 21-23 Wellington Street, Leeds LS1 4DL

First edition 2025

Editorial matter and selection © 2025 Jeroen Huisman and Malcolm Tight.
Published under exclusive licence by Emerald Publishing Limited.
Individual chapters © 2025 by Emerald Publishing Limited.

Reprints and permissions service
Contact: www.copyright.com

No part of this book may be reproduced, stored in a retrieval system, transmitted in any form or by any means electronic, mechanical, photocopying, recording or otherwise without either the prior written permission of the publisher or a licence permitting restricted copying issued in the UK by The Copyright Licencing Agency and in the USA by The Copyright Clearance Centre. Any opinions expressed in the chapters are those of the authors. Whilst Emerald makes every effort to ensure the quality and accuracy of its content, Emerald makes no representation implied or otherwise, as to the chapters' suitability and application and disclaims any warranties, express or implied, to their use.

British Library Cataloguing in Publication Data
A catalogue record for this book is available from the British Library

ISBN: 978-1-83608-717-5 (Print)
ISBN: 978-1-83608-716-8 (Online)
ISBN: 978-1-83608-718-2 (Epub)

ISSN: 2056-3752 (Series)

INVESTOR IN PEOPLE

CONTENTS

List of Contributors   *vii*

Editorial Introduction   *ix*

Autoethnography: Postgraduate Teaching Assistant Professional Development in the Academy   *1*
Kristyna Campbell

Studying Student Behaviour: Towards an Integrated Conceptual Framework   *19*
Victoria A. Bauer

Becoming Rhizome: Deleuze and Guattari's Rhizome as Theory and Method   *37*
Louise Drumm

Extending the Understanding of Gendered Career Choices in STEM: A Culture-rooted Theoretical Model   *57*
Irina V. Gewinner, Victoria A. Bauer and Mara Osterburg

Habitus(con)figuration in Higher Education: Diffracting Bourdieu Through Posthumanism   *77*
Nathalie Ann Köbli

Discontinuing, Fading Out or Just Simply Leaving? The Importance of Measuring Student Departure Behaviour in Different Ways   *95*
Elisabeth Hovdhaugen and Monia Anzivino

Beyond the Original: Exploring Replication Research in Higher Education   *113*
Karlijn Soppe and Jeroen Huisman

Autoethnography in Higher Education Research: A Marginal Methodology for the Marginalized? *131*
Malcolm Tight

Ubiquity Without Clarity? What do We Mean by the 'Higher Education Landscape'? A Systematic Review *147*
Richard Budd

LIST OF CONTRIBUTORS

Monia Anzivino	University of Trento, Italy
Victoria A. Bauer	Leibniz University Hannover, Germany
Richard Budd	Lancaster University, UK
Kristyna Campbell	University College London, UK
Louise Drumm	Edinburgh Napier University, UK
Irina V. Gewinner	Leibniz University Hannover, Germany
Elisabeth Hovdhaugen	Nordic Institute for Studies of Innovation, Research and Education, Norway
Jeroen Huisman	Ghent University, Belgium
Nathalie Ann Köbli	University of Vienna, Austria
Mara Osterburg	German Center for Higher Education and Science Research (DZHW), Germany
Karlijn Soppe	Utrecht University, The Netherlands
Malcolm Tight	Lancaster University, UK

EDITORIAL INTRODUCTION

This is the 2024 volume in the annual series *Theory and Method in Higher Education Research*, which we launched in 2013 in the belief that there was a need to provide a forum specifically for higher education researchers to discuss issues of theory and method.

Four contributions in this volume are theoretical or conceptual. Budd reflects on the use of the 'landscape' metaphor by higher education scholars; Bauer offers a holistic framework for analysing student behaviour; Gewinner, Bauer and Osterburg address gendered career choices in STEM; and Köbli argues that Bourdieu's theory could be enriched with insights from posthumanist theorising.

Methodological contributions include those of Hovdhaugen and Anzivino on measuring student departure, Soppe and Huisman on the use and pitfalls of replication studies, whereas both Campbell and Tight offer reflections on autoethnography in higher education research.

One contribution addresses both theoretical and methodological issues. Drumm explains the relevance of the rhizome perspective in higher education research.

As in previous years, this volume displays an international authorship, although this time we 'only' have contributions from European scholars. Authors stem from the United Kingdom (4), Germany (3), Belgium (1), the Netherlands (1), Austria (1), Norway (1) and Italy (1).

Anyone interested in contributing a chapter to a future volume is invited to get in touch with Malcolm Tight.

Jeroen Huisman and Malcolm Tight

AUTOETHNOGRAPHY: POSTGRADUATE TEACHING ASSISTANT PROFESSIONAL DEVELOPMENT IN THE ACADEMY

Kristyna Campbell

University College London, UK

ABSTRACT

This chapter explores the use of the qualitative research method autoethnography as a tool for early career researcher's professional development. In particular, the method is considered for postgraduate teaching assistants (PGTAs) working within higher education. Autoethnography has been conceptualised as a powerful reflexive tool, facilitating identity and transition work, something the author has explored in earlier scholarship examining role change, boundary crossing, and labelling in the academy. Following on from an introduction to the method and the role of the PGTA in the academy, the author explores a series of peer-reviewed autoethnographic articles, all of which are situated within higher education. These texts, in addition to the author's own, reveal themes pertaining to growth, interrelatedness and self-perception. This discussion portrays the significance of reflexive practice, the value of holding conversation with and of the self, and notably learning about the self in relation to other.

Keywords: Autoethnography; reflexive practice; postgraduate teaching assistant; higher education; professional development

INTRODUCTION: AUTOETHNOGRAPHY AND THE PGTA

In this chapter, I explore the use of the qualitative research method autoethnography in the context of higher education. In particular, I focus on its capacity to enrich the understanding of identity and personal development within the academy for PGTAs. This reflexive method is carried out by individuals to investigate the self in relation to other (Pithouse-Morgan et al., 2022) and is a means for exhibiting personal experience in the public sphere, by making connections between the personal and emotive with culture and the wider world. Autoethnography is often perceived as a story or conversation with the self about the self, with a recognition and synthesis of pertinent scholarship on emerging topics. As the growing field of autoethnography demonstrates, these accounts can be shared in abstract and creative ways, ranging from essays to plays (Vasconcelos, 2011).

I first encountered this method as I began work on a recent article on PGTAs in third space, a metaphorical terrain characterised by collaboration and participants from across different professional and academic domains sharing expertise (Veles, 2020; Whitchurch, 2015). Carrying out self-introspection in this way supported me to learn about the ways in which I perceived myself and others within this setting and how our interconnected beliefs and behaviours shaped who I was becoming whilst on the transitional path to early career academic. I will outline some of my discoveries later in the chapter, as I introduce three alternate cases of autoethnography in the academy to examine its value in developing identification.

The literature on PGTAs is growing gradually as this body of temporary workers expands in higher education. While they appear to offer significant benefits to the academy, including their being an affordable workforce, their existing membership in the organisation, and their closeness in experience to the students that they facilitate, a number of tensions also arise (Partin, 2018). PGTAs have expressed great issue with the temporary and precarious nature of their employment, often suggesting that they are not compensated fairly for their contributions to the teaching and learning experience. Researchers have also pointed to the lack of opportunities for feedback by PGTAs to their programmes and on their teaching, leading to insufficient support networks and training for these boundary practitioners (Park & Ramos, 2002; Slack & Pownall, 2023). That they are not often embraced by the existing community of staff within institutions is telling of the perceptions held by staff and students about the PGTA's role in the academy, and how they have trouble fitting into existing structures (Adefila, 2023; Sala-Bubaré & Castelló, 2017; Wald & Harland, 2018).

As an early career researcher, I have employed a variety of reflective practices throughout my doctoral studies in order to enrich my understanding of my experiences of teaching and learning. In earlier publications, I explored the use of autobiography to capture the renegotiation of identity through changing employment (Campbell, 2022), followed by a series of collaborative observations with colleagues through an ethic of care lens in higher education (Campbell et al., 2023), and of late, the use of autoethnography and vignettes has helped me to consider the PGTA as blended professional (Campbell, 2024), known predominantly to the literature on higher education as an individual that partially participates in multiple practices simultaneously due to the fusion of academic and professional roles (Whitchurch, 2015). This research has led me to discover new meanings pertaining to my professional development and unearthed strategies that have helped me to implement some of the skills acquired. The narratives depicted in my earlier publications can be illustrated through Ellis and Bochner's (2000: 737) conceptualisation, as they offer a process of gradual understanding through storytelling and meaning making. They state that

> I start with my personal life. I pay attention to my physical feelings, thoughts, and emotions. I use what I call systematic, sociological introspection and emotional recall to try to understand an experience I've lived through. Then I write my experience as a story. By exploring a particular life, I hope to understand a way of life.

Autoethnography is thought to be engaging and evocative, it draws in the reader using highly descriptive language that is both accessible and relatable. It uses the author as the insider, the tool, to root around and to self-discover. The experience of autoethnography is recognised as both a method and a process (Ellis et al., 2011); it demonstrates how one can be simultaneously a part of and apart from society, it involves looking in and looking out and ultimately tells intimate stories for readers to connect with and learn from (Denshire, 2014; Reed-Danahay, 2019). A key rationale for pairing the autoethnographic method with the PGTA practice stems from Pithouse-Morgan et al. (2022, pp. 219–220) claim that, 'Autoethnography offers marginalized academics a contained space to confront their unpleasant feelings, including anxiety, to negotiate a reflexive, ethical, and scholarly self'.

I explore the use of this method in enriching the experience and professional development of PGTAs and consider how other scholars have used this to develop their own understanding of identity and their surroundings. The chapter explores how to carry out autoethnography, what can be achieved by learning about and implementing this method, what significance this practice has to PGTAs and how established members of the academy can support the development of PGTAs by experimenting with this reflexive activity. I then introduce three pieces of autoethnography to the discussion in addition to my own experience with the method to explore how it has been implemented by academics to enrich their teaching and learning practices. The chapter is drawn to a close with acknowledgement of the limitations of the approach and the contributions it makes to the experience of PGTAs in the academy.

DOING AUTOETHNOGRAPHY

The field of autoethnography is full of articulations of how to carry out autoethnographic practice. Notably, the work of Ellis (2009) has offered an insightful conceptualisation, as a springboard for contemporary scholars looking to explore their inner-most feelings about the self and other in order to understand their connection with the world.

In a recent publication, Ellis et al. (2011: para 8) claim that

> When researchers do *autoethnography*, they retrospectively and selectively write about epiphanies that stem from, or are made possible by, being part of a culture and/or by possessing a particular cultural identity. However, in addition to telling about experiences, autoethnographers often are required by social science publishing conventions to analyze these experiences.

In this section, I will outline these stages as exhibited in the literature. The autoethnographic platform lays bare the vulnerabilities and subjectivities of an individual, enticing audiences in to view experience through a new lens, to create relationships with the stories and to consider the information in the context of their own lives.

In their seminal collection on autoethnography, Adams et al. (2015: 2) outline the rationale for carrying out this practice and how to determine whether it meets the intended objectives. They explain that autoethnography

- 'Uses a researcher's personal experience to describe and critique cultural beliefs, practices, and experiences.
- Acknowledges and values a researcher's relationships with others.
- Uses deep and careful self-reflection – typically referred to as 'reflexivity' – to name and interrogate the intersections between self and society, the particular and the general, the personal and the political.
- Shows 'people in the process of figuring out what to do, how to live, and the meaning of their struggles'.
- Balances intellectual and methodological rigour, emotion, and creativity and
- Strives for social justice and to make life better.'

Keles (2022) suggests a series of prerequisites for a successful autoethnography, as detailed by Bochner and Ellis (2016). They state that the accounts ought to be rich, with riveting descriptions to heighten the senses. Through the presence of time, characters and emotive language, they consider how the reader falls into the palms of the writer, believing in the micro-moments and the transformations. Accounts should exhibit periods of self-questioning and reflexivity, of discovery as the individual comes to determine who and how they are, and why (Ellis, 2004), based on how they perceive the insider and outsiders of the experience.

Existing literature conveys the diversified ways that autoethnography can be used to enrich professional development and practice, in particular, within the academy (Trahar, 2013; Pithouse-Morgan et al., 2022). Predominantly, this exercise supports a practitioner to peel open the many layers of experience and to not simply look around but to look inwards, to be inquisitive, and to make meaning of the multifaceted encounters that have shaped the ways they identify with their role. The knowledge generated from this self-analysis helps to inform the practitioner about their relation to culture and the wider setting in which their practice is situated (Boylorn & Orbe, 2020; Denzin, 1997).

While the experience of autoethnography has been conceptualised as both a method and a product (Ellis et al., 2011), it goes beyond consideration for the individual and their intimate involvement, capturing messages pertaining to culture, community and society (Reed-Danahay, 2019). This method supports the practitioner to observe and become conscious of their lived reality; in compiling these reflections, they are able to be critical, revealing how these encounters impress on their self-perception or self-definition, as well as understanding who they are and how they exist in the social world (Denshire, 2014).

While, historically, the significance of gathering unique reflections of experience has been disputed due to a lack of generalisability, scholars have begun promoting the use of autoethnography as a catalyst for transmitting relatable and untold stories that can connect to and with readers. Ellis' (2004) earlier work argues that autoethnographic accounts should speak to a reader. Similarly, Vasconcelos (2011: 418), in their reflections on the relationships and encounters that shape the student and teacher, develops evocative snapshots, contending that they fulfil this activity 'in the hope that the meanings embedded in my life stories might have relevance to other teachers' and students' memories, experiences, and practices'. These often empathetic and other times unspoken narratives can extend a branch towards another situated or contested facet of society (Adams et al., 2015, p. 103), expanding our understanding of prevailing conditions.

DOING AUTOETHNOGRAPHY: PGTAS

Throughout this chapter, I argue for the significance of autoethnographic practice for PGTAs. In an earlier article (Campbell, 2024), I contend that this exercise supported me to better understand my position and role within the academy, albeit revealing some dissatisfactory conditions and conflicts. Being reflexive in this way encouraged me to intimately explore micro-moments that have lingered, which have created a ripple effect, impressing upon wide-ranging areas of my practice as both a student and scholar. Engaging in autoethnography inspired me to look inwards at myself, and to consider my values, behaviours and beliefs, and how I transmit these in different spheres of practice. This process led me to ask questions about the way I am, the things I do and to connect these instances with spaces and the characters within. The cases I draw upon in this chapter by Vasconcelos (2011), Trahar (2013) and Kinchin and Thumser (2023), also portray the value of this method, as these scholars each explore the transition and transformation undertaken in their development within the academy. In their articles, common themes relate to the experience of belonging, becoming, emotion, documentation, tension and interconnection.

Knowledge of the PGTA positioning within the academy was unearthed as I placed an understanding of myself and my professional experiences in the context of the institutional culture (Adams et al., 2015). I considered the cultures and communities developed within this environment and the role that I played in those spaces, which seemed to be influenced considerably by the structures implemented as a result of social and historic implications. Although the PGTA role is widely understood as comprising multiple identities, due to its association with the doctoral candidate, being reflexive about this enabled me to grasp knowledge of the advantages that being situated on a boundary or in a liminal role can have.

A PGTA is often assigned hours in a week where they are required to fulfil their teaching duties. However emerging literature on this practice has revealed that PGTA duties can be wide-ranging and inconsistent throughout institutions, leading practitioners to have contrasting experiences of teaching, marking, material preparation and leading, amongst other skillsets (Clark et al., 2021). Arguably, the experience of teaching in this role can be informed by the relationships established in the academic community and with colleagues who are worked closely with. For instance, the PGTA might carry out their role alongside other PGTAs or alongside a module or programme leader. These relationships can influence the experience of belonging and identification. By integrating the autoethnographic method, the student-turned teacher can capture freeze-frames in which moments of activity changed the way they felt, understood or perceived their practice. This method gives voice to these undocumented moments (Kinchin & Thumser, 2023).

In Vasconcelos' (2011, p. 416) article, through snapshots that critically analyse their past and present selves, they explain how 'The teacher I am is impacted by the student I was'. This points to the significance of recognising the influence of the other on our understandings of self, through bringing together the emotional with the professional. Their memories of encounters in the classroom with their peers and the exchanges with staff who trained and challenged them underscore turning points and pivotal decisions taken as they moved closer to who they were becoming. Interestingly, Vasconcelos reflects on the impression of student–teacher–student in a continuum, suggesting that as a student they were influenced by their teachers who were influenced in their practices by them as a student and now as a teacher the students influence them. In this setting, the agents cannot be separated, nor can they be unaffected by the overarching culture of the space, whether this is thought to be inclusive or exclusive.

Contemporary literature demonstrates how identifying with the culture of the academy can be problematic for PGTAs as they are situated on the periphery of different memberships: the staff body and the doctoral community. This can lead the individual to crafting alternative versions of an academic identity to be carried out in the same setting; these can pertain to different roles and demands and can be mirrored in the behaviours of colleagues or peers (Slack & Pownall, 2023). The PGTA role however is widely recognised as being part of professional development; it is a steppingstone to a more secure academic position. Based on this, practicing autoethnography can be considered an effective way to self-examine and document the ways that these practices contributed to one another or have evolved simultaneously. Reflexively moving between experience in this way has been known to obscure the division between settings and periods in time (Ellis, 1999). This can be done in innovative and creative ways, not simply through diary entries or short extracts, nevertheless creating a map on which to plot the significant changes encountered over the teaching and learning experience (Phan, 2023).

PGTAs are an under-researched and under-acknowledged body of contributors to the teaching and learning experience in higher education; however, conducting autoethnography can reveal the transformative nature of our work. To ensure that this exercise creates impact, the writer must work to develop lived stories that are accessible (Adams et al., 2015); this is essential for practitioners to feel 'seen' (Pithouse-Morgan et al., 2022). Readers within the academy are offered insight into the conflicts and nuances of our practice, they are informed about the ways that our role is perceived by others and how this can impress on our ability and confidence to flourish in the setting, while our counterparts may feel noticed, valued, empathetic and not alone. In reading the experiences of others, strategies for coping can be developed, and this new social knowledge can be employed to inform the way that support is developed for novice academics (Keles, 2022; Kinchin & Thumser, 2023).

In terms of the PGTA experience, it is first important to consider that the label 'PGTA' is given to a particular role in the academy and thus does not capture the full set of identities held by an individual. As such, when this individual carries out reflexivity on their professional development and practice, it is probable that some of the listed features below will help to structure their accounts:

- Consideration for relationships with others in the academy: supervisors, line-managers, fellow PGTAs, and students under PGTA supervision.
- Development of teaching practice: autonomy in the classroom, teaching/learning interventions, responsibility/accountability, confidence and self-perception in the role.
- Negotiation of academic identity: feelings of belonging to the academic community, modelling the behaviours, values and beliefs of collective identity, and socialisation into wider institutional structures.

In order to effectively and critically discuss the aforementioned encounters in the academy, the PGTA might consider engaging with existing research and synthesising this with their own experience. Indeed, they might also open up the dialogue on uncommunicated encounters from within the space through accessible and intimate language to draw in a much-needed audience with whom change may be instigated.

DOING AUTOETHNOGRAPHY: THE ACADEMIC COMMUNITY

In my research on the PGTA role in higher education, specifically on the impact of labelling in the academy, and in an attempt to address some of the conflicts encountered by PGTAs, I have come to believe that use of the autoethnographic method by established members of the academic community could have significant implications for the professional development of PGTAs, even indirectly. Here, I underscore the ways that others might utilise this reflexive activity to enrich their understanding of the cultures within which they are situated and also of the relationships formed within – in particular, revealing the perceptions held of the PGTA in relation to the staff and student populations.

Indeed, as the number of autoethnographers in the academy grows, it is probable that there will be greater acknowledgement of the inconsistencies and discrepancies between academic practices and positions. This is where autoethnography thrives, unearthing the subjectivities of experience (Ellis et al., 2011), and indeed through this style of storytelling, issues of power, exclusion, oppression and difference may be unearthed. These stories can be rich, descriptive and vastly different from one another, broadening our understanding of growth within the academy and through the life course (Vasconcelos, 2011). Existing literature points to the ambiguity of the PGTA role, as these early career individuals pursue a variety of responsibilities and demands (Wald & Harland, 2018), though this is not widely reported on by individuals outside of the PGTA community. Bringing members of the community like early career staff into the discussion on identity politics and power discourses experienced by PGTAs may well help to address the injustices encountered in the academy (Pithouse-Morgan et al., 2022).

Acknowledgement of the contributions made by these temporary workers by others in the community might help to bring a conversation about liminality in the academy to the table. This may help to address PGTA experiences with institutional structures and the issues they face with fitting in to these, ultimately enriching the understanding of how PGTAs might be supported to identify more closely with a collective. Vasconcelos (2011, p. 432) in their autoethnography reports that 'My sweetest memories come from the moments and times when my presence was acknowledged and my voice was heard by my teachers'. Indeed, as argued in Mills (1959, p. 3), 'neither the life of an individual nor the history of a society can be understood without understanding both' and thus it stands to reason that, in considering the individual experience of academic practice, the extensive tapestry of interconnected others and situational characteristics working in this environment should also be examined (Adams et al., 2015).

In sharing reflective methods that support practitioners to enrich the way they engage with and make sense of the interactions in their professional settings, autoethnography may create space for PGTAs to be thought about in relation to others, to be bought in from the periphery, to be considered in the wider frame of activity and society, and to become a part of the language of the setting. In turn, it is possible that enhanced awareness of the role that these early career individuals play in the academy may reshape the support structures provided to them, tailoring the way that they target identity development and community building. Undertaking autoethnography enables the practitioner to connect their personal self with their multifaceted surroundings; from the knowledge developed during this process, individuals may feel compelled to respond to and reshape their relational practice (Campbell et al., 2023).

THE CASE OF AUTOETHNOGRAPHY

In earlier work (Campbell, 2024), I employed the autoethnographic method to explore my experience of being a PGTA employed at a research-intensive Russell Group university. In this, vignettes were developed to convey a selection of turning points in my professional development. Through these, I was able to convey the role of the blended professional working in third space and to describe the impact that labelling within the academy can have on self-perception and how one feels that they fit into existing institutional structures. Based on Adams et al. (2015, p. 5) conceptualisation of autoethnographic work, through my reflections I worked at

- 'Recognising the limits of scientific knowledge (what can be known or explained), particularly regarding identities, lives, and relationships and creating nuanced, complex, and specific accounts of personal/cultural experience,
- Connecting personal (insider) experience, insights, and knowledge to larger (relational, cultural, and political) conversations, contexts, and conventions,
- Answering the call to narrative and storytelling and placing equal importance on intellect/knowledge and aesthetics/artistic craft, and
- Attending to the ethical implications of their work for themselves, their participants, and their readers/audiences'.

The three vignettes I developed were each captioned with one line that summarised the feature theme. These prepared the reader, while simultaneously creating ambiguity and an element of curiosity. The language used within aimed to be vivid, detailing the intricacies of the interactions within changing settings, and the influence that subtle yet significant symbolic acts had on the shifting shape I took in the academy. These interpretations of my data revealed various experiences with society and culture, which supported me to grasp enriched knowledge of others, and the myriad identities within the space, as well as my relationships with the surroundings (Boylorn & Orbe, 2020). This experience is modelled on Pithouse-Morgan et al. (2022, p. 224) belief that 'In thinking and working autoethnographically, we choose to understand the academic self and vocation as personal, social, emotional, embodied, and mindful'.

The vignettes revealed the ways in which PGTAs are supported to integrate into the community and culture of the organisation and to what extent the discontinuities in the boundaries of their role both help and hamper their understanding of who and how to be in higher education. Through hindsight, I was able to portray the significance of lived experiences in shaping my understanding of how I came to be perceived by others. To achieve this, I needed to analyse each encounter from the inside out; to consider the meanings I had assigned to experience based on my internal definitions, but to also look outward at the interactions and exchanges, at the characters that moved in and out of my lived experience, and to consider how the behaviours, values and norms of a space had impressed on my understanding (Boylorn & Orbe, 2020). These reflections do not simply transmit the concealed felt experience of the author, but the author too becomes a researcher from the inside, as they report from the eye of the storm (Adams et al., 2015). The experience of autoethnography was one of continued inquiry; to first draw out some of the key issues faced by PGTAs, to ask how these connect with existing scholarship on the matter, and to be critical about the environments and social structures that inform these encounters (Pithouse-Morgan et al., 2022).

To curate the vignettes, I was inspired by Pitard's (2016) 'structured vignette analysis'. They propose a series of key stages to ensure a rich and insightful representation; these include consideration for the context, anecdote, emotional response, reflexivity, strategies developed and conclusive comments on layers. The vignettes exhibit what Adams et al. (2015) describe as an epiphany, moments of realisation that stem from the ordinary and the mundane but very much writing-as-inquiry (Poulos, 2020). Bringing these to the printed page was felt to be an effective way to capture the subjectivities of the PGTA experience by conceptualising the role in a way that is neglected in existing literature. My autoethnography attempted to convey some of the challenges and accomplishments of early career individuals, documenting their professional development, something I perceive as being of utmost importance as these individuals become a rapidly growing temporarily employed figure in the academy. As Poulos (2020) explains, in order for our readers to go beyond feeling and in order for our readers to span beyond the qualitative community, we must find ways as writers to unite and to consider the implications of our lived experience for others. While for a long time autoethnographic work was considered simply as non-generalisable storied information about an individual, frequently conceptualised as 'me-search', work by Boylorn and Orbe (2020, p. 4) points to the changing views of scholars on the individual experience, suggesting that these contributions bring us closer to wisdom 'relationally, personally, and culturally'.

I felt that the power of the autoethnographic experience was in capturing and calling attention to the challenges and inconsistencies of the PGTA role; by employing an accepted reflexive practice that functioned in accordance with the language of the academy, the PGTA voice might be afforded a seat at the table. For every unique story conveyed by a PGTA, a more holistic and transparent view of teaching in this liminal role is unearthed. I write to reveal the insecurities and uncertainties that fester within our community, which can become more intense or problematic over time if left unspoken. While there is great opportunity for strengthening the sense of belonging and community under these conditions, acting as the sounding board or mentor for one another can create difficulty with finding a resolution; I considered, if we are only supported by one another in our roles, who will support us to grow beyond this space (Boylorn & Orbe, 2020)? The autoethnographic examples drawn upon in this chapter portray the significance of the moments of connection shared with others in the academy, but if we are only trained to exist outside the structure of the institution how can we be sure that we are taking on the identity of the setting? As such, if the problems we encounter are left to infiltrate our marginalised community, these issues will remain. The development and dissemination of PGTA narratives can and will highlight the need for greater recognition, acknowledgement and support for this overlooked population (Adams et al., 2015).

Much of my own reflexive work is centred on transition and identity renegotiation, a framework that I have formerly used to explore the experiences of postgraduate students in higher education, and this can also be sensed in the overview of articles to follow. By bringing together scholarship on common matter, for instance the experience of identity and transition, I am better able to exhibit 'the interconnectedness of the human experience' (Boylorn & Orbe, 2020, p. 3). These texts not only convey the unique encounters of practitioners, but underscore their commonalities, their subjectivities, and the significance of reflection on professional development, channelling an ethos of care at the core (Adams et al., 2015). Through this approach, readers are invited in through our snapshots and windows, to look around, to get a sense of the space and the moments framed within.

THREE CASES IN THE ACADEMY

To explore the power of autoethnography in higher education research, three peer-reviewed articles have been selected to identify the various approaches that have been taken in order to convey the unique and transformative moments encountered in professional development. Ellis et al. (2011: para 1) conceptualise autoethnography as a process in which the author must 'describe and systematically analyze personal experience in order to understand cultural experience'. Notably, these are explored by individuals on the periphery, those having transitioned from a student or support role to an integrated member of the academic community or by members of the academy that are identified by their multimembership.

The first article '*I Can See You*': *An Autoethnography of My Teacher-Student Self* by Vasconcelos (2011) delves into the multiplicity of roles and identities one can hold within the academy. Through their writing, a series of pivotal moments are bought together to represent a timeline of becoming. The article intermittently poses questions for the reader to connect with, sensing the author's internal dialogue as they undertake a self-examination. As the article progresses, so too does the story of the writer, moving from an investigation through the lens of a student to that of a member of staff. They place themselves in the social context of the academy through their remembered interactions with peers, their own students, and representations of the academic community; these each draw the reader into the changing shape of the author's world, where stories layered upon another depict their emotions and altering self-perception. The movement of the author's narrative throughout the article, between past and present, confirms Muncey's (2005, p. 71) line of thought that 'life must be lived forward but can really be understood only backward'.

Within this text, Vasconcelos (2011) draws on confrontation, on conflict, but also inspiration and modelling. They point to the lasting impact of interactions with others and how the longevity and emotional response has shaped them as a professional. What is particularly interesting about their autoethnography is their connection with the subject of translation, as a learner and then teacher of translation, followed by the act of translating felt experience for the reader through their reflections. Throughout the excerpts, the author identifies the space between agents, between teachers–teachers, students–students, students–teachers, addressing the interconnections and the tensions that resist and facilitate their merging identities.

In this article, the author chose to use 'snapshots' to depict their autoethnography. In describing their closeness to moments captured on a camera, the short texts are arranged in an album. Like an old photograph or recording, the snapshots are often dated, sometimes with a location, situating the encounter. The text-based images are bought to life through storytelling, much like concrete poetry, introducing the reader to various meaningful characters, and illustrations of relationships fostered between the author and their surroundings. Vasconcelos creates very evocative, emotional and compelling narratives for each frame. Characters talk to one another, the setting of the event is intimately described, the position of the writer moves about in the moment – through this the author has captured a sense of pace, of stillness and, at other times, urgency. As each facet of a frame is bought back to life, we find ourselves stepping into their lived reality, peering through their lens (Pithouse-Morgan et al., 2022). While the author provides reflections that seem to move back and forth in time, the extra details like dates and captions cleverly guide the reader's deeper engagement with the story.

The use of autoethnography in this article transports the reader to bygone frames and events. Through the captions of the snapshots, the author offers information about the 'unsaid', they clarify and insert the wisdom acquired through hindsight. Each fixed moment details a juncture at which change was encountered, pulling the reader into the eye of the emotional impact. While the snapshots summarise moments caught in wider frames, the storytelling nature of autoethnography has enabled the author to gradually alter the reader's perspective, setting their discoveries into the context of real life that can be connected with.

The second paper, *Mapping the 'becoming-integrated-academic': an autoethnographic case study of professional becoming in the biosciences* by Kinchin and Thumser (2023) documents the path from researcher to teacher. In this, the authors describe the multiplicity of roles undertaken by individuals in the academy in the present day, depicting the regular horizontal transitions undertaken where identities overlap, influence and evolve. This article reveals critical incidents that impressed upon the practitioner's professional development and the intricacies of challenges, conflicts and compromises made in order to embrace the vision of the possible self.

Throughout the paper, the authors curate the reflective excerpts and pair these with descriptive themes. Critical discussions follow, opening up the illustrations to interrogate the practitioner's changing sense of self with relation to the academic community and the society in which the work is framed. The incidents are incredibly focused, they comprise esoteric knowledge of the classroom and pedagogical practice, and sometimes questions are posed, which demonstrates how they uncover thoughts and responses about their experience. Notably, there were instances of citations appearing in the excerpts, contextualising the tacit knowledge; these somehow de-personalised the writing a little, not necessarily making the experience appear more general, but by using the language of the academy the practitioner's encounters could be more transparently felt by the reader. Kinchin and Thumser (2023) note in their article that value can be attributed to autoethnography when a sense of 'context similarity' is projected, something that they appear to achieve by using relatable terminology.

The use of autoethnography to detail the experience of identity development and transition within the academy has offered a series of well-organised encounters that eloquently communicate the 'tensions' of professional development. The authors contend that opportunity to reflect on this is a rarity and suggest that there would be benefits to both practitioners and the academy to document and listen to these unique trajectories in order to account for the often-overlooked challenges and power-dynamics faced. Creating this space from the inside can be a helpful way of gathering new understandings about personal experience in social spaces.

The third paper, *Autoethnographic Journeys in learning and teaching in Higher Education* by Trahar (2013), interrogates their teaching and learning practice through reflections on interactions held between themselves and others in the academic community – these are predominantly their experiences of research, supervision and offering feedback in an international European higher education context. In their writing, Trahar (2013, p. 367) places significance on an autoethnographic practice in order to 'enable greater sensitivity to our diverse constituencies'; their desire to carry this out is evidenced in the multiplicity of relationships fostered with individuals across the academic community.

This article comprises lengthy introspections, in which different characters are introduced. The first-person reflections appear to be the author in conversation with the self, through which they are wildly descriptive, contemplative and somewhat critical. Many of the incidents are thoroughly contextualised and further synthesised with scholarship to indicate to the reader where these experiences exist in a wider frame, predominantly linking their enquiries to Freire (2005), as they critique and interrogate their pedagogical positioning.

Throughout the article, Trahar (2013) also looks towards their earlier experience of learning to understand how this impressed on their approach to teaching. Simultaneously, they consider the learning experiences of their students as influenced by Trahar their supervisor and by the various institutional styles encountered from around the globe. Trahar's reflections point to some of the conflicts and challenges that emerge in a supervisory relationship when the participants are positioned with contrasting beliefs or academic conventions. Amongst these issues, they outline critical thinking and substance as being most contentious for them. Much of the writing is grounded in pedagogical scholarship which has supported them to contextualise some of the lived experience.

Existing autoethnography points to its significance in exploring identity, something Trahar (2013) also channelled in this article. They took this process a step further, in order to learn from and about others too. The excerpts draw on how individuals within a diversely populated academy portray their identities in their solitary practices and to their communities; their article explores the layering of identities, and how strands of this are digested by in-lookers. They draw on the act of writing for their students as a means for portraying a true identity, something that they also appear to seek out in their own reflections.

Based on these three articles, while it is evident that the outcome is similar and that the act of reflexivity in autoethnography can support an individual to reach rich meaning about their unique experience placed in social settings, there are indeed different ways to achieve this. Vasconcelos (2011) depicts the changing nature of their role within academia, how this alters their self-perception and the influence that the actions of others had on their professional development. Through snapshots they convey detailed micro-moments, poetically revealing narratives with the benefit of hindsight. In Kinchin and Thumser (2023), while more theoretically driven, the path towards becoming is documented through a series of critical and reflective excerpts. The authors report on their experience of transition through the language of the academy. Finally, Trahar's (2013) experience of identity renegotiation and continual growth is captured in their excerpts. Much of their writing is immersed in the context of international schooling, which supports them to critique their interconnectivity with others and the space they inhibit.

LIMITATIONS OF THE APPROACH

While I believe autoethnography is a powerful exercise and tool for PGTAs working in higher education to grasp a richer understanding of the academic identity and the perceived roles of contributors to teaching and learning, I also recognise that there are a number of existing criticisms and limitations of the method. In the context of a PGTA's professional development, one might consider the implications that reflecting openly might have on others involved in the re-telling of a story or simply on the PGTA themselves as they unearth areas of contention in the academy.

An overarching issue of the approach is the way that it focuses on the individual experience, which while highlighting the subjectivities of wider issues, also risks overlooking larger matters (Boylorn & Orbe, 2020; Reed-Danahay, 2019). On the contrary, it is possible too that through sharing experience, exchange and connection can inspire political and collective action.

The honesty conveyed in autoethnographic works has been identified as risky by scholars, who recognise that by revealing relationships with culture, society and self, we make ourselves vulnerable. We can learn much about ourselves which is felt to be simultaneously enriching and possibly quite harmful. Indeed, the spaces in which we inhabit will have expectations of us, and assumptions will have been made about us, as such, by sharing our internal voices we risk these perceptions being altered (Adams et al., 2015; Armstrong, 2008), which may be either a positive or negative thing.

The examples of autoethnography I have referred to within this chapter reveal much about the experience of change and transition as they do about the author and those moving in and out of their shared spaces. That said, autoethnography historically has been thought of as self-indulgent, and coined 'me-search' by many (Boylorn & Orbe, 2020). Reed-Danahay (2019) goes further, suggesting that research of this nature not only illuminates the author, but those associated with them too, posing ethical dilemmas (Denshire, 2014).

CONCLUSION

This chapter has identified various rationales for carrying out autoethnography in the field of higher education, in particular for those fulfiling the role of PGTA. It provides space for early career individuals to articulate their lived realities in conjunction with many of the unspoken power imbalances and dynamics at play within the academy. Autoethnography also serves to help individuals better understand their relationship with identity and culture, enriching their knowledge of who and how they are in the world and how this has been shaped (Adams et al., 2015). The intricate details afforded in autoethnography have been known to support writers to develop eloquent and engaging stories of subjectivity, which emphasises the distinctions between and diversity of roles in the academy, based on how they fit into existing structures along with their unique circumstances.

By encouraging this method as a means to interrogate and nurture professional development, a greater awareness of lived realities will be revealed, unearthing other ways that individuals relate to one another, can empathise with one another, and can eventually support one another (Ellis et al., 2011). As these collections of experience grow, the more capacity we have to spread these subjectivities to collect allies and activists from wider audiences; this method has the capacity to unearth issues from within the academy and to share them with a wider social world. Hence, this is so important for the marginalised members of our community (Muncey, 2005; Pithouse-Morgan et al., 2022). By revealing the mistreatment of PGTAs in the academy, practitioners may reconsider their own actions towards colleagues or how they support and participate through unions.

The PGTA is known to feature heavily in the teaching and learning experience of undergraduate students, in which their responsibilities and demands are wide-ranging and often eat away at valuable research time. Despite their commitment to and care for their students and the experience of the academy they strive to provide, they are frequently left on the periphery of the academic and student communities, belonging everywhere and nowhere (Turner, 1987). While this liminality has proved to be a learnable space for some, it can be a disorientating and uncertain space for others who strive to become and identify as an established member of the staff body. I have argued for the autoethnographic approach to be utilised for these marginalised participants in order to help them to better understand the ways that the university simultaneously helps and hinders their ability to assimilate into the culture of the institution in order to unveil practices and to develop resources that will support the PGTA on their journey of professional development.

REFERENCES

Adams, T. E., Jones, S. H., & Ellis, C. (2015). *Autoethnography*. Oxford University Press.

Adefila, A. (2023). GTAs negotiating development trajectories in the modern edu-factory. *Postgraduate Pedagogies Journal, 3*, 6–11.

Armstrong, P. (2008). Towards an autoethnographic pedagogy. In *Paper presented at the 38th Annual SCUTREA Conference*. Edinburgh, UK. July 2–4.

Bochner, A., & Ellis, C. (2016). *Evocative autoethnography: Writing lives and telling stories*. Routledge.

Boylorn, R. M., & Orbe, M. P. (2020). Introduction: Critical autoethnography as method of choice/choosing critical autoethnography. In *Critical autoethnography* (2nd ed.). Routledge.

Campbell, K. (2022). 'Shape Shifting - Autobiography as a tool for exploring boundary practices: A GTA's perspective.' *Postgraduate Pedagogies Journal, 2*, 212–238.

Campbell, K. (2024). Labelling in the academy: Identity renegotiation among postgraduate teaching assistants. *London Review of Education, 22*(1), 16. https://doi.org/10.14324/LRE.22.1.16

Campbell, K., Gurini, P., O'Sullivan, S., & Trollope, R. (2023). The significance of care in a global higher education institution: An insight from the periphery. *Postgraduate Pedagogies Journal, 3*, 52–62.

Clark, L. B., Hansen, J., Hastie, A., Kunz, S., Standen, A., & Thorogood, J. (2021). Introduction to postgraduate pedagogies: Centring graduate teaching assistants in higher education. *Postgraduate Pedagogies, 1*(1), 7–25.

Denshire, S. (2014). On auto-ethnography. *Current Sociology, 62*(6), 831–850. https://doi.org/10.1177/0011392114533339

Denzin, N. K. (1997). *Interpretive ethnography: Ethnographic practices for the 21st century*. Sage.

Ellis, C. (1999). Heartful autoethnography. *Qualitative Health Research, 9*(5), 669–683.

Ellis, C. (2004). *The ethnographic I: A methodological novel about autoethnography*. AltaMira Press.

Ellis, C. (2009). Telling tales on neighbors: Ethics in two voices. *International Review of Qualitative Research, 2*(1), 3–28.

Ellis, C., Adams, T. E., & Bochner, A. P. (2011). Autoethnography: An Overview. *Forum Qualitative Sozialforschung Forum: Qualitative Social Research, 12*(1). https://doi.org/10.17169/fqs-12.1.1589

Ellis, C., & Bochner, A. P. (2000). Autoethnography, personal narrative, reflexivity. In N. K. Denzin & Y. S. Lincoln (Eds.), *Handbook of qualitative research* (2nd ed., pp. 733–768). Sage.

Freire, P. (2005). *Teachers as cultural workers: Letters to those who dare teach*. Westview.

Keleş, U. (2022). Writing a "good" autoethnography in educational research: A modest proposal. *Qualitative Report*. https://doi.org/10.46743/2160-3715/2022.5662. [Preprint].

Kinchin, I. M., & Thumser, A. E. (2023). Mapping the "becoming-integrated-academic": An autoethnographic case study of professional becoming in the biosciences. *Journal of Biological Education, 57*(4), 715–726. https://doi.org/10.1080/00219266.2021.1941191

Mills, C. W. (1959). *The sociological imagination*. Oxford University Press.

Muncey, T. (2005). Doing autoethnography. *International Journal of Qualitative Methods, 4*(1), 69–86. https://doi.org/10.1177/160940690500400105

Park, C., & Ramos, M. (2002). The donkey in the department? Insights into the Graduate Teaching Assistant (GTA) experience in the UK. *Journal of Graduate Education, 3*, 47–53.

Partin, C. M. (2018). *Investigating transformation: An exploratory study of perceptions and lived experiences of graduate teaching assistants*. University of South Florida.

Phan, A. N. Q. (2023). "Dear Epsom": a poetic autoethnography on campus as home of an international doctoral student in Aotearoa New Zealand. *London Review of Education, 21*(1), 28. https://doi.org/10.14324/LRE.21.1.28

Pitard, J. (2016). Using vignettes within autoethnography to explore layers of cross-cultural awareness as a teacher. *Forum for Qualitative Social Research, 17*(1).

Pithouse-Morgan, K., Pillay, D., & Naicker, I. (2022). Autoethnography as/in higher education. In T. E. Adams, S. Holman Jones, & C. Ellis (Eds.), *Handbook of autoethnography* (2nd ed., pp. 215–227). Routledge. https://doi.org/10.4324/9780429431760-22

Poulos, C. N. (2020). The perils and the promises of autoethnography: Raising our voices in troubled times. *Journal of Autoethnography, 1*(2), 208–211. https://doi.org/10.1525/joae.2020.1.2.208

Reed-Danahay, D. (2019). *Autoethnography*. SAGE Research Methods Foundations. https://doi.org/10.4135/9781526421036815143. [Preprint].
Sala-Bubaré, A., & Castelló, M. (2017). Exploring the relationship between doctoral students' experiences and research community positioning. *Studies in Continuing Education*, *39*(1), 16–34. https://doi.org/10.1080/0158037X.2016.1216832
Slack, H. R., & Pownall, M. (2023). "treat GTAS as colleagues, rather than spare parts": The identity, agency, and wellbeing of graduate teaching assistants. *Journal of Further and Higher Education*, *47*(9), 1262–1275. https://doi.org/10.1080/0309877x.2023.2241392
Trahar, S. (2013). Autoethnographic journeys in learning and teaching in higher education. *European Educational Research Journal*, *12*(3). https://doi.org/10.2304/eerj.2013.12.3.367
Turner, V. (1987). Betwixt and between: the liminal period in rites of passage. In L. C. Mahadi, S. Foster, & M. Little, (Eds.), *Betwixt between: Patterns of masculine and feminine initiation* (pp. 3–19). Open Court.
Vasconcelos, E. F. (2011). "I Can See You": An autoethnography of my teacher-student self. *The Qualitative Report*, *16*(2), 415–440.
Veles, N. (2020). *University professional staff in collaborative third space environments: a multiple case study of the Australian and Singapore campuses of one university*. PhD thesis, James Cook University.
Wald, N., & Harland, T. (2018). Rethinking the teaching roles and assessment responsibilities of student teaching assistants. *Journal of Further and Higher Education*, *44*(1), 43–53. https://doi.org/10.1080/0309877x.2018.1499883
Whitchurch, C. (2015). The rise of third space professionals: Paradoxes and dilemmas. In U. Teichler & W. C. Cummings (Eds.), *Recruiting and managing the academic profession*. Springer.

STUDYING STUDENT BEHAVIOUR: TOWARDS AN INTEGRATED CONCEPTUAL FRAMEWORK

Victoria A. Bauer

Leibniz University Hannover, Germany

ABSTRACT

The concept of student behaviour provides a tool for describing and understanding the underlying mechanisms between academic success as a dependent variable and individual determinants of students and the institutional context of study as independent variables. Defined as the micro-level characteristics that encompass students' actual behaviour and transitions within higher education, student behaviour influences the outcomes of academic performance, learning outcomes, the duration of studies, completion rates and future career paths. Student behaviour therefore serves as an intermediary construct between inputs and student outcomes. This chapter provides a comprehensive heuristic framework of student behaviour, drawing on insights from a range of disciplinary theoretical perspectives, including education, psychology, sociology, economics and political science. The conceptual model outlines the central role of student behaviour within the student life cycle and its implications for higher education research. In doing so, the chapter offers a conceptual panorama that encompasses both the factors that explain student behaviour and the phenomena that student behaviour itself influences, including its relationship to the concept of student engagement. The framework is not limited to conceptual delineation but invites further theoretical development.

Keywords: Higher education; student behaviour; academic success; framework; attendance rates

INTRODUCTION

High dropout rates and student persistence are challenges facing higher education institutions worldwide (Behr et al., 2020; Witteveen & Attewell, 2021). In order to gain a comprehensive understanding of the dynamics that influence persistence and attrition, researchers face several methodological challenges when studying dropout rates and student retention in higher education. On the one hand, student surveys are subject to self-report bias (Bowman & Hill, 2011; Gewinner et al., 2022). On the other hand, longitudinal studies of individual subjects lack generalisability and face huge panel attrition, especially after dropouts (Harris-Huemmert, 2015; Neugebauer et al., 2019). Despite these complexities, researchers still mainly focus on individual determinants to explain student outcomes, while institutional factors are under-researched (Vossensteyn et al., 2015), and a comprehensive understanding of educational pathways is lacking (Bahr, 2013; Haas, 2022). As a result, the mechanisms behind the generation of academic success in the context of a complex student lifecycle cannot yet be fully explained.

One possible approach to exploring this is through the study of student behaviour. Student behaviour in higher education has long been described as a 'black box' (Bahr, 2013, p. 144), but its relevance has become increasingly apparent in recent years. This is largely due to the availability of new data sources, such as administrative data (Bauer et al., 2023) or digital behavioural data (Hewson, 2018), which have led to a proliferation of student-centred big data analytics in higher education research (Cantabella et al., 2019; Prinsloo & Slade, 2016). These student data allow new behavioural insights, which enable the previously hidden mechanisms in explaining academic success to be illuminated. Student behaviour thus stands as an intermediary construct at the interface between input factors and student outcomes. It allows for a holistic view of academic success that brings together the micro-, meso- and macro-levels, highlighting the role of institutional governance in student outcomes.

The increasing performativity of educational institutions has led to a greater focus on predicting performance and at-risk students, for example through learning analytics tools. The shift towards using these tools to improve student learning, performance and success is evident in higher education institutions worldwide and is growing rapidly (Shepard et al., 2021). Institutions are now tracking trends and patterns in student behaviour using rich and complex educational datasets, enabling analysis that informs different aspects of student outcomes (McBroom et al., 2020). However, this trend is not without its critics. Ethical concerns around privacy and data management issues have been associated with the use of learning analytics (cf. Chinsook et al., 2022; Slade & Prinsloo, 2013), as well as administrative data (cf. Bauer et al., 2023) and data mining of big data on higher education in general (cf. Johnson, 2014).

Nevertheless, the audience for student behaviour data has expanded beyond higher education practitioners and stakeholders to include the scientific community. As the new data sources offer many opportunities to analyse trends in student behaviour, researchers are using them for studies on student attrition, automated feedback provision, peer learning and student equity (McBroom et al., 2020). When published for external purposes, the choice of indicators depends heavily on the intended audience, as particularly the input and process variables of student behaviour can be easily misinterpreted (Beerkens, 2022). Despite the growing body of research, a comprehensive conceptual framework for understanding student behaviour in higher education is lacking. The current state of research resembles a patchwork quilt, with the conspicuous absence of a strong theoretical background hindering the full potential of recent studies.

This chapter seeks to fill these gaps by introducing an interdisciplinary and adaptable heuristic framework for the study of student behaviour in higher education. By bringing together similar ideas and perspectives from different contexts and disciplines, including education, psychology, sociology, economics, and political science, it advances the current approaches to the study of student behaviour. The chapter aims to provide a basis for future developments in the analysis of student behaviour and its impact on academic success.

In the following, I will discuss the definition of student behaviour and illustrate a conceptual framework of student behaviour by synthesising the surrounding theories. These links are then explained in the next two sections: the first of which theorises the relationship between student behaviour and upstream input characteristics (the effectors of student behaviour) and the second of which theorises the relationship between student behaviour and downstream outcomes (the effects of student behaviour), supplemented with empirical evidence. The section on input factors argues from the macro- to the meso- to the micro-level in order to better bring the theories into the discussion. The theoretical approaches are not structured by discipline, but by possible links to other theories and approaches, thus enabling the interdisciplinarity of the framework. The final section concludes and discusses possible links to the conceptual framework and its applicability to further studies in higher education.

A DEFINITION AND FRAMEWORK OF STUDENT BEHAVIOUR

Student behaviour encompasses the micro-level process characteristics of students' behaviour throughout their higher education journey. It represents a continuous accompaniment to the academic pathway, capturing not only specific transitions and events but every single observable behaviour taken by students in the context of their academic progress during the student life cycle. This behaviour is influenced both by the context of institutional arrangements and by the cross-level effects of individual socio-economic and psychological determinants. The concept of student behaviour therefore links the student experience to student learning at the micro-level, to course design at the meso-level, and even to system policy at the macro-level. At its core, variation in student behaviour leads to differences in outcomes such as overall performance in programmes, length of study, progress within programmes, completion rates and attrition (Chen & Ward, 2022; McBroom et al., 2020). In the long term, these outcomes have a profound impact on individuals' future career trajectories and the development of human capital (Wilson et al., 2019; Wollscheid & Hovdhaugen, 2021).

Student behaviour means the actual behaviour of students as they interact in and with educational systems, showing the exact frequency and duration of different types of behaviour. In a tautological sense, it refers to behaviour that may be unconscious but also to meaningful behaviour that is action as defined by Weber (1981). Student behaviour can be observed as digital behavioural data in digital learning environments, such as e-learning platforms, learning management systems, and other tools that facilitate and record online learning activities in which students can participate and collaborate (Cantabella et al., 2019; Kadoić & Oreški, 2018), such as their actual amount of reading. However, forms of student behaviour do not only relate to learning behaviour but also include information on students' examination behaviour, their course-taking behaviour and detailed pathways through higher education, structured by institutional regulations and module plans (Haas & Hadjar, 2020).

These can be captured as administrative or registry data through indicators such as attendance, participation in formal and independent learning, examination registration and withdrawal, credit accumulation, and module grades. In their system architecture of big data on student behaviour in higher education, Chinsook et al. (2022) distinguish four data sources: (1) traditional databases, such as data warehouses and other administrative systems, (2) personal data, such as emails, paper documents and handwritten notes, (3) digital traces on the web, such as behaviour on university networks and Wi-Fi zones, and (4) data on outdoor activities, e.g. observed via GPS tracking. Macfarlane and Tomlinson (2017) caution against focussing solely on easily observable behaviours, such as class attendance, and encourage the expansion of indicators that are more difficult to capture, such as note taking behaviour, which can only be collected by observation in non-digital classrooms.

Yet, there are also competing definitions of student behaviour. In educational research, student behaviour is often characterised as an aspect or dimension of student engagement, measured by activity, time and effort (Macfarlane & Tomlinson, 2017; Tight, 2020). This limits the full potential of the concept of student behaviour and also leads to a complex and diffuse definition of student engagement. Given the need to look more closely at both the explanatory factors and the explained effects of student behaviour, the conceptual model presented in this paper also helps to define and explain the diffuse construct of student engagement, embedded in a broader context of student inputs and outcomes.

Another limited but common definition of student behaviour in higher education is its meaning as deviance, misbehaviour, (un-)ethical behaviour or (non-)compliance with social rules, with examples including passive or dominant attitudes towards teachers or noncompletion of tasks in the classroom (cf. Fredricks et al., 2004) or ethical issues on campus such as reporting crimes (cf. Janosik & Gehring, 2003). Student behaviour as study team behaviour refers to the way students interact with each other in relation to their studies, for example, by meeting in study groups or by meeting to discuss lectures (cf. Senior et al., 2012). This multifaceted understanding of student behaviour highlights its complex and interdisciplinary nature and underlines the need for a comprehensive conceptual framework to holistically capture and analyse the intricacies of student behaviour in higher education in future research.

In order to understand the complex interplay of factors that influence student behaviour and its ultimate impact on academic success, I introduce a heuristic conceptual framework that synthesises different theoretical perspectives. The framework incorporates insights from educational research, political science, psychology, sociology, and economics, providing a comprehensive lens through which to examine the intricate dynamics of student behaviour in higher education. While the model provides a unifying framework for the study of student behaviour, it is important to recognise that it does not represent a coherent body of theory. Rather, it reflects a synthesis of different theoretical approaches, each with its own conceptual underpinnings and assumptions.

Elements of student behaviour include a wide range of learning and examination behaviour, such as class attendance, course registration and participation, note taking, writing style, examination registration and attempts, performance and completion of exercises and examinations, study and preparation time, and process grades. Therefore, student behaviour can vary in space, but the space must relate to the higher education environment, so student behaviour can be campus behaviour, in-class behaviour, or digital behaviour. Fig. 1 visually models the integrated conceptual framework around student behaviour and provides a concise representation of the key elements involved (dashed arrows) and the factors and links that extend beyond them (dotted arrows).

The conceptual framework takes into account various inputs that shape student behaviour, including teaching practices, course formats, curricular conditions, examination rules, and institutional norms. These inputs interact and create a dynamic and evolving educational environment, which is why the student behaviour framework operates with overlap, where certain categories of inputs

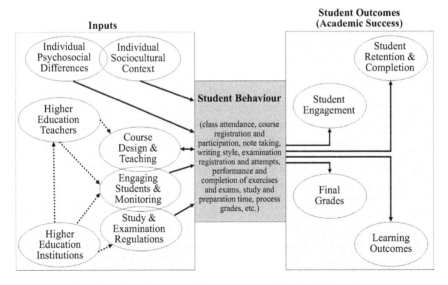

Fig. 1. The Conceptual Framework of Student Behaviour.

may share a number of characteristics. These are framed by economic approaches and draw on psychological and sociological theories. The influence of institutional governance, derived from political science perspectives, also affects the student experience. The resulting student behaviour then leads to various student outcomes as dependent variables, including learning outcomes, completion, and grades, which contribute to overall academic success. The heuristic construction of the upstream inputs and downstream student outcomes of student behaviour is illustrated next.

THE EXPLANATION OF DIFFERENCES IN STUDENT BEHAVIOUR

At a macro-level, student behaviour is influenced by governance structures, so administrative processes and operational procedures can be used as control mechanisms in higher education governance (Kleimann, 2019). Policy theory on educational institutionalism and policy convergence emphasises the role of national contexts and institutions in shaping educational policy and practice (Knill et al., 2013). Students may adapt their behaviour in response to a country's higher education policy tradition (Clark, 1983), educational policy structures, and institutional norms and rules that influence student behaviour, such as enrolment policies, academic standards or disciplinary procedures. Policy convergence theory suggests that policies in different contexts tend to converge over time due to globalisation, international benchmarking and the diffusion of best practice (Humphreys, 2002), leading to standardised expectations and practices across educational settings (e.g. Huisman & Van der Wende, 2004). However, recent research suggests that globalisation and internationalisation have little impact on the core elements of national education systems (Garritzmann & Garritzmann, 2023). National and institutional policies can therefore have a significant impact on how students engage with their studies and interact with peers and teachers.

Despite its definition as an indicator of student engagement (Macfarlane & Tomlinson, 2017; Tight, 2020), student behaviour can also be influenced by institutional agendas of student engagement. As such, policymakers and higher education institutions set behavioural expectations for students (Macfarlane & Tomlinson, 2017) and assess increases and decreases in engagement by observing student behaviour (Thomas, 2012), comparing a student's behaviour to that of others or to the student's previous behaviour (Wilson et al., 2019). From a political theory perspective, student engagement can be seen as an externally imposed agenda for government efficiency and institutional effectiveness. In terms of Foucault, it is a means of disciplining students towards conformity and desired behaviour. Institutional rules and processes, such as examinations, make it possible to regulate the student body (Foucault, 1995). In highly performative institutional cultures, student engagement is an overt manifestation of the regulated student subject, with institutions guiding student behaviour (Macfarlane & Tomlinson, 2017). An example of institutional arrangements of engagement used to change student behaviour is the gamification approach, which comes from marketing economics and works by applying game elements to non-game situations (Rivera & Garden, 2021).

Thus, while student engagement has been argued to embody student behaviour, it is also constructed to change it. Kahu (2013) highlights this lack of clear distinction between the factors that influence student engagement, its measurement and the factors that student engagement influences and suggests that engagement should be defined as an outcome. Drawing on Bryson et al. (2010), engagement is not only an outcome but also a process. They distinguish between 'engaging students', which refers to the process, and 'students engaged', which refers to the outcome. In relation to their 'engaging students' definition of student engagement, student behaviour is not part of student engagement; student behaviour is influenced by student engagement agendas. Institutions that 'engage students' lead to changes and thereby differences in student behaviour.

The underlying values and hidden curriculum of the academic field not only construct students but also regulate their behaviour (Hewson, 2018). Forms of student behaviour, such as class attendance, are influenced by institutional and contextual factors, including institutional rules, institutional norms, course design, and teaching style (Credé et al., 2010). It has been shown that the distribution of examinations and the number of examination periods in the first year, as well as fewer opportunities to repeat examinations, can have a positive effect on students' academic progress and duration (Jansen, 2004), while assessment designs with multiple attempts and timely feedback can lead to better grades (Faulconer et al., 2021). The provision of soft commitment devices, such as automatic registration for examinations, has a positive effect on participation and passing, especially for procrastinators, and leads to a lower risk of dropping out (Behlen et al., 2021; Himmler et al., 2019). Differences between higher education institutions at the level of curricula, study and examination regulations therefore lead directly to differences in observable student behaviour.

Macro-sociological theory can also be taken into account when considering adaptation to institutional rules. According to Bourdieu's (1986) concept of habitus and field, the possession of capital leads to the structural position of individuals in social space, which the habitus transforms into forms of practice and thus into unconscious patterns of action (Barlösius, 2011), which one could call behaviour. There are three types of capital: economic, social, and cultural. Economic capital includes everything that can be directly converted into money. Social capital includes the availability of certain social contacts that can be used to one's advantage. Cultural capital can be divided into material capital, such as the ownership of books and paintings; institutionalised capital, such as certificates or educational degrees; and embedded capital, such as educational aspirations, certain vocabulary and other forms of knowledge. Embedded cultural capital is rooted in the practices of social actors and is acquired through social acceptance, interaction, and shared thinking over time and through engagement with a particular habitus (Barlösius, 2011; Bourdieu, 1986). Therefore, embedded cultural capital is necessary to adapt to the rules and processes of the university field so that they can be understood and followed behaviourally

(Bourdieu & Passeron, 1977), which in turn leads to student success (DiMaggio, 1982; Jæger, 2011) or otherwise to study non-completion due to self-selection (Schmitt, 2006).

Besides the macro- and meso-perspectives on the effectors of differences in student behaviour, a number of theoretical approaches apply to the micro-level. In their theory of student development, Pascarella and Terenzini (1991) argue that structural characteristics of institutions intervene with students' pre-college characteristics such as attitudes, ethnicity, and personality. Both then influence student behaviour in the form of student interactions with socialisation agents such as faculty and peers, which in turn lead to a wide range of student outcomes in terms of student learning, cognitive and psychosocial development, satisfaction, and socio-economic status.

In contrast to the passive conception of students in higher education, the relationship between higher education institutions and students can be seen as institutions as providers and students as customers, due to the global competition for students as stakeholders (Leišytė & Westerheijden, 2013). From this point of view, students are seen as active subjects and decision-makers rather than passive objects (Hewson, 2018). From the perspective of the sociology of education, educational choices (Becker, 1993) represent trade-offs between short-term gains in terms of time spent on more enjoyable activities and long-term gains in terms of better learning outcomes. Studying in higher education presents individuals with a variety of different decision-making situations, such as how best to structure their studies, planning in which semester to take which examination, when to start preparing for examinations, etc. (Brade et al., 2019).

In the behavioural economics of education, long study periods and lack of student success are explained by behavioural biases that lead to deviations from rational decisions (Himmler et al., 2019; Koch et al., 2015). On the one hand, behavioural biases can be time-inconsistent preferences (Ericson & Laibson, 2019), which occur for actions with current costs and no current benefits, but only future returns that are considered distant. For example, the costs of successfully passing an examination (studying) are incurred immediately, while the benefits (passing the examination, better grades) are only realised in the future. Even when both costs and benefits lie in the future, e.g. registering for an examination that is scheduled to take place in four months' time, so that the learning can only take place in three months' time, this may be considered less costly than at a later point in time when the student actually has to study.

On the other hand, behavioural biases also imply limited attention, which means that tasks that are initially highly salient, such as registering for examinations and starting to study on time, become less salient over the course of a semester as the number of tasks increases, leading students to register and take examinations later, to overlook them, or to forget about them altogether (Behlen et al., 2021). In educational nudging studies in behavioural economics, which is research on changing behaviour through interventions in the form of environmental changes, late task completion is associated with procrastination (cf. Damgaard & Nielsen, 2018), which consists of both cognitive and behavioural components (Rahimi & Hall, 2021). Academic procrastination is a common and well-explained psychological concept. Approximately 80% of students tend to procrastinate to varying degrees (Fentaw et al., 2022; Steel, 2007).

Another bias that has developed its own theoretical approach is the status quo bias, known in microeconomic theory as the endowment effect. It suggests that people place a higher value on things that they own than on a similar item that they do not own (Thaler, 1980). Therefore, when faced with a complex choice, individuals do not make an active decision, but default to the status quo and passively choose the path of least resistance (Kahneman et al., 1991). Applied to higher education and student behaviour, the endowment effect explains why students have higher examination participation when the default setting for registration is changed to opt-out (cf. Behlen et al., 2022, pp. 1–60). Faulk et al. (2019) show that this concept also applies to students' endowment of credit points.

Self-regulation problems are responsible for several behavioural barriers, including limited attention and procrastination (Damgaard & Nielsen, 2017). Differences in student behaviour are therefore due to psychosocial factors such as self-control (Credé et al., 2010) and self-efficacy (Bandura, 1986). Psychological approaches draw in particular on self-determination theory (Ryan & Deci, 2000), which explains student success by personal growth, well-being and intrinsic motivation (Niemiec & Ryan, 2009). Therefore, individual psychological characteristics are suggested to play a crucial role for the behaviour of higher education students.

Not only the characteristics of the teaching staff (Kuh et al., 2004; Marlina et al., 2021), but also their educational values, practices and monitoring shape student behaviour. Teaching styles and methods can also influence and change student behaviour, especially if they are not culturally neutral (McDonald, 2014). The assignment of higher-order cognitive and academically challenging tasks, facilitation of collaborative learning activities, and diverse perspectives in the classroom emphasise greater student experience and engagement with these practices and aspects (Kuh et al., 2004).

In many ways, behaviour is influenced by social-psychological processes of comparison (Festinger, 1954). In sociology, Weber's theory of social action suggests that individuals adapt certain meaningful behaviours based on the expected behaviour of others and the subjectively assessed probabilities of success of their own actions (Weber, 1981). In this way, it may be not only institutional governance itself, but also students' perceptions of institutional governance, that influence their behaviour. For example, Dawson (2006) finds that students' awareness of monitoring techniques in online teaching and learning can change their behaviour, including their browsing behaviour, the range of topics discussed and their writing style. With regard to social reference points, students' evaluation of their own behaviour in relation to that of other students changes their behaviour. Reference points set by institutions, e.g. standard settings in examination and study processes, lead individuals to try to minimise deviations and make efforts to actually reach the reference point (Kahneman et al., 1991).

Drawing on sociological theory, Tinto's (1957, 1993) student integration model suggests that persistence in higher education is maintained not by reference points but by the commitments that students have to their course, programme and institution. These commitments are part of students' sociocultural context and are mediated by their interactions with the academic and social systems of the institution. Accordingly, students who become part of their campus academically and socially are more likely to persist in their programme, with much of this attachment coming through engagement in learning communities. Learning communities in this context are groups of students who attend seminars and courses together or otherwise engage in academic and social exchange (Chrysikos et al., 2017).

THE EFFECT OF STUDENT BEHAVIOUR ON STUDENT OUTCOMES

Student behaviour influences several factors associated with academic success. Looking at grade outcomes, studies in educational machine learning show that students' midterm performance is a large and appropriate explanatory factor for the variance in final examination performance (Chen & Ward, 2022). Regarding student behaviour in the form of class attendance, a meta-analytic review of research shows that it makes a contribution to grades that is independent of individual characteristics such as personality traits (Credé et al., 2010). In addition, students who start their examination preparation too late also tend to perform less well in their studies (Beattie et al., 2018).

Student behaviour as both an effector and an indicator of grades may seem paradoxical at first, but it becomes clear when one considers that student outcomes are never fixed during the student lifecycle and that one has to distinguish between process grades and final grades as outcomes. Academic success is process-oriented, can be assessed on and between any number of trajectories, and can vary throughout the student journey, for example in terms of drop-out intentions (Heinze, 2018). Often, it is the final state of the student outcome dimensions that defines final academic success, for example students' final grade point average. This broad definition of academic success is comparable to the definition of dropout, which can only be completed by looking at the whole life course of the individual and observing that they never re-enter higher education (cf. Tieben, 2023).

Just as course design and teaching methods influence student behaviour, so does student behaviour influence course design and teaching methods. This is not only true of the behavioural feedback that students give on tasks, which informs practitioner reflection and helps to improve course and curriculum design (Dawson, 2006). New technologies are also enabling flexible teaching strategies based on student behaviour. For example, artificial intelligence algorithms can identify homogeneous groups of students with similar student behaviour on e-learning platforms to help instructors and teachers create heterogeneous groups to improve student performance in collaborative activities (Nalli et al., 2021). In this way, student behaviour leads to variation in curriculum and teaching, which in turn changes student behaviour and ensures better learning outcomes.

Also connected with learning outcomes, such as critical thinking and grades, is student engagement in forms of educational practice (Carini et al., 2006). Kahu (2013) argues that student engagement is a student outcome that manifests as an individual psychological state consisting of affect, cognition and behaviour. Educational research shows that it is student activity rather than student engagement that is associated with student outcomes such as retention and completion rates (Thomas, 2012), which are critical to academic success. Previous research has argued that regulating student behaviour can also create student engagement, as student identity is not a fixed state (Hewson, 2018).

Organisational behaviour theory in management studies further defines (work) engagement not only as a cognitive-affective state but also as a phenomenon that manifests itself through behaviour (Balwant, 2018; Kahn, 1990). Applied to higher education, student behaviour induces student engagement and is itself one of the indicators of engaged students when compared to previous student behaviour. Drawing on Bryson et al.'s (2010) definition of student engagement, student behaviour is an effector of student engagement, linking student engagement agendas ('engaging students') to observed student engagement as outcome ('students engaged').

CONCLUSION AND DISCUSSION

In conclusion, the integrated conceptual framework of student behaviour proposed in this chapter offers a distinct perspective on the complex relationship between input characteristics and resulting educational outcomes. In contrast to existing models, the framework proposed here delves deeper into the micro-level behaviours of students in higher education settings, including digital behaviour, examination behaviour and course-taking behaviour. By incorporating these nuanced aspects of student behaviour, the model provides a more detailed understanding of how individual actions and transitions influence educational outcomes. In addition, the student behaviour framework provides interdisciplinary integration by drawing on insights from education, psychology, sociology, economics, and political science. This interdisciplinary approach allows for a comprehensive analysis of student behaviour, taking into account the multiple influences that shape students' experiences and outcomes in higher education.

The concept of student behaviour is needed as an intermediary construct because not enough different perspectives on input factors have been used to explain academic success. It is important to understand what is going on in the black box in between, and this can be made visible through the analysis of student behaviour, as it sheds light on the hidden mechanisms during the student lifecycle and thus also on trajectories. The model could therefore explain student outcomes better than models that work only with input and output variables, without treating student behaviour as a useful intermediary construct between the inflows and outflows of academic education. The student behaviour framework provides a comprehensive way of examining process characteristics, mechanisms, and dynamics during the study process and their impact on academic success in higher education. Considering study pathways as a student lifecycle adds depth to the framework, as it addresses the limitations of current analytical models (Bahr, 2013; Haas & Hadjar, 2020) and provides a conceptual tool that focuses on the bridge between entry and exit from higher education.

With the aim of encouraging researchers to unravel the underlying mechanisms of student engagement (cf. Tight, 2020), the framework also addresses a broader understanding of engagement by considering a variety of factors that contribute to variation in student behaviour in higher education. Thus, a distinction needs to be made between student engagement agendas ('engaging students'), which are an input to student behaviour, and student engagement outcomes as 'students engaged', which is often measured in the literature by student behaviour throughout the student lifecycle, but is also a static outcome from an end-of-study perspective.

The framework highlights the importance of institutional governance, the impact of which on student outcomes remains under-researched (Vossensteyn et al., 2015). It allows for a closer examination of the institutional context, moving away from the traditional line of studying individual factors towards a new paradigm of evaluating institutional governance in the study of academic success and assessing whether particular educational policies actually work. The framework can even be used as an instrument of power critique beyond the study of student success when, for example, Foucault is used to reconstruct the power structures between actors in higher education and actors in the various situations and spaces of scholarship.

By acknowledging the data-driven nature of studies of student behaviour and taking into account empirical evidence, the framework promises analytical applicability. Looking ahead, the analysis of student behaviour will become increasingly possible through new access to data, such as big data and administrative data. These types of data are closely related to the future study of student behaviour. Whereas for a long time the collection of indicators of student behaviour was only possible ethnographically, the new digital universities allow for computerised mass collection. Even in bricks-and-mortar universities, the number of digital traces is increasing significantly, for example through new teaching concepts such as the flipped classroom (cf. Dooley & Makasis, 2020), not least as a result of the switch to online teaching in the wake of the COVID-19 pandemic in the early 2020s (Lutfiani & Meria, 2022) or the encounter with the 'digital generation' (Marlina et al., 2021).

As a result of different approaches and heterogeneous perspectives on behaviour, the framework has shortcomings in the theorisation of the value and importance of individual psychosocial characteristics and sociocultural resources for student behaviour. However, the weighting of each input factor is not consistent across institutional contexts. Differences in individual psychosocial characteristics and sociocultural resources may have a greater impact on student behaviour when the institutional environment is less regulated and a smaller impact when the environment is highly regulated. For example, if students study in an institution that allows them to resit an examination that they have not passed three times, we might see differences in student behaviour (in terms of number of resits) between psychosocially different groups of students. If students study in an institution that does not allow resits of failed examinations, we cannot observe variation in student behaviour and differences by psychosocial factors; we can only observe these differences in student outcomes in terms of completion, retention, and failure.

Another limitation of the framework is its complexity. The large number of factors outlined in the model can pose practical challenges for researchers and make it difficult to operationalise and test empirically. While the integrated model provides a conceptual framework for understanding student behaviour, researchers may face challenges in translating it into concrete research designs and data collection instruments. Understanding how different inputs and aspects of student behaviour influence each other and ultimately affect student outcomes would require lengthy surveys and further extensive data collection efforts. Researchers using the model should approach it with a critical attitude, acknowledging the diversity of theoretical perspectives involved and carefully considering how they intersect and diverge in their implications for understanding student behaviour in higher education.

Despite these limitations, the framework provides a valuable starting point for theoretical exploration and empirical research in higher education. The different theoretical approaches in the literature provide a selection from which future researchers can draw, while facilitating reflection and integration of opposing positions and different schools of thought. By acknowledging its complexity and limitations, researchers can work towards refining and adapting the model to better capture the intricacies of student behaviour and its implications for educational practice and policy. In this way, the proposed heuristic conceptual framework serves as a foundation for future research efforts.

One of the key features of the model is its focus on digital behaviour, which is becoming increasingly important in modern educational settings. Furthermore, the emergence of performance measurement as a distinct research area in the higher education literature (Beerkens, 2022) has increased the emphasis on more theory-driven research on student behaviour, which is consistent with the approach and relevance of the framework. By capturing students' interactions with digital learning environments and online tools, the framework recognises the challenges and opportunities presented by technology-enhanced learning.

Although there is an emphasis on quantitative methods and computational social science due to new big data sources, the analytical agenda of the model is not intended to be limited to quantitative analyses, as qualitative research can provide valuable insights into the mechanisms underlying the observed relationships and further develop the model presented. For example, Deil-Amen and Rosenbaum (2002) show how knowledge of institutional rules can influence student behaviour. There are also forms of student behaviour that cannot be observed digitally, such as the taking of pen and paper notes during lectures, and that need to be observed through ethnographic data collection.

By complementing traditional measures with a holistic view of micro-level behaviour, student life and pathways, the concept of student behaviour can improve future studies and help develop policies to improve student success.

However, much practical application is needed to unlock the black box of student behaviour and to assess the interplay of the different dimensions. This chapter invites scholars to engage in further empirical studies and theoretical developments with the aim of refining and extending the framework for a comprehensive understanding of student behaviour in higher education.

REFERENCES

Bauer, V. A., Hönnige, C., & Jungbauer-Gans, M. (2023). Opportunities and challenges of higher education administrative data (HEAD) analysis: An empirical example from a large German university. *Qualität in der Wissenschaft*, *17*(2), 56–62.

Bahr, P. R. (2013). The deconstructive approach to understanding community college students' pathways and outcomes. *Community College Review*, *41*(2), 137–153. https://doi.org/10.1177/0091552113486341

Balwant, P. T. (2018). The meaning of student engagement and disengagement in the classroom context: Lessons from organisational behaviour. *Journal of Further and Higher Education*, *42*(3), 389–401. https://doi.org/10.1080/0309877X.2017.1281887

Bandura, A. (1986). The explanatory and predictive scope of self-efficacy theory. *Journal of Social and Clinical Psychology*, *4*(3), 359–373. https://doi.org/10.1521/jscp.1986.4.3.359

Barlösius, E. (2011). *Pierre Bourdieu. Eine Einführung*. Campus.

Beattie, G., Laliberté, J. W. P., & Oreopoulos, P. (2018). Thrivers and divers: Using non-academic measures to predict college success and failure. *Economics of Education Review*, *62*, 170–182. https://doi.org/10.1016/j.econedurev.2017.09.008

Becker, G. S. (1993). *Human capital. A theoretical and empirical analysis with special reference to education* (3rd ed.). University of Chicago Press.

Beerkens, M. (2022). An evolution of performance data in higher education governance: A path towards a 'big data' era?. *Quality in Higher Education*, *28*(1), 29–49. https://doi.org/10.1080/13538322.2021.1951451

Behlen, L., Brade, R., Himmler, O., & Jäckle, R. (2021). Verhaltensökonomisch motivierte Maßnahmen zur Sicherung des Studienerfolgs (VStud). In M. Neugebauer, H.-D. Daniel, & A. Wolter (Eds.), *Studienerfolg und Studienabbruch* (pp. 393–419). Springer.

Behlen, L., Himmler, O., & Jaeckle, R. (2022). *Can defaults change behavior when post-intervention effort is required?*. Munich Personal RePEc Archive (MPRA) Working Paper No. 113398. https://mpra.ub.uni-muenchen.de/113398/

Behr, A., Giese, M., Teguim Kamdjou, H. D., & Theune, K. (2020). Dropping out of university: A literature review. *The Review of Education*, *8*(2), 614–652.

Bourdieu, P. (1986). The forms of capital. In J. G. Richardson (Ed.), *Handbook of theory and research for the sociology of education* (pp. 241–258). Greenwood.

Bourdieu, P., & Passeron, J.-C. (1977). *Reproduction in education, society and culture*. Sage.

Bowman, N. A., & Hill, P. L. (2011). Measuring how college affects students: Social desirability and other potential biases in college student self-reported gains. *New Directions for Institutional Research*, *150*, 73–85.

Brade, R., Himmler, O., & Jäckle, R. (2019). Können Ansätze aus der Verhaltensökonomik den Studienerfolg erhöhen? Das Forschungsprojekt VStud. *Qualität in der Wissenschaft*, *13*(3/4), 108–115.

Bryson, C., Cooper, G., & Hardy, C. (2010). Reaching a common understanding of the meaning of student engagement. Paper presented at *The society for research in higher education (SRHE) conference*. Celtic Manor, Wales, 14–16 December.

Cantabella, M., Martínez-España, R., Ayuso, B., Yáñez, J. A., & Muñoz, A. (2019). Analysis of student behavior in learning management systems through a big data framework. *Future Generation Computer Systems*, *90*, 262–272. https://doi.org/10.1016/j.future.2018.08.003

Carini, R. M., Kuh, G. D., & Klein, S. P. (2006). Student engagement and student learning: Testing the linkages. *Research in Higher Education*, *47*, 1–32. https://doi.org/10.1007/s11162-005-8150-9

Chen, H., & Ward, P. (2022). Clustering students using pre-midterm behaviour data and predict their exam performance. In *Proceedings of the 15th international conference on educational data mining* (pp. 1–6). International Educational Data Mining Society.

Chinsook, K., Khajonmote, W., Klintawon, S., Sakulthai, C., Leamsakul, W., & Jantakoon, T. (2022). Big data in higher education for student behavior analytics (Big data-HE-SBA system architecture). *Higher Education Studies*, *12*(1), 105–114.

Chrysikos, A., Ahmed, E., & Ward, R. (2017). Analysis of Tinto's student integration theory in first-year undergraduate computing students of a UK higher education institution. *International Journal of Comparative Education and Development*, *19*(2/3), 97–121. https://doi.org/10.1108/IJCED-10-2016-0019

Clark, B. R. (1983). *The higher education system: Academic organization in cross-national perspective.* University of California Press.

Credé, M., Roch, S. G., & Kieszczynka, U. M. (2010). Class attendance in college: A meta-analytic review of the relationship of class attendance with grades and student characteristics. *Review of Educational Research*, *80*(2), 272–295. https://doi.org/10.3102/0034654310362998

Damgaard, M. T., & Nielsen, H. S. (2017). *The use of nudges and other behavioural approaches in education.* Publications Office of the European Union.

Damgaard, M. T., & Nielsen, H. S. (2018). Nudging in education. *Economics of Education Review*, *64*, 313–342. https://doi.org/10.1016/j.econedurev.2018.03.008

Dawson, S. (2006). The impact of institutional surveillance technologies on student behaviour. *Surveillance and Society*, *4*(1/2), 69–84.

Deil-Amen, R., & Rosenbaum, J. E. (2002). The unintended consequences of stigma-free remediation. *Sociology of Education*, 249–268. https://doi.org/10.2307/3090268

DiMaggio, P. (1982). Cultural capital and school success: The impact of status culture participation on the grades of U.S. high school students. *American Sociological Review*, *47*(2), 189–201.

Dooley, L., & Makasis, N. (2020). Understanding student behavior in a flipped classroom: Interpreting learning analytics data in the veterinary pre-clinical sciences. *Education Sciences*, *10*(10), 1–14, 260 p. https://doi.org/10.3390/educsci10100260

Ericson, K. M., & Laibson, D. (2019). Intertemporal choice. In B. D. Bernheim, S. DellaVigna, & D. Laibson (Eds.), *Handbook of behavioral economics: Foundations and applications* (Vol. 2, pp. 1–67). Elsevier. https://doi.org/10.1016/bs.hesbe.2018.12.001

Faulconer, E., Griffith, J. C., & Frank, H. (2021). If at first you do not succeed: Student behavior when provided feedforward with multiple trials for online summative assessments. *Teaching in Higher Education*, *26*(4), 586–601. https://doi.org/10.1080/13562517.2019.1664454

Faulk, L. H., Settlage, D. M., & Wollscheid, J. R. (2019). Influencing positive student behaviour using the endowment effect. *e-Journal of Business Education and Scholarship of Teaching*, *13*(1), 20–29.

Fentaw, Y., Moges, B. T., & Ismail, S. M. (2022). Academic procrastination behavior among public university students. *Education Research International*, 1–8, 1277866. https://doi.org/10.1155/2022/1277866

Festinger, L. (1954). A theory of social comparison processes. *Human Relations*, *7*(2), 117–140. https://doi.org/10.1177/001872675400700202

Foucault, M. (1995). *Discipline and punish* (2nd ed.). Vintage Books.

Fredricks, J. A., Blumenfeld, P. C., & Paris, A. H. (2004). School engagement: Potential of the concept, state of the evidence. *Review of Educational Research*, *74*(1), 59–109. https://doi.org/10.3102/00346543074001059

Garritzmann, J. L., & Garritzmann, S. (2023). Why globalization hardly affects education systems: A historical institutionalist view. In P. Mattei, X. Dumay, É. Mangez, & J. Behrend (Eds.), *The Oxford handbook of education and globalization* (pp. 554–575). Oxford University Press.

Gewinner, I. V., Hauschildt, K., Keute, A. L., Lagerstrøm, B. O., & Mandl, S. (2022). A total survey error perspective on cross-national student surveys. In G. Brandt & S. de Vogel (Eds.), *Survey-Methoden in der Hochschulforschung* (pp. 453–475). Springer VS.

Haas, C. (2022). Applying sequence analysis in higher education research: A life course perspective on study trajectories. In J. Huisman & M. Tight (Eds.), *Theory and method in higher education research* (Vol. 8, pp. 127–147). Emerald Publishing Limited. https://doi.org/10.1108/tmher

Haas, C., & Hadjar, A. (2020). Students' trajectories through higher education: A review of quantitative research. *Higher Education, 79*, 1099–1118.

Harris-Huemmert, S. (2015). Student attrition: A search for adequate definitions and initial findings from a university-wide student survey. *Qualität in der Wissenschaft, 9*(3+4), 81–86.

Heinze, D. (2018). *Die Bedeutung der Volition für den Studienerfolg: Zu dem Einfluss volitionaler Strategien der Handlungskontrolle auf den Erfolg von Bachelorstudierenden*. Springer. https://doi.org/10.1007/978-3-658-19403-1

Hewson, E. R. (2018). Students' emotional engagement, motivation and behaviour over the life of an online course: Reflections on two market research case studies. *Journal of Interactive Media in Education, 1*(10), 1–13. https://doi.org/10.5334/jime.472

Himmler, O., Jäckle, R., & Weinschenk, P. (2019). Soft commitments, reminders, and academic performance. *American Economic Journal: Applied Economics, 11*(2), 114–142.

Huisman, J., & Van der Wende, M. (2004). The EU and Bologna: Are supra- and international initiatives threatening domestic agendas?. *European Journal of Education, 39*(3), 349–357. https://doi.org/10.1111/j.1465-3435.2004.00188.x

Humphreys, P. (2002). Europeanisation, globalisation and policy transfer in the European Union: The case of telecommunications. *Convergence: The International Journal of Research into New Media Technologies, 8*(2), 52–79. https://doi.org/10.1177/135485650200800204

Jæger, M. M. (2011). Does cultural capital really affect academic achievement? New evidence from combined sibling and panel data. *Sociology of Education, 84*(4), 281–298.

Janosik, S. M., & Gehring, D. D. (2003). The impact of the Clery Campus Crime Disclosure Act on student behavior. *Journal of College Student Development, 44*(1), 81–91. https://doi.org/10.1353/csd.2003.0005

Jansen, E. P. (2004). The influence of the curriculum organization on study progress in higher education. *Higher Education, 47*, 411–435.

Johnson, J. A. (2014). The ethics of big data in higher education. *International Review of Information Ethics, 21*, 3–10. https://doi.org/10.29173/irie365

Kadoić, N., & Oreški, D. (2018). Analysis of student behavior and success based on logs in Moodle. In *2018 41st International convention on information and communication technology, electronics and microelectronics (MIPRO)* (pp. 0654–0659). IEEE.

Kahn, W. A. (1990). Psychological conditions of personal engagement and disengagement at work. *Academy of Management Journal, 33*(4), 692–724. https://doi.org/10.2307/256287

Kahneman, D., Knetsch, J. L., & Thaler, R. H. (1991). Anomalies: The endowment effect, loss aversion, and status quo bias. *The Journal of Economic Perspectives, 5*(1), 193–206.

Kahu, E. (2013). Framing student engagement in higher education. *Studies in Higher Education, 38*(5), 758–773. https://doi.org/10.1080/03075079.2011.598505

Kleimann, B. (2019). (German) Universities as multiple hybrid organizations. *Higher Education, 77*, 1085–1102. https://doi.org/10.1007/s10734-018-0321-7

Knill, C., Vögtle, E. M., & Dobbin, M. (2013). *Hochschulpolitische Reformen im Zuge des Bologna-Prozesses: Eine vergleichende Analyse von Konvergenzdynamiken im OECD-Raum*. Springer.

Koch, A., Nafziger, J., & Nielsen, H. S. (2015). Behavioral economics of education. *Journal of Economic Behavior & Organization, 115*, 3–17. https://doi.org/10.1016/j.jebo.2014.09.005

Kuh, G. D., Laird, T. F. N., & Umbach, P. D. (2004). Aligning faculty activities & student behavior: Realizing the promise of greater expectations. *Liberal Education, 90*(4), 24–31.

Leišytė, L., & Westerheijden, D. F. (2013). Students as stakeholders in quality assurance in eight European countries. *The Quality of Higher Education, 10*, 12–27.

Lutfiani, N., & Meria, L. (2022). Utilization of big data in educational technology research. *International Transactions on Education Technology, 1*(1), 73–83. https://doi.org/10.33050/itee.v1i1.198

Macfarlane, B., & Tomlinson, M. (2017). Critiques of student engagement. *Higher Education Policy, 30*, 5–21. https://doi.org/10.1057/s41307-016-0027-3

Marlina, E., Tjahjadi, B., & Ningsih, S. (2021). Factors affecting student performance in e-learning: A case study of higher educational institutions in Indonesia. *The Journal of Asian Finance, Economics and Business, 8*(4), 993–1001. https://doi.org/10.13106/jafeb.2021.vol8.no4.0993

McBroom, J., Yacef, K., & Koprinska, I. (2020). DETECT: A hierarchical clustering algorithm for behavioural trends in temporal educational data. In *Artificial intelligence in education: 21st International conference, AIED 2020, Ifrane, Morocco, July 6–10, 2020, Proceedings, Part I* (Vol. 12163, pp. 374–385). https://doi.org/10.1007/978-3-030-52237-7_30

McDonald, I. (2014). Supporting international students in UK higher education institutions. *Perspectives: Policy and Practice in Higher Education*, *18*(2), 62–65. https://doi.org/10.1080/13603108.2014.909900

Nalli, G., Amendola, D., Perali, A., & Mostarda, L. (2021). Comparative analysis of clustering algorithms and Moodle plugin for creation of student heterogeneous groups in online university courses. *Applied Sciences*, *11*(13), 1–21, 5800 p. https://doi.org/10.3390/app11135800

Neugebauer, M., Heublein, U., & Daniel, A. (2019). Studienabbruch in Deutschland: Ausmaß, Ursachen, Folgen, Präventionsmöglichkeiten. *Zeitschrift für Erziehungswissenschaft*, *22*, 1025–1046. https://doi.org/10.1007/s11618-019-00904-1

Niemiec, C. P., & Ryan, R. M. (2009). Autonomy, competence, and relatedness in the classroom: Applying self-determination theory to educational practice. *Theory and Research in Education*, *7*(2), 133–144. https://doi.org/10.1177/1477878509104318

Pascarella, E. T., & Terenzini, P. T. (1991). *How college affects students: Findings and insights from twenty years of research*. Jossey-Bass.

Prinsloo, P., & Slade, S. (2016). Big data, higher education and learning analytics: Beyond justice, towards an ethics of care. In B. K. Daniel (Ed.), *Big data and learning analytics in higher education: Current theory and practice* (pp. 109–124). Springer. https://doi.org/10.1007/978-3-319-06520-5

Rahimi, S., & Hall, N. C. (2021). Why are you waiting? Procrastination on academic tasks among undergraduate and graduate students. *Innovative Higher Education*, *46*, 759–776. https://doi.org/10.1007/s10755-021-09563-9

Rivera, E. S., & Garden, C. L. P. (2021). Gamification for student engagement: A framework. *Journal of Further and Higher Education*, *45*(7), 999–1012. https://doi.org/10.1080/0309877X.2021.1875201

Ryan, R. M., & Deci, E. L. (2000). Self-determination theory and the facilitation of intrinsic motivation, social development, and well-being. *American Psychologist*, *55*(1), 68–78. https://doi.org/10.1037/0003-066X.55.1.68

Schmitt, L. (2006). *Symbolische Gewalt und Habitus-Struktur-Konflikte. Entwurf einer Heuristik zur Analyse und Bearbeitung von Konflikten*. Universität Marburg, Zentrum für Konfliktforschung.

Senior, C., Howard, C., Reddy, P., Clark, R., & Lim, M. (2012). The relationship between student-centred lectures, emotional intelligence, and study teams: A social telemetry study with mobile telephony. *Studies in Higher Education*, *37*(8), 957–970. https://doi.org/10.1080/03075079.2011.556719

Shepard, L., Rehrey, G., & Groth, D. (2021). Faculty engagement with learning analytics: Advancing a student success culture in higher education. In M. Shah, S. Kift, & L. Thomas (Eds.), *Student retention and success in higher education* (pp. 89–107). Palgrave Macmillan. https://doi.org/10.1007/978-3-030-80045-1_5

Slade, S., & Prinsloo, P. (2013). Learning analytics: Ethical issues and dilemmas. *American Behavioral Scientist*, *57*(10), 1509–1528. https://doi.org/10.1177/0002764213479366

Steel, P. (2007). The nature of procrastination: A meta-analytic and theoretical review of quintessential self-regulatory failure. *Psychological Bulletin*, *133*(1), 65–94. https://doi.org/10.1037/0033-2909.133.1.65

Thaler, R. (1980). Toward a positive theory of consumer choice. *Journal of Economic Behavior & Organization*, *1*(1), 39–60.

Thomas, L. (2012). *Building student engagement and belonging in higher education at a time of change*. Paul Hamlyn Foundation.

Tieben, N. (2023). Dropping out of higher education in Germany: Using retrospective life course data to determine dropout rates and destinations of non-completers. In S. Weinert, G. J. Blossfeld, & H. P. Blossfeld (Eds.), *Education, competence development and career trajectories. Methodology of educational measurement and assessment* (pp. 225–248). Springer. https://doi.org/10.1007/978-3-031-27007-9_10

Tight, M. (2020). Student retention and engagement in higher education. *Journal of Further and Higher Education, 44*(5), 689–704. https://doi.org/10.1080/0309877X.2019.1576860

Tinto, V. (1975). Dropout from higher education: A theoretical synthesis of recent research. *Review of Educational Research, 45*(1), 89–125. https://doi.org/10.3102/00346543045001089

Tinto, V. (1993). *Leaving college: Rethinking the causes and cures of student attrition* (2nd ed.). University of Chicago Press.

Vossensteyn, H., Kottmann, A., Jongbloed, B., Kaiser, F., Cremonini, L., Stensaker, B., & Wollscheid, S. (2015). *Dropout and completion in higher education in Europe: Main report.* Luxembourg Publications Office.

Weber, M. (1981). Some categories of interpretive sociology. *The Sociological Quarterly, 22*(2), 151–180.

Wilson, C., Broughan, C., & Marselle, M. (2019). A new framework for the design and evaluation of a learning institution's student engagement activities. *Studies in Higher Education, 44*(11), 1931–1944. https://doi.org/10.1080/03075079.2018.1469123

Witteveen, D., & Attewell, P. (2021). Delayed time-to-degree and post-college earnings. *Research in Higher Education, 62*, 230–257. https://doi.org/10.1007/s11162-019-09582-8

Wollscheid, S., & Hovdhaugen, E. (2021). Study success policy patterns in higher education regimes: More similarities than differences?. *Higher Education Policy, 34*, 499–519. https://doi.org/10.1057/s41307-019-00147-z

BECOMING RHIZOME: DELEUZE AND GUATTARI'S RHIZOME AS THEORY AND METHOD

Louise Drumm

Edinburgh Napier University, UK

ABSTRACT

This chapter explores Deleuze and Guattari's rhizome as a multifaceted approach within educational research, suggesting it as an alternative way of mapping complexities, limiting structures and messiness which may not always be surfaced in more traditional theoretical frameworks, methods, and methodologies. Despite its potential to enrich higher education scholarship through non-linear and interconnected perspectives, adoption has been hindered by the perceptions of its dense philosophical language and ideas and the fear of 'doing it wrong'. By offering a primer on rhizome theory and its potential for methodological and theoretical frameworks, this chapter seeks to demystify it for scholars new to Deleuze and Guattari, acknowledging and building upon previous work in this field. A case study illustrates the rhizome's capacity to challenge traditional epistemological assumptions, presenting a more holistic and connected view of teaching with technologies in universities. The chapter concludes with a critical discussion on the limitations of rhizome theory and suggests opportunities for its broader application in higher education research. This exploration recommends rhizome's potential in reflecting the dynamic, complex nature of educational scholarship and practices.

Keywords: Rhizome; Deleuze; Guattari; rhizoanalysis; philosophy

Deleuze and Guattari (1988) propose the rhizome as a concept to understand the world which challenges traditional linear and hierarchical modes of thought. It has been put to work in education research in the decades since they wrote and lectured together about this multiplicitous and frequently dense philosophy. Yet, it is often still viewed as controversial (Fenwick et al., 2011a) and indeed with fear of not doing it 'right' (Strom, 2017), so calls for rhizome-infused research have mostly not resulted in more widespread uptake. Some well-intentioned work promoting the rhizome may have backfired in its purpose by reproducing elitist and inaccessible language found in the original works by Deleuze and Guattari. Undoubtedly, there is a balance to be struck between accessibility, on the one hand, and the rich complexity to be found in the rhizome, on the other hand. This chapter offers the reader multiple routes into the rhizome (as theory, philosophy, and method), pointing the curious scholar towards its affordances of alternative approaches to conventional methods, methodologies and theoretical frameworks, while also acknowledging issues and limitations.

While perhaps daunting for those new to Deleuze and Guattari's work, and possibly oversimplified for those well-versed in their work, the chapter starts with a modest primer in rhizome theory, followed by an overview of where it might sit as a theoretical framework and method in higher education research. The chapter continues with an appraisal of the debates about rhizome's potential use within educational research and the epistemological considerations. A case study follows which maps how rhizome theory infected and re-shaped a research project and brought a critical eye to its philosophical underpinnings. Briefly, it will discuss: (a) how rhizome probed traditional epistemological and ontological assumptions behind qualitative educational research methods; (b) how rhizome theory and methods allowed for a more comprehensive, less structured picture of teaching practice to be viewed and analysed, and (c) rhizome as a way of understanding the research process itself, especially in contrast to the static nature of how research is represented in text.

The chapter will conclude with a critical discussion, including limitations of the rhizome, and recommendations for how higher education scholarship could benefit from its wider use.

A RHIZOME PRIMER

Deleuze and Guattari's rhizome can be described and applied in multiple ways, but one starting position is to see it as a theory; that is as a framework or model for understanding knowledge, culture, society and various forms of organisation to varying degrees of abstraction. Within that understanding, the rhizome is imbued with a philosophical position which challenges traditional Western thought. As such, the rhizome has been called a philosophy (or more accurately, *part* of Deleuze and Guattari's philosophy), a theory, a conceptual framework and a method. In calling it 'rhizome theory' here, I do not wish to conflate the purpose of each of these important aspects of scholarship, but rather to try to capture the multiple levels – from the highly abstract to the applied – of scholarship where rhizome can be put to work.

Taking inspiration from the botanical rootstalk, this element of Deleuze and Guattari's (1988) philosophy seeks out and celebrates organic and experimental growth which can, and does, connect with anything. At every turn, the rhizome challenges any assumptions that there is a centre, from which everything else derives, or that binaries are the only natural order. Instead, the rhizome has no centre, adapts to its context, never stays still nor reaches its 'potential'. As with a map, it can be entered and exited at any point. The rhizome is juxtaposed with the idea of the *tree*. This *arborescence*, as they term it, is seen as the limiting structure behind traditional Western thought, which is characterised by hierarchical growth from a central root or trunk, reproduction through binary division to create branches and is only capable of tracing a delimited, prescribed journey. As such, rhizome is a challenge to individualistic, patriarchal and colonising thought.

Their work, *A Thousand Plateaus* (1988), is recognised as the volume in which they refine and provide most examples of how rhizome may manifest. However, it is also a dense, erudite and, at times inaccessible text (Harris, 2016). Taking St. Pierre's counsel on how to read their work may help:

> But if we keep reading, the concepts begin to pile up and wash over us, producing a jamming effect that infiltrates and destroys the being we were told was real so we might be ready for another image of thought. That is the lure of their work, their invitation - thinking differently. Being different. St. Pierre (2016, p. 1,082)

Helpfully, they enumerate six principles of the rhizome in their first chapter, itself a seemingly 'un-rhizomatic' thing to do (see Strom, 2017), but typical of their movement in and out of rhizomatic forms:

1. and 2. *'Principles of connection and heterogeneity*: any point of a rhizome can be connected to anything other, and must be' (Deleuze & Guattari, 1988, p. 7). The nature of the rhizome means that as it grows, it endlessly makes connections to itself and to other entities which are different from itself.
3. *The Principle of multiplicity:* A multiplicity cannot be reduced or divided into a single unit. Therefore, the positions of subjectivity or objectivity are incompatible with being rhizomatic:

> It is only when the multiple is effectively treated as a substantive, "multiplicity", that it ceases to have any relation to the One as subject or object, natural or spiritual reality, image and world. Multiplicities are rhizomatic, and expose arborescent pseudomultiplicities for what they are. There is no unity to serve as a pivot in the object, or to divide in the subject. (p. 8)

4. *The Principle of asignifying rupture:* 'A rhizome may be broken, shattered at a given spot, but it will start up again on one of its old lines, or on new lines' (p. 9). Unlike the *tree*, the rhizome can grow successfully from these breakages. However, the rhizome is in constant productive dialogue with the *tree*; indeed, the rhizome can contain *arborescent* properties:

> Every rhizome contains lines of segmentarity according to which it is stratified, territorialized, organized, signified, attributed, etc., as well as lines of deterritorialization down which it constantly flees. There is a rupture in the rhizome whenever segmentary lines explode into a line of flight, but the line of flight is part of the rhizome. (p. 8)

This endless connectedness makes dualist or binary thinking impossible:

> These lines always tie back to one another. That is why one can never posit a dualism or a dichotomy, even in the rudimentary form of the good and the bad. (p. 8)

5. and 6. *The Principles of cartography* and *decalcomania*: 'a rhizome is not amenable to any structural or generative model. It is a stranger to any idea of genetic axis or deep structure' (p. 12). The logic of the *tree* is a sequence of growth along a pre-determined path with a definite endpoint. The rhizome does not follow such a path but forges its own pathway:

> What distinguishes the map from the tracing is that it is entirely oriented toward an experimentation in contact with the real[...] The map is open and connectable in all of its dimensions; it is detachable, reversible, susceptible to constant modification. It can be torn, reversed, adapted to any kind of mounting, reworked by an individual, group, or social formation[...] Perhaps one of the most important characteristics of the rhizome is that it always has multiple entryways[...] The map has to do with performance, whereas the tracing always involves an alleged "competence". (pp. 12–13)

Deleuze and Guattari employ many other images, stories and terminology from an eclectic range of literature, art and history to portray the rhizome in different contexts. Like the rhizome itself, there are links out to many of their other concepts contained in their other writings. The following is a selection of a few which may offer the researcher a 'way in' to the rhizome, but it is by no means comprehensive of all their works.

A rhizomatic conception of unbounded fluid space, *smooth space*, is made up 'of intensities constructed through a proliferation of connections' (Roy, 2003, p. 73). *Smooth* space allows unfettered movement from one point to another where movement itself is more important than the arrival. *Becoming* is such movement, simultaneously *deterritorialising* (becoming rhizome) and *reterritorialising* (*becoming arborescent* or tree-like). Deleuze and Guattari present non-urban sites, like the sea or a field as smooth space:

> A field, a heterogeneous smooth space, is wedded to a very particular type of multiplicity: nonmetric, acentered, rhizomatic multiplicities that occupy space without "counting" it and can "be explored only by legwork". (1988, p. 371)

Striated space, on the other hand, is structured and hierarchical, where movement is regulated and defined by arrival. In contrast to *smooth* space, Deleuze and Guattari use urban imagery: 'sedentary space is *striated*, by walls, enclosures, and roads between enclosures' (p. 381). *Smooth* and *striated* spaces are not separate physical locations, but forces which are acting and interacting within spaces. Therefore, *smooth* space can be *reterritorialised* into *striated* space and vice versa.

Smooth space is seen as the habitat of the *nomad*, a figure used frequently in *A Thousand Plateaus* to stand for pure rhizomatic *becoming*. The *nomad*, who is self-sufficient, sits outside ordered society and operates organically and efficiently, regardless of boundaries or territories. The *nomad* forges their own pathways experimentally. In contrast to the *nomad* is the *Roman Empire* and moving between the two is the *barbarian*:

> On one side, we have the rigid segmentarity of the Roman Empire, with its center of resonance and periphery, its State, its *pax romana*, its geometry, its camps, its *limes* (boundary lines). Then, on the horizon, there is an entirely different kind of line, the line of the nomads who come

in off the steppes, venture a fluid and active escape, sow deterritorialization everywhere, launch flows whose quanta heat up and are swept along by a Stateless war machine. The migrant barbarians are indeed between the two: they come and go, cross and recross frontiers, pillage and ransom, but also integrate themselves and reterritorialize. At times they will subside into the empire, assigning themselves a segment of it, becoming mercenaries or confederates, settling down, occupying land or carving out their own State (the wise Visigoths). At other times, they will go over to the nomads, allying with them, becoming indiscernible (the brilliant Ostrogoths). (pp. 222–223)

Thus, the *Roman Empire* is a regulating force, concerned with boundaries, territories, responsibility, and hierarchy. The *barbarian* plunders the formal system when useful to them, exploits it, even attacks it, then assimilates into it as it suits them, or, alternatively, reintegrates into nomadic life. As with the rhizome, Deleuze and Guattari do not set these conceptualisations in opposition – like the rhizome is not *against* the *arborescent* tree – but in a sort of uneasy entanglement, with movement between free and *smooth* spaces into bound *striated* space not only possible, but necessary.

'THINKING DIFFERENTLY' IN HIGHER EDUCATION RESEARCH

Informed as it is by many other disciplines, higher educational research has been viewed as fragmented in approaches (Macfarlane, 2012), though representation of theories has been shown to be improving in a slowly maturing field (Hamann & Kosmützky, 2021; Macfarlane, 2022; Tight, 2019, 2023). Research in this area tends to operate within silos, sometimes seemingly being conducted without the knowledge of alternative methods and conceptions of research (Tight, 2019) or even what ontological and epistemological stances accompany proscribed methods (St. Pierre, 2016). Understandably, transdisciplinarity informs much higher education research, with researchers moving into the field from elsewhere and bringing with them the philosophies and methodologies of their home disciplines (Tight, 2014). Publications such as this book series have made strides in assembling potential approaches and shedding light on the rich possibilities open to researchers. Yet the broader swathe of higher education research published year on year continues to be dominated by a narrow range of methods, rare use of theoretical frameworks (Tight, 2020) and a seeming reluctance to engage with theory (Kinchin & Gravett, 2022). This is not to say the methods, particularly quantitative ones, are not appropriate for exploring certain research questions. However, the acknowledged 'messiness' of education practices (Jones, 2011) can often be more fully explored within looser, more open paradigms, and the rhizome has been previously proposed as just such a means to 'open up' scholarly inquiry (McKay et al., 2014).

The rhizome can serve as a counterpoint to some of the methodological strictures which come with mimicking positivist claims for truth (Richardson & St. Pierre, 2008) or as Oliver puts it, the misapplication of the scientific method (2016). This situates the rhizome as a method within post-structural (Lather, 1993) and post-qualitative (Lather & St. Pierre, 2013) spaces which require researchers to 'operate within and against tradition' (p. 629). Within higher education, many educational and pedagogical theories and methods are rooted in linear and hierarchical models which simplify the complexity of educational phenomena, leading to reductive understandings of learning and teaching. The rhizome offers the researcher principles to guide how to conduct inquiries, organise information, and understand relationships in a manner that reflects the non-linear, interconnected and multiplicitous nature of reality. Rhizomatic methods may, on the surface, look similar to other methods but are undertaken with the purpose of opening up nuanced and holistic understandings which acknowledge the complexity and multiplicity of pathways through educational fields of inquiry, and are aligned with epistemological and ontological positions coherent with Deleuze and Guattari's philosophy.

As a theoretical framework, the rhizome can provide a context which allows for the flow of ideas across different areas, including disciplinary boundaries, which could overcome the lack of intradisciplinary communication and insights. With its emphasis on decentring dominant hierarchies and structures, the rhizome can be put to work alongside critical theories which challenge and seek change in existing practices and knowledge in higher education, for example decolonising work, student co-construction of the curriculum, and critical pedagogies. The interplay of process-bound activities and informal agents within higher education can be reflected within the rhizome's *striated* and *smooth* spaces; formal structures and informal practices can be acknowledged and recognised as tree-like and rhizome-like respectively. Moving understanding beyond cause and effect, rhizome's emphasis on interconnectedness allows for the complex interplay of various factors, some of which may be informal and previously unacknowledged or invisible. It can also account for a holistic understanding of education, especially learning which happens informally or outwith quantifiable spaces with metricised outputs. Learning, and indeed teaching, can occur in spaces which are not classrooms and between actors who may not hold roles formally ascribed to 'learner' or 'teacher'.

While rhizome theory can provide an alternative lens, not in opposition to, but in juxtaposition to other more established approaches to researching higher education, treading this balance is not straightforward nor without issues, as will be discussed later. However, taking Deleuze and Guattari's own recommendation to 'plug-in' to see 'what works', thinking and analysis can pursue exploratory lines. Mazzei and Jackson's frame this methodological approach so that "theory and data 'constitute one another and in doing so resist (over) simplification'" (2012 quoted in Nelson, 2017, p. 186); in other words, the data collected influence theoretical understanding, and vice versa, with mutual enrichment. With thoughtful use, rhizome theory may provide an approach which is reflective of the complex, dynamic and interconnected nature of scholarship in higher education.

THE THEORETICAL FRAMEWORK OF THE RHIZOME

Like the subterranean weed that it is, rhizome theory and its permutations have no beginning and no end in how they can infiltrate scholarly work. In line with

Hamann and Kosmützky's proposal of 'theory work' as a craft which needs to be illuminated (2021), the rhizome may be 'a small machine' which is 'plugged in' to 'think differently' in a discrete area, or *lines of flight* connecting points of difference with each other, or rhizomatic and *nomadic* perspectives on research itself (Brown & Leigh, 2018). As a research philosophy in higher education, the rhizome can be put to work as an epistemology which, for example, challenges hierarchical and Western understandings of knowledge. It chimes with Haraway's 'antagonistic dualisms' (2007) and post-humanist thought which counter the valorising of the individual and subjective, and Platonic binaries and dualisms which perpetuate patriarchal and colonial views of the world. As such, to attempt to insert it into Burrell and Morgan's somewhat *arborescent* categorisation of paradigms (1994), the rhizome may sit within both social theory paradigms of regulation or radical change, i.e. it can be put to work to map the status quo of 'what is' or it can challenge and activate towards emancipatory practices.

Rhizomatic understandings of the research process itself can provide the educational researcher with forms for developing research questions which do not assume dichotomies or orderly underlying structures. The field of higher education can therefore be viewed as an *assemblage* (another word which manifests rhizome) of *smooth* and *striated* spaces, constantly *becoming*, as learners, academics and administrators move through and across boundaries. Data can be understood as *multiplicities*, with no unifying or essentialist principle to be interpreted though an objective eye of the researcher. Indeed, differences within data are to be welcomed and connected to one another. The choice for the researcher is how far to allow rhizomatic approaches to *deterritorialise* research conventions, and when to stay within, or return (*reterritorialise*) to, the familiar ground of *striated* tree-like spaces underpinned by research traditions. Reading a map can take experience and skill, so there is an argument to say that going 'full rhizome' risks alienating audiences which are less familiar with Deleuze and Guattari's work and terminology. For the higher education researcher, moving knowingly between research structures and *lines of flight*, while observing philosophical and methodological coherence may prove challenging.

Of the practical applications of rhizome, rhizomatic analysis or 'rhizoanalysis' can be found in higher education research (Honan & Sellers, 2006; McKay et al., 2014; Sellers, 2015; Strom & Martin, 2013). This takes Deleuze and Guattari's adage that 'any point of a rhizome can be connected to anything other and must be' (1988, p. 7) and implements it as data analysis. However, detailed accounts in the literature of what this looks like in practice are few and most argue that formulating protocols and processes for rhizoanalysis is itself impossible (Honan & Sellers, 2006). Indeed, Lather states, 'This inquiry cannot be tidily described in textbooks or handbooks. There is no methodological instrumentality to be unproblematically learnt. In this methodology-to-come, we begin to do it differently wherever we are in our projects' (2013, p. 635). Cumming (2015) recognises the difficulties of rhizoanalysis when there is a lack of models which can be followed, instead outlining her own reflexive examples to fill in the gaps. Offering transparency in lieu of procedures is a common approach (Honan & Sellers, 2006; McKay et al., 2014; Sellers, 2015; Strom & Martin, 2013). The case study within this chapter is offered in a similar vein, as a 'light touch' rhizoanalysis to elucidate rather than mandate.

A WORD ON VOCABULARY

Deleuze and Guattari's works provide a vocabulary palette which affords the scholar opportunities to express and interrogate their thinking through and even against the rhizome. This jargon can be challenging for both writer and reader (therefore the key terms which may cause the reader to pause have been italicised in this chapter). In their original writings in French, they co-opt existing terms and spin them into an adjacent meaning. This can be further complicated through translation from the original French, where approximations add another layer of obscurity. There are no shortcuts through this difficulty other than following St. Pierre's advice to let it wash over us. We can also make use of multiple sources to connect multiple points of connection to aid understanding and the judicious use of works such as the Deleuze Dictionary (Parr, 2010) even though some may argue its existence is 'not very Deleuzian'! Questioning and reflecting on academic conventions is no bad thing, so even if a choice is made ultimately to not go 'full rhizome' in order to make work more within reach of an early career researcher (and their PhD examiners) and accessible to a wider audience, the rhizome can be broken off and left to sit dormant within work, laying a seed of an idea which may later sprout for the reader. This is not to say that rhizome-informed terminology can be liberally sprinkled through a work to make it 'rhizomatic', but I maintain that readers and researchers/writers are also rhizome and should be seen as constantly in motion through ideas and positionalities.

It is none-the-less challenging for the scholar. For example, within a philosophical position aligned with rhizome theory, there is an understanding that all is continuation and there is nothing 'new' to be discovered, no interpretation to be made; within this context, the research convention of 'findings' does not stack up. The common label 'Findings' for a section of writing was rejected by Honan and Sellers (2006), Grellier (2013), and Strom and Martin (2013) for this very reason. Yet, there are also claims for rhizoanalysis that are represented in texts which unproblematically include sections called 'findings', such as work by Wohlwend and Handsfield (2012). Is this doing Deleuze 'wrong'? There are numerous trip hazards when making claims for rhizomatic approaches. For example, Deleuze and Guattari rejected the idea of representation which separated words and their meanings as observed by St. Pierre (2016), who makes a robust argument against qualitative methods which make claims for representation or lack of understanding of the 'transcendental empiricism' (p. 1,081) of employing the rhizome. Indeed, Deleuze and Guattari pathologise the quest for meaning as 'interpretosis'. Once the rhizomatic thread is pulled on the vocabulary conventions for describing what is done in educational research, the familiar methods of coding, interpretive inquiry, and thematic analysis and categorization (that which we are 'well trained in' according to St. Pierre (2016)) all fall away, leaving researchers without methods nor a means to describe them.

I take the position that getting to grips with rhizome is like stepping through a never-ending series of threshold concepts (Meyer & Land, 2005); every portal into Deleuze and Guattari's ideas is irreversibly transformational, albeit sometimes painful. However, inhabiting a pure 'rhizome' state is impossible, as there is, and should always be, movement through liminality. Some of that movement is incremental, just as Deleuze and Guattari often start with dualisms to step beyond them into pluralistic understandings which *deterritorialise* dualism. As Strom (2017) eloquently argues, there are times when being un-rhizomatic is very 'Deleuzian'.

Finally, rhizome can extend into the presentation and communication of higher education research. Employing the principle of 'no beginning and no end', formats and structural conventions for writings such as articles, books and theses can be upended, with readers invited to enter at will through any point 'as if a map'. Providing a key can offer the uninitiated reader a lifeline, but presenting scholarly work in this way can reconfigure the author–reader relationship, distributing agency back upon the reader, connecting them onwards to Deleuze and Guattari's original works. It is not only structure which can be upended by a rhizomatic presentation but also modalities and genres like poetry (Charteris et al., 2019). Why must we represent research through text? The growing creative methods movement has tapped into such approaches, some explicitly to rhizome theory (de Vries et al., 2023; Honan & Sellers, 2006).

A LITERATURE REVIEW ON RHIZOME THEORY IN EDUCATION

In recent years, examples of rhizoanalysis have been employed to examine the messy complexity of students' experiences of transitions into university (Gravett, 2019; Gravett & Winstone, 2021; Taylor & Harris-Evans, 2018). Gravett (2019) suggests that, unlike thematic or discourse analysis, rhizomatic analysis does not aim to identify patterns nor collapse complexity, but instead allows a focus on the multiplicities of 'hot spots' of interest. Taylor and Harris-Evans (2018) draw more heavily on the imagery and language of rhizome theory to reconceptualise transitions away from students fitting into pre-existing structures, but into assemblages which incorporate a holistic account of elements in space and time. In more recent work, Gravett and Winstone (2021) connect rhizome theorisations of student transitions with Meyer and Land's threshold concepts (2005) to deepen understanding of their diverse and rich experiences through troublesome, liminal and *becoming* lenses.

Smith McGloin (2021) examines doctoral journeys through mapping students' reflective diaries to 'moorings, spaces and rhizomes', combining Deleuze and Guattari's work with Sheller and Urry's (2006) mobilities paradigm although the article itself demonstrates little or no follow-through on using rhizome theory for analysis, discussion or conceptualisation, having only cited it as a paradigm that was used. This is not uncommon, perhaps as multiple paradigms must compete for space within constricted word counts.

CASE STUDY: RHIZOME THEORY TO MAP THEORY AND PRACTICE IN TEACHING WITH DIGITAL TECHNOLOGIES AT UNIVERSITIES

The case study presented here concerns a qualitative research project on teaching with digital technologies in universities in Scotland and Ireland, specifically questioning the role of theory in these practices (Drumm, 2015, 2019). Rhizome theory was originally conceived as an overarching theoretical framework to conceptualise the complex relationships between lecturers, technologies, teaching practices, and theories of learning and technology. However, once inserted into the project, the rhizome grew, weed-like, infiltrating aspects of the research, presenting challenges and opportunities such as

- problematising dichotomies found in this field such as theory/practice, digital/human, online/in-person, novice/expert user, and good/bad uses of technology,
- crosscutting connections and questioning hierarchies between theories and other theories and practices with practices,
- enabling a philosophical position on the nature of what is 'real' and what is 'knowable' within the context of the field and placing it within the post-structuralist tradition,
- as means to map how lecturers create *lines of flight* from institutionally sanctioned teaching methods and technologies, into innovative or subversive digital education practices to benefit student learning,
- a method of assembling, analysing and connecting data, while recognising the multiplicities inherent in the data through a 'light-touch' rhizoanalysis, and
- questioning how to present the research, specifically the static, structured and linear conventions of text vs the fluid and dynamic nature of the topic.

While I am not claiming this research as 'fully' rhizomatic, the idea of presenting it as a case study here is to demonstrate how the project moved into, and out of, the rhizome. It is just this interaction between conventions (methods, terminology, and academic writing) and rhizome which could be seen as more rhizomatic than 'pure' rhizome, as in Strom's (2017) words, 'Although lines of flight are always fleeting and will be recaptured by the molar line, they shuffle normative systems, structures, or discourses and thus can reshape the status quo in unpredictable ways' (p. 6). The result, in both process and product, was a balancing act between observing scholarly conventions to ensure validity, readability, and accessibility of the work, while maintaining rhizomatic congruence (itself something of an oxymoron when one considered it is a philosophy of difference!). As a text, the nature of academic writing about research is linear. It flows hierarchically, building an argument through successive elements and evidence. As a book, *A Thousand Plateaus* eschews a traditional linear framework and instructs the reader to enter the text at any point with multiple possibilities of reader engagement. Some publications employing rhizomatic methodologies for the analysis of teaching have re-framed the linear language of scholarship into less *arborescent* terms (Sellers & Gough, 2010; Strom & Martin, 2013). Braver scholars than I have claimed to have written a rhizomatic PhD thesis (Honan & Sellers, 2006; Sellers, 2015) complete with poetry and art. This was not such a piece of work.

Discourses about, for example, theory and practice are steeped in terminology which imply underlying, perhaps even determining structures: e.g. theory 'underpinning practice' as explored at the end of this chapter. As discussed earlier, research conventions, methods and terminology such as interviews, interpretation or presenting 'findings' can be problematic due to accompanying essentialist assumptions which contradict, not just rhizomatic thinking but also ontological and epistemological positions (St. Pierre, 2016). Yet there is a dearth of ways to communicate alternative approaches which readily trip off the tongue and do not require more explanation than they provide clarity. As a result, I find myself resorting to conventional terminology, but do so with circumspection. Nevertheless, the strength in a rhizomatic approach is not in its opposition to linear *arborescence*, but in its coexistence with it. The rhizome is dependent on the existence of the tree in order to define itself in juxtaposition to it.

Rather than talking to ourselves, I favour inviting in readers who may not be familiar with rhizome theory, whereas a more post-qualitative approach could, as Greene (2013) posits, result in loss of systematicity and clarity of communication. I acknowledge that not all *lines of flight* were pursued (this would be impossible), although I have, in my experimental use of rhizoanalysis described next, attempted to move 'beyond current scripts and their conventional codifying and disciplining of inquiry' (Lather, 2013, p. 638).

Rhizoanalysis

> However, while there may be different approaches to rhizoanalysis, the ontology remains the same: subject decentered, immanence, and difference. Masny (2016, p. 669)

The process of rhizoanalysis can be difficult to discern within scholarship, as its very nature eschews regimented processes. This makes for double the frustration for would-be rhizoanalysts who are used to conventional methods described in familiar terms. Though it is worth remembering Strom and Martin's (2013) assertion that rhizoanalysis is unique to the researcher, so trustworthiness may be evidenced through transparency. The researcher themselves must embody Masny's quote above and challenge themselves to think differently:

> It is a challenge to think nomadically after decades and centuries of Cartesian logic and transcendent empiricism. A nomadic thinking is important to qualitative research because it is a game-changer: transforming life. Masny (2013, p. 345)

Within the case study presented here, rhizoanalysis was employed with a 'light touch'. To give the methodological background first; data were collected via semi-structured interviews with lecturers on their reported practices and beliefs on using digital technologies for teaching, with the understanding that no participant was a singular voice but a multiplicity of experiences. From the first interview onward, the process was planned as an iterative cycle of data collection and analysis, where each part would be revisited, and a growing understanding would allow for connections to be made between the different parts of the process. Thus, the methods chosen, and the very structure of the research process itself, aligned with the theoretical approach of the research. In short, the research design's methods and process enabled a rhizomatic approach on my part as the researcher where 'any point of a rhizome can be connected to anything other, and must be' (Deleuze & Guattari, 1988, p. 7). Following Silverman's (2006) recommendations for constant comparison for similarities and deviations, a rhizomatic view allowed me to generate an overview of the data which embraced multiplicities and differences, as much as similarities and patterns. As Cumming (2015) states, 'rhizoanalytic approaches offer opportunities to engage with, and disrupt the sometimes limiting strictures of qualitative research methodologies' (p. 138). In the same spirit, I employed rhizome theory, not so much in pure *nomadic* form, but as a *barbarian* would: weaving into and out of *striated* spaces and escaping as needed into *smooth* space.

Initially, analysis traced the conventional thematic coding of the data for emergent patterns, targeting sections which addressed the a priori research question and stratifying the data. In parallel to this approach, I engaged in 'data walking' (Strom & Martin, 2013) through the transcripts, embracing a lack of researcher 'distance' from the data, or any illusion that I could 'interpret' what I read as 'representing' anything other than what was said. As can be seen elsewhere in more conventionally reported terms (Drumm, 2019), these points of interest were collated and categorised within spreadsheets though not without the knowledge of irony of using true/false binaries in spreadsheets for rhizoanalysis! However, as multiple points on the flat plane of a spreadsheet, which were then mapped back on to every participant, it became possible to connect any point within the data directly to any other, no matter where it occurred. Instead of hierarchies of codes and themes, this flat plane could fold upon itself into a multidimensional form, with lines of flight breaking out in any direction and spaces where there was no connectivity thrown into sharp relief. For example, through colour coding joins and disconnects on the spreadsheet, heterogenous aspects could be connected such as

- not having a teaching qualification *joined* to teacher-centred descriptions of teaching,
- using a variety of teaching methods *connected* to rationales for personalised learning,
- not mentioning explicit theories of learning or pedagogical terms still *connected* to descriptions of teaching which were social constructivist, and
- lecturers found it easier to describe what 'shouldn't be done' with technology in education than describing their own practices.

Throughout this process of mapping points of connection and disconnection within the data, I employed a rhizomatic lens to view what the participants were saying, constantly asking whether rhizomatic understandings could be plugged in to illuminate the concepts, structures and spaces through which they were navigating their teaching with technologies. The technologies themselves were seen by lecturers as both *smooth* and *striated spaces*, with multiple efficiencies and ease of use contrasting with the embarrassment of facing a lecture theatre full of students when the technology (or the user) fails. This seemingly contradictory belief could be held by the same person, indicating multiplicities were at play. Some lecturers preferred to work like *nomads*, using their own devices, servers or accounts rather than use institutionally run technologies. Others put strict boundaries between their personal and professional use of technology, teaching only within the *Roman Empire* walled garden of university systems. A few acted as *barbarians*, selectively engaging and subverting the intended use of provisions for other means, such as co-opting computer labs for examinations without official sanction.

Some digital education practices reinscribed structured and hierarchical pedagogies, such as controlling means and access to online learning materials for students through bound spaces such as virtual learning environments where learners were offered little choice and could only follow the prescribed pathway. Those lecturers who demonstrated more pedagogically informed practices often used self-completion learning activities, like multiple choice questions which provide immediate and automatic feedback, and they appeared to be informed theoretically by disciplinary understandings of knowledge, particularly those in 'hard' disciplines where knowledge could be described as hierarchical, atomistic and ultimately *arborescent*. However, these student activities seemed to be most effective when blended or *connected* with other teaching methods, creating what could be described as a *line of flight* out of striated spaces. In contrast, lecturers who used technology to broadcast content to students provided means for students to connect in multiple ways to learning experiences, thereby accommodating student differences. For lecturers who used technologies in low stakes learning activities, these were playful experiments to test *lines of flight* to see where they would take them, which, if successful, would be reterritorialised into formal learning or assessment methods.

THE LIMITATIONS OF RHIZOME THEORY

Rhizome theory has, by definition, no structure or formulaic procedures to follow, which can make it challenging to employ, particularly for novice researchers. As a method, rhizoanalysis does not have a canon of examples of what it looks like in practice. For researchers or readers conditioned to educational research being conducted under the conditions of validity, replicability, and generalisability, rhizomatic work could be potentially accused of lack of rigour as it appears not to be systematic nor objective. Da Silva Lopes et al. propose that validation is better evidenced through a minimisation of invalidity, and that making decisions transparent through an iterative and interactive approach can tell a fuller story of a research project (2016). A further risk is that peer reviewers may be either unaware or prejudiced against rhizome theory, and this may prevent researchers from using it as a theoretical or methodological framework.

While the case study presented here demonstrates the layers and depths to which rhizome theory can be employed, that is not to say that rhizome theory is appropriate for every context or audience. The epistemological challenges of putting rhizome theory to work in educational research are not insignificant. While rhizome theory may be 'plugged in' as if a 'little machine', without an appreciation of its coherence – or incoherence – with the rest of the research's ontological and epistemological propositions, there is a risk of contradiction and ultimately a reterritorialisation of rhizome into philosophical positions which negate the benefits of the rhizome. Most importantly, St. Pierre warns of importing rhizome terms into research without comprehending the ontological structures that come with Deleuze and Guattari's concept (2016). St. Pierre argues that, for example, a method which centres the phenomenological voice is fundamentally incompatible with the post-humanist decentring of the human subject in rhizome theory, where there is no singular and no meaning to interpret.

There is also the question of whether it is possible to maintain rhizomatic congruence while also being accessible. Engaging with *A Thousand Plateaus* and the ideas can take time and effort and of course may not be to all readers' tastes. There is a growing body of higher education scholarship using and, in the case of Strom (2017), debating rhizome theory, yet no assumptions can be made that the majority of readers will be familiar with it and the original works. Often limited word counts in publications mean authors have little space to give a fully rounded and nuanced explanation and background to complex theory, philosophy, and methodologies used (hence this chapter). What assumption, if any, can be made that readers are aware of, say, Deleuze and Guattari's unique lexicon? The challenges of understanding their ideas start with their repurposing of existing words into nuanced new meanings, further compounded by refraction through translation from French into English.

As a culture, we are steeped in textual practices which seek out representation, but Deleuze and Guattari were emphatic in their denial of any hidden meaning; the rhizome, or any other term or story within their work, is not a metaphor (1988). Yet, many published works which lean on their work use the term 'metaphor' to explain the rhizome to their readers. The gatekeepers of 'being Deleuzian' so effectively described by Strom (2017) would mostly likely condemn these works as naïve, but there is an argument to say that to take a line of flight into *smooth, rhizomatic space*, one must begin in the middle of a *striated, arborescent* place; the researcher–author themselves is moving from point to point, taking their readership with them. We are all *becoming*.

Engaging with rhizome as theory and method is to step into a contested space, opening oneself to accusations ranging from naïveté, bastardisation and ignorance to over-intellectualism. A small flurry of Anglophone scholarly work employing rhizome in the decades following the translation of *A Thousand*

Plateaus into English, emerging rhizome-like within educational research in areas such as teacher training (Strom, 2015), thesis writing workshops (Jusslin & Hilli, 2023), virtual reality (Keskitalo, 2011), curriculum development (Sidebottom, 2021), sustainability in Higher Education (Le Grange, 2011), and as previously discussed, student transitions (Gravett, 2019; Gravett & Winstone, 2021; Taylor & Harris-Evans, 2018). An interesting and accessible off-shoot was Cormier's proposition of rhizomatic learning, which framed a type of learning where there are no correct answers, no curriculum, and no pre-defined end point (2008) although he has since questioned it as an all-encompassing learning theory (Bali & Honeychurch, 2014). Rhizomatic learning was an antidote to the reduction of online learning to controlled, hierarchical and, for the most part, quite solitary experiences for the learner, as exemplified with the didacticism of extended massive open online courses (xMOOCs). The embodiment of rhizomatic learning were experimental online courses where 'The community is the curriculum' (Honeychurch et al., 2016). These brought a lighter interpretation of Deleuze and Guattari's ideas to a wider higher education audience although a rupture within those cohorts between those who wanted to engage with Deleuze and Guattari's writings and those who did not is a lesson in how theory within higher education contexts can prove divisive (Bell et al., 2016).

CONCLUSION

In the decade since the development of these online communities, rhizome has subsided in higher education research, with the exception of continued lines of flight from the work of Strom (Strom, 2015, 2017; Strom, Haas, et al., 2018; Strom & Martin, 2013; Strom, Mills, et al., 2018) in particular and some more recent new generative shoots (Jusslin & Hilli, 2023; Sidebottom, 2021). Paradigm-shifting theoretical lenses such as posthumanism (Braidotti, 2019), agential realism and entanglement (Barad, 2007), post-qualitative approaches (Lather & St. Pierre, 2013), sociomaterialism (Fenwick et al., 2011b, 2012) and feminist pedagogies (Beetham et al., 2022) present equally exciting opportunities for research. In many respects, rhizome theory within higher education research has yet to reach a maturity of debate and critique, and this chapter is intended to contribute to, and provoke, such discussion. Indeed, how rhizome sits in alignment or misalignment with other philosophical positions and theories can be difficult to discern for the novice researcher and is an area crying out for contributions from experienced thinkers.

An informed use of Deleuze and Guattari's ideas is an opportunity to de-centre essentialist assumptions and open up opportunities for 'nomadic subjectivity that allows thought to move across conventional categories and disturb "settled" concepts, signs, and theories' (Gough, 2007, p. 282). This chapter has shown how the use of rhizome theory and a 'light touch' rhizoanalysis can lead to profound and generative lines of flight within a research project. Higher education research is developing (Tight, 2019, 2020, 2023), and rhizome can challenge and expand our understanding of what can be known within this field and the methods we use to explore and question those boundaries. As methods and theories pass in and out of vogue and educational researchers cast about for the new, the rhizome has lain dormant, challenging the very idea of *newness* in a world in which all can only be seen as *becomings*.

REFERENCES

Beetham, H., Drumm, L., Bell, F., Mycroft, L., & Forsythe, G. (2022). Curation and collaboration as activism: Emerging critical practices of #FemEdTech. *Learning, Media and Technology, 47*(1), 143–155. https://doi.org/10.1080/17439884.2021.2018607

Bali, M., & Honeychurch, S. (2014). Key pedagogic thinkers-Dave Cormier. *Journal of Pedagogic Development, 4*(3). http://www.beds.ac.uk/jpd/volume-4-issue-3/key-pedagogic-thinkers-mahabali

Barad, K. (2007). *Meeting the universe halfway: quantum physics and the entanglement of matter and meaning.* Duke University Press.

Bell, F., Mackness, J., & Funes, M. (2016). Participant association and emergent curriculum in a MOOC: Can the community be the curriculum? *Research in Learning Technology, 24.* https://doi.org/10.3402/rlt.v24.29927

Braidotti, R. (2019). A Theoretical framework for the critical posthumanities. *Theory, Culture & Society, 36*(6), 31–61. https://doi.org/10.1177/0263276418771486

Brown, M. N., & Leigh, J. (2018). Creativity and playfulness in higher education research. In *Theory and method in higher education research* (pp. 49–66). Emerald Publishing Limited.

Burrell, G., & Morgan, G. (1994). *Sociological paradigms and organisational analysis.* Heinemann.

Charteris, J., Nye, A., & Jones, M. (2019). Posthumanist ethical practice: Agential cuts in the pedagogic assemblage. *International Journal of Qualitative Studies in Education, 32*(7), 909–928. https://doi.org/10.1080/09518398.2019.1609124

Cormier, D. (2008). Rhizomatic education: Community as curriculum. *Innovate, 4*(5). https://nsuworks.nova.edu/innovate/vol4/iss5/2

Cumming, T. (2015). Challenges of 'thinking differently' with rhizoanalytic approaches: A reflexive account. *International Journal of Research and Method in Education, 38*(2), 137–148. https://doi.org/10.1080/1743727X.2014.896892

da Silva Lopes, B., Pedrosa-de-Jesus, H., & Watts, M. (2016). The old questions are the best: Striving against invalidity in qualitative research.In *Theory and method in higher education research* (pp. 1–22). Emerald Group Publishing Limited. https://doi.org/10.1108/S2056-375220160000002002

de Vries, E. W., Delnooz, P., Velthuijsen, H., & Pinxten, R. (2023). Addressing creativity in higher education from a rhizomatic perspective. *Innovations in Education & Teaching International, 60*(6), 906–917. https://doi.org/10.1080/14703297.2022.2103583

Deleuze, G., & Guattari, F. (1988). *A thousand plateaus: Capitalism and schizophrenia.* Bloomsbury Publishing.

Drumm, L. (2015). Is there theory behind practice? Theorising university teaching with digital technologies. In *14th European conference on e-learning* (pp. 670–676).

Drumm, L. (2019). Folk pedagogies and pseudo-theories: How lecturers rationalise their digital teaching. *Research in Learning Technology, 27*(0). https://doi.org/10.25304/rlt.v27.2094

Fenwick, T., Edwards, R., & Sawchuk, P. (2011a). *Emerging approaches to educational research: Tracing the socio-material,* (1st ed., Vol. 5(Oct), p. 232). Routledge. https://doi.org/10.4324/9780203817582

Fenwick, T., Edwards, R., & Sawchuk, P. (2011b). *Emerging approaches to educational research: Tracing the socio-material.* Taylor & Francis.

Fenwick, T., Nerland, M., & Jensen, K. (2012). Sociomaterial approaches to conceptualising professional learning and practice. *Journal of Education and Work, 25*(1), 1–13. https://doi.org/10.1080/13639080.2012.644901

Gough, N. (2007). Changing planes: Rhizosemiotic play in transnational curriculum inquiry. *Studies in Philosophy and Education, 26,* 279–294. https://doi.org/10.1007/s11217-007-9034-6

Gravett, K. (2019). Story completion: Storying as a method of meaning-making and discursive discovery. *International Journal of Qualitative Methods, 18,* 1–8. https://doi.org/10.1177/1609406919893155

Gravett, K., & Winstone, N. E. (2021). Storying students' becomings into and through higher education. *Studies in Higher Education, 46*(8), 1578–1589. https://doi.org/10.1080/03075079.2019.1695112

Greene, J. C. (2013). On rhizomes, lines of flight, mangles, and other assemblages. *International Journal of Qualitative Studies in Education, 26*(6), 749–758. https://doi.org/10.1080/09518398.2013.788763

Grellier, J. (2013). Rhizomatic mapping: Spaces for learning in higher education. *Higher Education Research and Development, 32,* 83–95. January 2015. https://doi.org/10.1080/07294360.2012.750280

Hamann, J., & Kosmützky, A. (2021). Does higher education research have a theory deficit? Explorations on theory work. *European Journal of Higher Education, 11*(S1), 468–488. https://doi.org/10.1080/21568235.2021.2003715

Haraway, D. (2007). A cyborg manifesto: Science, technology, and socialist-feminism in the late 20th century. *The International Handbook of Virtual Learning Environments, 80*(80), 117–158. https://doi.org/10.1007/978-1-4020-3803-7_4

Harris, D. (2016). Rhizomatic education and Deleuzian theory. *Open Learning: The Journal of Open, Distance and e-Learning, 31*(3), 219–232. https://doi.org/10.1080/02680513.2016.1205973

Honan, E., & Sellers, M. (2006). *So how does it work? – Rhizomatic methodologies.* Paper presented at the Australian Association for Research in Education Annual Conference, Adelaide, Australia. http://www.aare.edu.au/publicationsdatabase.php/5086/so-how-does-it-work-rhizomatic-methodologies

Honeychurch, S., Stewart, B., Bali, M., Hogue, R. J., & Cormier, D. (2016). How the community became more than the curriculum: Participant experiences in # RHIZO14. *Current Issues in Emerging eLearning, 3*(1).

Jones, A. (2011). Seeing the messiness of academic practice: Exploring the work of academics through narrative. *International Journal for Academic Development, 16*(2), 109–118. https://doi.org/10.1080/1360144X.2011.568282

Jusslin, S., & Hilli, C. (2023). Supporting bachelor's and master's students' thesis writing: A rhizoanalysis of academic writing workshops in hybrid learning spaces. *Studies in Higher Education,* 1–18. https://doi.org/10.1080/03075079.2023.2250809

Keskitalo, T. (2011). Teachers' conceptions and their approaches to teaching in virtual reality and simulation-based learning environments. *Teachers and Teaching: Theory and Practice, 17*(1), 131–147.

Kinchin, I. M., & Gravett, K. (2022). *Dominant discourses in higher education: Critical perspectives, cartographies and practice.* Bloomsbury Publishing.

Lather, P. (1993). Fertile obsession: Validity after poststructuralism. *The Sociological Quarterly, 34*(4), 673–693.

Lather, P. (2013). Methodology-21: What do we do in the afterward?. *International Journal of Qualitative Studies in Education, 26*(6), 634–645. https://doi.org/10.1080/09518398.2013.788753

Lather, P., & St. Pierre, E. A. (2013). Post-qualitative research. *International Journal of Qualitative Studies in Education, 26*(6), 629–633. https://doi.org/10.1080/09518398.2013.788752

Le Grange, L. L. L. (2011). Sustainability and higher education: From arborescent to rhizomatic thinking. *Educational Philosophy and Theory, 43*(7), 742–754. https://doi.org/10.1111/j.1469-5812.2008.00503.x

Macfarlane, B. (2012). The higher education research archipelago. *Higher Education Research and Development, 31*(1), 129–131. https://doi.org/10.1080/07294360.2012.642846

Macfarlane, B. (2022). A voyage around the ideological islands of higher education research. *Higher Education Research and Development, 41*(1), 107–115. https://doi.org/10.1080/07294360.2021.2002275

Masny, D. (2013). Rhizoanalytic pathways in qualitative research. *Qualitative Inquiry, 19*(5), 339–348. https://doi.org/10.1177/1077800413479559

Masny, D. (2016). Problematizing qualitative research: Reading a data assemblage with rhizoanalysis. *Qualitative Inquiry.* https://doi.org/10.1177/1532708616636744

Mazzei, L. A., & Jackson, A. Y. (2012). Complicating voice in a refusal to "let participants speak for themselves". *Qualitative Inquiry*, *18*(9), 745–751. https://doi.org/10.1177/1077800412453017

McKay, L., Carrington, S., & Iyer, R. (2014). Becoming an inclusive educator: Applying Deleuze & Guattari to teacher education. *Australian Journal of Teacher Education*, *39*(3). http://ro.ecu.edu.au/ajte/vol39/iss3/10

Meyer, J. H. F., & Land, R. (2005). Threshold concepts and troublesome knowledge (2): Epistemological considerations and a conceptual framework for teaching and learning. *Higher Education*, *49*(3), 373–388. https://doi.org/10.1007/s10734-004-6779-5

Nelson, E. (2017). Re-thinking power in student voice as games of truth: Dealing/playing your hand. *Pedagogy, Culture & Society*, *25*(2), 181–194. https://doi.org/10.1080/14681366.2016.1238839

Oliver, M. (2016). What is technology?. In N. Rushby & D. Surry (Eds.), *Wiley handbook of learning technology*. John Wiley & Sons.

Parr, A. (Ed.) (2010), *Deleuze Dictionary*. Edinburgh University Press.

Richardson, L., & St. Pierre, E. A. (2008). Writing: A method of inquiry. In *Collecting and interpreting qualitative materials* (3rd ed.). Sage.

Roy, K. (2003). *Teachers in nomadic spaces: Deleuze and curriculum* (Vol. 5). Peter Lang Pub Incorporated.

Sellers, M. (2015). …working with (a) rhizoanalysis…and…working (with) a rhizoanalysis…. *Complicity: An International Journal of Complexity and Education*, *12*(1), 6–31. https://doi.org/10.29173/cmplct23166

Sellers, W., & Gough, N. (2010). Sharing outsider thinking: Thinking (differently) with Deleuze in educational philosophy and curriculum inquiry. *International Journal of Qualitative Studies in Education*, *23*, 589–614. January 2015. https://doi.org/10.1080/09518398.2010.500631

Sheller, M., & Urry, J. (2006). The new mobilities paradigm. *Environment and Planning A*, *38*(2), 207–226. https://doi.org/10.1068/a37268

Sidebottom, K. (2021). *Rhizomes, assemblages and nomad war machines-re-imagining curriculum development for posthuman times*. Lancaster University.

Silverman, D. (2006). *Interpreting qualitative data: Methods for analysing talk, text and interaction* (3rd ed.). Sage.

Smith McGloin, R. (2021). A new mobilities approach to re-examining the doctoral journey: Mobility and fixity in the borderlands space. *Teaching in Higher Education*, *26*(3), 370–386. https://doi.org/10.1080/13562517.2021.1898364

St. Pierre, E. A. (2016). Deleuze and Guattari's language for new empirical inquiry. *Educational Philosophy and Theory*, *1857*(October), 1–10. https://doi.org/10.1080/00131857.2016.1151761

Strom, K. J. (2015). Teaching as assemblage: Negotiating learning and practice in the first year of teaching. *Journal of Teacher Education*, *66*(4), 321–333. https://doi.org/10.1177/0022487115589990

Strom, K. J. (2017). "That's not very Deleuzian": Thoughts on interrupting the exclusionary nature of "high theory". *Educational Philosophy and Theory*, *1857*(July), 1–10. https://doi.org/10.1080/00131857.2017.1339340

Strom, K. J., Haas, E., Danzig, A., Martinez, E., & McConnell, K. (2018). Preparing educational leaders to think differently in polarized, post-truth times. *The Educational Forum*, *82*(3), 259–277. https://doi.org/10.1080/00131725.2018.1458361

Strom, K. J., & Martin, A. D. (2013). Putting philosophy to work in the classroom: Using rhizomatics to deterritorialize neoliberal thought and practice. *Studying Teacher Education*, *9*(3), 219–235. https://doi.org/10.1080/17425964.2013.830970

Strom, K. J., Mills, T., & Ovens, A. (2018). Introduction: Decentering the researcher in intimate scholarship. *Advances in Research on Teaching*, *31*(October), 1–8. https://doi.org/10.1108/S1479-368720180000031002

Taylor, C. A., & Harris-Evans, J. (2018). Reconceptualising transition to higher education with Deleuze and Guattari. *Studies in Higher Education*, *43*(7), 1254–1267. https://doi.org/10.1080/03075079.2016.1242567

Tight, M. (2014). Discipline and theory in higher education research. *Research Papers in Education*, *29*(1), 93–110. https://doi.org/10.1080/02671522.2012.729080

Tight, M. (2019). *Higher education research: The developing field.* Bloomsbury Publishing.
Tight, M. (2020). *Syntheses of higher education research: What we know.* Bloomsbury Academic.
Tight, M. (2023). The development of higher education journals, 2000–2020. In J. Huisman & M. Tight (Eds.), *Theory and method in higher education research* (Vol. 9, pp. 153–170). Emerald Publishing Limited. https://doi.org/10.1108/S2056-375220230000009009
Wohlwend, K. E., & Handsfield, L. J. (2012). Twinkle, twitter little stars: Tensions and flows in interpreting social constructions of the techno-toddler. *Digital Culture & Education, 4*(2), 185–202.

EXTENDING THE UNDERSTANDING OF GENDERED CAREER CHOICES IN STEM: A CULTURE-ROOTED THEORETICAL MODEL

Irina V. Gewinner[a], Victoria A. Bauer[a] and Mara Osterburg[b]

[a]*Leibniz University Hannover, Germany*
[b]*German Center for Higher Education and Science Research (DZHW), Germany*

ABSTRACT

The conceptual "model of cultural stereotypes" offers a comprehensive understanding of gendered career choices of higher education students. Rooted in socio-cultural perspectives, the model integrates socialization effects, individual gender ideology and internalized cultural stereotypes to provide a nuanced understanding of career-related orientations. The model addresses the limitations of existing theories by recognizing the interplay between individual, institutional and cultural factors. It emphasizes the impact of societal values, norms and prevailing gender roles on career decisions. Empirical validation through a large-scale survey at a German research university underscores the efficacy of the model. The chapter also explores theoretical, methodological and practical implications to guide researchers and practitioners in advancing a contextually informed approach to understanding and addressing gender disparities in career decisions and differences regarding certain occupational fields.

Keywords: Career choices; gender; cultural stereotypes; STEM; conceptual model

INTRODUCTION

Career choices of higher education students are an extensively researched topic. Previous studies elaborated on individual factors of career choices of higher education students, mainly focusing on personal interests, abilities or self-efficacy. However, the commonly used theoretical frameworks explaining gendered career choices often lack culture-rooted theoretical perspectives or consider them arbitrary. Under the factors rooted in culture, we include stereotypes, internalized cultural values, social norms, individual beliefs and prevailing gender role models in a society, as well as cultural capital. Existing conceptualizations treat individual characteristics as constants so that latent mechanisms of career choices are glimpsed and under-researched in empirical studies.

The lack of models that incorporate culturally rooted theoretical perspectives hinders a comprehensive understanding of the mechanisms that shape career choices. Socialization effects and individual gender ideology (Davis & Greenstein, 2009) may shed light on gendered choices of study programmes. Drawing upon these considerations, we address the outlined gap by introducing the "*model of cultural stereotypes,*" a conceptual framework that seeks to enhance our understanding of gendered career choices by integrating social psychological, sociological and culturally rooted perspectives.

At the core of this effort is the recognition that career choices are not isolated decisions made in a vacuum; rather, they are deeply embedded in the cultural fabric and shaped by a complex interplay of socialization effects, individual gender ideology and internalized cultural stereotypes. The new model integrates the micro- and macro-levels, bridging individual cognitive processes with institutional and cultural influences, thereby providing a comprehensive framework for unravelling the complexities of gendered career choices. By moving beyond the limitations of traditional models that either isolate individual factors or ignore broader cultural and social contexts, our model aims to provide a more nuanced lens through which researchers can explore the intricate mechanisms that influence gendered career choices among higher education students.

In this chapter, we describe a novel culture-rooted theoretical model and empirically validate its effectiveness in explaining gendered career choices among higher education students. As we embark on this exploration, we will navigate not only the historically developed landscape of career choice theories but also investigate disciplinary boundaries, dissecting prominent psychological and sociological frameworks that have shaped our understanding to date. From Parsons' trait-factor approach to Holland's typology and from Eccles' expectancy-value model to gender role theory, we will examine the strengths and limitations of these theories, setting the stage for the emergence of the "*model of cultural stereotypes.*" In doing so, we expect not only to enrich the theoretical discourse but also to provide practical insights for educational institutions and policymakers aiming to foster more inclusive and equitable career landscapes.

THE PREVIOUS CONCEPTUALIZATIONS OF GENDERED CAREER CHOICES

There is no genuine career choice theory that explicitly incorporates external influences, such as stereotypes or individual cultural/societal norms, apart from well-established factors. In the following, we present the concepts that are commonly used in the literature (and in career counselling practice) to explain career choices. These theoretical frameworks are rarely geared to a research subject, i.e. the career choice itself, but more frequently address explanations of gendered preferences regarding fields of study, learn motivations and occupational segregation. We discuss the most prominent conceptualizations related to disciplines and delve into psychological, sociological and culturally-rooted approaches.

Social-Psychological Approaches

Previous theories of career choice have focused primarily on individual and cognitive factors. Psychologists such as Parsons (1909) and Williamson (1939) developed significant theories in the first half of the 20th century that emphasized that active engagement in identifying job-related strengths and aptitudes leads to career satisfaction. Parsons accentuates the importance of self-awareness and knowledge of professional requirements for a successful career choice. These theories, particularly Parsons' trait-and-factor approach, found application in psychological career counselling, where the categorization of personality traits enabled easier career recommendations. Twentieth-century approaches underlined matching character traits with specific occupations to increase job satisfaction. However, later theories recognized that career decisions often involve compromise and adjustment. Holland (1959) coined the idea that career choice is a match between personal characteristics and job content.

Based on Holland's theory, Gottfredson presented her *"theory of circumscription, compromise and self-creation"* (1981). This theory assumes that people make their career choices based on subjective criteria such as gender roles, prestige and interests. The original focus was on gender differences in career decisions, although later developments also included other dimensions.

Gottfredson's theory is based on the assumption that individual inherent cognitive strengths influence success in school, professional and social areas. She emphasizes the importance of career-related aspirations as a reflection of self-concept, since people choose careers that align with how they see themselves and reflect their knowledge of different careers. The theoretical model uses notions such as "conceptions of professions" and "cognitive map of professions" to tackle individual career choice decisions. In addition, Gottfredson posits a "zone of acceptable alternatives" that reflects an individual's perception of where one best fits into society. Overall, she believes that the genetically anchored general intelligence and related cognitive abilities play a central role in individual career development, which offers little space for external circumstances and cultural factors within the career choice explanations.

In her four-phase model of career development, Gottfredson describes the gradual process through which young people discover their own strengths. The phases range from the simple perception of jobs as adult roles in early childhood to the formation of final career preferences in adolescence. The phases include the recognition of gender-specific stereotypes, the perception of class differences and an orientation towards one's own uniqueness.

Gottfredson highlights that idealized career preferences often cannot be realized, and young people sometimes have to give up their preferred alternatives. She calls this adaptation process a compromise, which takes the external reality of life into account. The limiting factors for placement in society are the sex type, social prestige and areas of interest of the individuals. Gottfredson elaborates four principles of adaptation that suggest that people are more interested in developing a "good enough" public self as the private self-gains meaning later in life.

The empirical evidence validating Gottfredson's theory is mixed. Some studies partially support the theory (Cochran et al., 2011; Jones & Hite, 2021), while others criticize it or provide different results (Hesketh et al., 1990; Junk & Armstrong, 2010). Overall, the theory remains controversial, although it is partially supported by various researchers. Although Gottfredson's theory brings new perspectives to the career choice debate, it has some limitations for sociological research. She neglects the differentiation of gender-specific professional characteristics between masculine and feminine, and sexual type is viewed as a rigid, unchangeable construction. The deterministic stance regarding the impact of mental ability and intelligence on career success appears conservative and not up to date with the latest research. The conceptual positioning in relation to racial theories is also viewed critically, as her differentiation of world races based on intelligence criteria is reminiscent of questionable historical patterns of argumentation.

Further points of criticism concern the assumptions of Gottfredson's theory. First, it assumes that young people can choose from an unlimited pool of possible careers, which is unrealistic due to the limited labour market and life experiences of young people. Second, it views career choices as linear, final and uncorrectable, which ignores the reality of adjustments, abandonments and other life events. Third, the theory neglects social change and new professional fields. Fourth, it understands the career path as a gradual, linear process, which is problematic in times of career breaks and uncertainty in the constantly changing world full of new challenges and crises. These aspects raise doubts about the validity of Gottfredson's thesis.

Lent et al. (1994) social cognitive career theory (SCCT) integrates the concept of self-efficacy from social psychology to more comprehensively capture the process of career development and advancement. The SCCT is based on Bandura's social cognitive theory (1986), which connects mental abilities with social factors and learning processes. Bandura's triadic reciprocal determinism posits that person, behavior and environment are inextricably linked. Two central elements of social cognitive theory are model learning and self-efficacy. While model learning involves acquiring knowledge through observation, transfer and influence, self-efficacy refers to the subjective belief that one can successfully perform a certain behavior.

In Bandura's theorizing, perceived self-efficacy is crucial for the implementation of human actions. Self-efficacy is based on individual experiences, including coping experience, vicarious experience, verbal communication mediation and physiological states. Research in the context of social cognitive theory has primarily examined performance in various areas, such as academic performance, work and health behavior. These studies largely support Bandura's argument by showing that high self-efficacy is associated with higher self-motivation and better performance (Code, 2020; Dogan, 2015; Schunk, 1995). Feedback about performance also influences self-efficacy, with positive feedback increasing self-efficacy and negative feedback decreasing it.

Lent et al. (1994) extended Bandura's social cognitive theory, particularly the concept of self-efficacy, and developed the model of the development of career-related interests over time. Its focus lies in explaining the intention to pursue a specific highly qualified profession, especially in an academic context. The authors claim that individual career interests reflect subjective self-efficacy and outcome expectations.

Despite its contribution to the study of career intentions, SCCT has limited potential to explain career choice. The approach emphasizes learning but doesn't fully address how skills learned in one context are applied in actual work settings nor does it consider external factors that influence career choices over time and due to which mechanisms individuals establish career related interests and choose certain professions (Zola et al., 2022). A number of studies posed concerns about infinite self-efficacy and underestimation of other factors influencing career decisions. The SCCT does not make gender-specific statements about the effects of self-efficacy and career choice. While the authors consider some barriers such as race and gender, they do not discuss the general applicability of their model to different cultural contexts. It remains an open question to what extent SCCT can be applied to cultural environments outside of the dominant white (male) middle class with rather linear careers.

In an attempt to address such limitations more precisely and systematically address them, a team led by Eccles took on this challenge. Eccles et al. (1983) first examined gender differences in the choice of mathematics courses in a school context and developed a causality model. This model takes into account not only the expected outcome but also the value (interest) and usefulness (instrumental function) of corresponding tasks from the perspective of the individual. Eccles integrated important contextual dimensions such as behavior, (gender) stereotypes and the perceptions of significant others (socializers) into her model. She concluded that these factors significantly influence young people's self-concept, (future) behavior, expectations and attitudes.

Eccles' expectancy-value model of achievement motivation is an often-cited theoretical concept in studies addressing gendered career or particularly STEM (science, technology, engineering and mathematics) choices of young people. It takes up the concept of motivation and argues that persistence, performance and ultimately the choice of activities to be carried out are determined by individuals' belief that they can do these tasks well and by their placing a certain value on overcoming these problems (Eccles et al., 1983; Wigfield & Eccles, 1992, 2000). According to this argumentation, young people are more likely to choose later career paths and professions depending on the experiences with subjects they had previously. Eccles integrated gender, individuals' gender role identifications and personal values into her theorizing, thereby giving new impetus to the existing body of knowledge about motivation and (career) decision-making. Her empirical findings underscored that individual values, previous emotional experiences and attributions based on gender can relativize career expectations. These findings were based on extensive research in which school children's expectations of success were measured in both the short and long term (Eccles et al., 1983).

Eccles' expectancy-value model has been (at least partly) validated in numerous studies. Research on the transition from primary to secondary school showed how different choices can influence the decision-making process. However, most studies focused on the school context and the learning process in general. The challenge is that many analyses targeted homogeneous groups of students, particularly white, middle-class children. The question, therefore, arises to what extent alternative social groups, especially in relation to gender and cultural stereotyping, would lead to different research results. Moreover, the conceptualization is based on measuring gendered stereotypes by a handful of statements on traditional beliefs (Dicke et al., 2019), for instance "*In general, men are more reliable on the job than women.*" Such a methodological approach, based on general society observations and self-reporting (Drake et al., 2018), does not fully capture and explain career choices based on gender stereotypes in young individuals.

In summary, the psychological theories on career choice and decision-making discussed here sharpen the focus on the primacy of cognitive abilities and intelligence. These approaches emphasize the priority of subjective perceptions and personal characteristics, which should be assigned as precisely as possible to specific existing professional fields. However, despite their prevalence in the scientific literature, it is often disregarded that the nub of psychological approaches rests upon the standard life course of white, middle-class individuals, a reflection that partly triggered the so-called replication crisis (Shrout & Rodgers, 2018). This raises not only individual but also economic and socio-political implications and appears to be insufficient for theory development in view of current social developments foregrounding diversity and inclusion. Seen against the background of professional uncertainty, the crisis of work and further technological progress, the predictability and linearity of career paths and the substance of professions themselves cannot be fully assumed. Although the presented psychological approaches pursue this goal, there remains a desideratum regarding the consideration of contextual and cultural dimensions in which individuals are embedded. These dimensions could potentially better explain individual decision-making processes and career trajectories and enable more precise predictions.

Sociological Approaches

Contrary to the mainstream theoretical considerations of social status, acquisition processes (Blau & Duncan, 1967; Erikson & Goldthorpe, 1992), Musgrave (1967, 1970, 2017) contributed to theorizing on career choices and decision-making by drawing on the structural–functionalist approach. He postulated that socialization is a key concept for theorizing career choices. He understood socialization to be a dynamic process of role acquisition in which individuals join social groups and identify with them. This process also extends to career choice, and Musgrave identified four stages of development: pre-occupational socialization, transition to the labor market, in-work socialization and job transition.

Musgrave argued that an interaction between initial social situation, individual performance level and aspirations maximizes status attainment. In later work, he contended that career choice is irrational because socialization processes restructure individual preferences according to economic demand. His theoretical contribution embraces identification of micro- and macro-factors that influence career choices, including family background, school context, friends and anticipatory socialization. This refers to the adjustment of educational and professional aspirations from idealized to realistic aspirations while becoming aware of one's own possibilities. Musgrave emphasized economic factors such as wages and the hierarchizing function of educational institutions. He highlighted the basic attitude towards work as a decisive role in career choice and raised the question of how genders differ or converge in this respect.

In "The Second Shift: Working Families and the Revolution at Home," Hochschild (1989) argued that a significant portion of working women in dual-career households not only face the demands of their jobs but also shoulder an additional "second shift" of domestic responsibilities at home. Hochschild contends that despite changes in women's workforce participation, traditional gender roles persist within the domestic sphere. Women often find themselves responsible for a disproportionate share of household tasks and childcare, creating a situation where they effectively work a "second shift" when they return home from their paid employment.

Hochschild contends that the challenges posed by the second shift have implications for marital relationships, family dynamics and individual well-being. Hochschild also accentuates the structural and cultural factors that perpetuate this unequal distribution of labor, including workplace policies and societal norms. Ultimately, Hochschild calls for a re-evaluation of gender roles both at home and in the workplace. She advocates for societal changes and policy reforms that address the second shift, aiming to create a more equitable division of labor between men and women within families. Sadly, the described circumstances have not lost their relevance 35 years later, which makes the book serve as a powerful critique of the persistent gender inequalities embedded in both the professional and domestic spheres of modern life. These inequalities have also had a striking impact on the career choices of young people, since both women and men internalize the gendered division of unpaid labor in parental homes. As a result, the choices remain gendered, especially with regard to the STEM fields (Gewinner & Esser, 2021, pp. 25–44).

In line with the conceptualizations of Musgrave and Hochschild, gender role theory, as a narrower frame of the social role theory (Eagly & Wood, 2012), posits that societal expectations and cultural norms associated with gender roles significantly influence individuals' behavior, including career choices. This theory suggests that predefined roles and stereotypes assigned to men and women shape their occupational preferences and decisions. For example, women may be steered toward nurturing professions due to cultural expectations regarding caregiving roles, while men may face pressure to pursue careers associated with dominance and leadership. The theory highlights how occupational segregation, family expectations, media representations, educational guidance and leadership norms contribute to the perpetuation of gendered career choices (Correll et al., 2007; Eagly & Carli, 2007; Eccles, 2007; England, 2010; Gauntlett, 2008).

Occupational segregation, where certain professions are dominated by one gender, is a manifestation of gender role expectations (England, 2010). Family expectations reinforce traditional gender norms, leading women to face a "motherhood penalty" in the workforce (Correll et al., 2007). Media representations contribute to the perpetuation of gender stereotypes, shaping individuals' perceptions of suitable careers (Gauntlett, 2008; Kay et al., 2015). Educational systems may guide boys and girls towards different academic paths based on gender expectations, influencing future career choices (Eccles, 2007). Leadership roles often reflect gendered expectations about leadership styles, contributing to the under-representation of women in leadership positions (Eagly & Carli, 2007).

In summary, gender role theory provides a framework for understanding how societal expectations, perpetuated through various channels, play a crucial role in shaping gendered career choices, influencing individuals' aspirations and decisions throughout their lives. Overall, sociological approaches to gendered career choices accentuate the macro-level of agency, foregrounding the predominant societal expectations towards certain (career) roles. In line with these expectations, men are found more traditional than women in their aspirations towards fields of study and professions (Murdoch et al., 2010; Shin et al., 2019), whereas women with traditional beliefs in adolescence are less likely to pursue STEM fields of study. Although these insights provide a sound ground for understanding persisting gendered career choices, they lack tangible mechanisms explaining how exactly the internalization takes place.

Culturally Rooted Approaches

Demarcating sociological and culturally rooted approaches with regard to gendered career choices is a fairly difficult task, since a number of conceptualizations mention culture as explanatory or context factor. Indeed, gender and/or gender role understandings bound to gender are occasionally addressed in studies foregrounding STEM education, disciplinary segregation and gendered leadership development. To enrich and substantiate the existing perspectives, under culture we understand not only gender and the associated internalized roles but also concrete internalized values and views on role distribution, broadly known as gender ideology (Davis & Greenstein, 2009). What precedes here is whether people see employment as a fulfilling part of their life or not and what associated roles and life scenarios they attach importance to.

Various studies have already provided evidence that young people's career choices can lead to horizontal gender segregation and, later in life, vertical gender segregation. The findings of these studies go back to the two factors that have a particularly strong influence on career choice: gender and the socioeconomic status of the parents (Achatz, 2008; Maaz et al., 2010, pp. 11–46; Ratschinski, 2009). These categories of influence play a decisive role in determining whether a career choice is gender-typical or gender-atypical (Alm & Bäckman, 2015; Driesel-Lange & Hany, 2005; Holland Iantosca & Lemke, 2022; Jaoul-Grammare, 2023; Makarova & Herzog, 2014; Shen-Miller & Smiler, 2015; Tokar & Jome, 1998). The term "typicality" is understood as a congruence between the person and the gender type of a profession.

Different studies showed no direct connection between gender roles and traditionalism regarding career aspirations. However, career interests suggest that there is a relationship between these variables (Tokar & Jome, 1998). In research on atypical career choices, some scholars (Funk & Wentzel, 2014, p. 192; Makarova & Herzog, 2013, 2014, 2015) concluded that men prefer traditional career models, while women tend to choose atypical careers if their family role models are typically male or pursued mixed-gender jobs. Based on studies in Switzerland, Buchmann and Kriesi (2012) show that parents' gender-specific attributions have a positive influence on their children's later choice of corresponding women's and men's professions. This effect has also been proven to be reinforced by teachers in the form of a fulfilling prophecy (Friedrich et al., 2015; Lorenz et al., 2016; Retelsdorf et al., 2015).

Despite the softening of the breadwinner model as a conservative gender arrangement, an opposite trend can be observed in Germany, which reflects the consolidation of traditional life patterns and trajectories through the choice of typically male and female professions (Gewinner & Esser, 2020; Wetterer, 2002). A similar ambivalence can also be observed in Eastern Europe (Gewinner, 2016; Haller & Hoellinger, 1994; Lobodzinska, 1996). The finding that young people tend to choose gender-typical careers is all the more astonishing when one takes into account that women have been seen as the winners of educational expansion in recent decades (Hadjar & Becker, 2017; Helbig, 2012a, 2012b; Konstantinovsky & Popova, 2015; Lörz & Schindler, 2011). Studies show that although women stay in the education system longer and obtain higher qualifications through better access to education, they are not likely to overcome gender-specific barriers when choosing a career (Bothfeld et al., 2005; Hecken, 2006, pp. 123–155; Zafar, 2013).

While international research shows a consensus on the question that gender can predetermine career choice, the investigation of the role of gender-specific and cultural stereotypes as a context in this process has received little attention so far (Chaxel, 2015; Deemer et al., 2014; Gianettoni et al., 2015; Heilman, 2015; Reuben et al., 2014; Shen, 2015; Shu et al., 2022). However, the social construction of gender occurs, among other things, through a (latent) mediation or internalization of stereotypes or individual ideas, which can create a persistent character in the long term. Studies have shown, for example, that an outdated, stereotypical perception of subjects such as STEM as supposedly more cognitively demanding deters women from studying them (Aeschlimann et al., 2016; Ertl et al., 2014; Kessels, 2015; Trauth et al., 2016). Similarly, perceived exclusivity, male dominance and high-performance expectations deter women from choosing science as a career (Cheryan et al., 2015; Dasgupta et al., 2015; Deemer et al., 2014; Reuben et al., 2014).

Investigations on explicit and implicit individual career preferences revealed discrepancies between the two, which indicates an impact of the socially acceptable, or wished, male and female occupations on individual career related decisions (Gadassi & Gati, 2009). Other studies also delve deeper into stereotypes and argue that the persistence of gender-specific career choices and, consequently, the reproduction of gender segregation in the labor market is culturally determined (Seron et al., 2016). They explain this by the external influence of female counterparts during the development of professional socialization during studies: gender segregation can be traced back to informal communication with peers as well as everyday sexism in study groups and during internships. In the course of this socialization, norms, interpretations and practices are conveyed that are recognized and common among people in the same profession (Xie & Shauman, 2003). If these norms, etc. do not correspond to cultural ideas and individual values, they silently reinforce the exit of the so-called "troublemakers" from the respective profession (Seron et al., 2016).

This refreshing perspective establishes a connection between (professional) cultural and gender-specific stereotypes and the structural persistence of occupational segregation. The core of the study, however, lies in researching the professional socialization of individuals who are already studying and met a decision regarding a particular career track. Those who are one step further in their life courses are included, while those who are still in the decision-making process, such as school leavers, are left out. The focus on the professional orientation of young individuals before their professional socialization is central because it provides insights into the coupling between culture and the structure of a society. This is crucial for research into cultural influences on individual decisions as well as on class reproduction.

In summary, it can be stated that none of the presented approaches addresses the theorization of the cultural impact on career choice. This existing gap might be caused social psychological but also sociological, explanations of career choice often being located in a positivist, i.e. measurable, tradition and usually capture the micro-factors of career orientation that are quantifiable. (Social) psychological theories emphasize the importance of cognitive skills for career choice, while sociological approaches either address social mobility patterns and establish the connection between origin and status attainment, or assume the impact of the dominant values on individual career choices, yet lack methodological rigor to demonstrate it.

Many approaches create the impression of plannability and normative linearity of the professional biography, which gives room for individual fears of existence and failure even with a small deviation. Institutional components such as labor market segmentation or even the popularity or prestige of certain professions are rarely used to explain the process of professional orientation. However, this harbors the fallacy that all social classes enjoy the same prestige on the occupational scale. The basic assumption of the influential approaches presented here, that professional development is structured similarly for all professional groups, is also problematic, which is why theoretical statements have a uniform character. They also aim to compare professional aspirations with actual professional success, which can be difficult to measure and compare because both concepts allow for different semantic interpretations at different stages of life of individuals.

Gender typing mechanisms receive little consideration when theorizing career choice. Approaches and studies replicate each other in their agreement on the influence of gender on career choice, which is why this category is included as a standard variable in studies. However, the background of cultural socialization that shapes gender typing in this process, as well as the cultural differences within and between different societies, is poorly reflected on. Most problematic are the methodological shortcomings of many studies that are likely to measure scattered individual beliefs based on self-reporting, but not rigorously conceptualized values.

THE NEW MODEL OF CULTURAL STEREOTYPES

Conceptualization

Recognizing the strengths and weaknesses of previous theoretical explanations of gendered career choices, we developed "*the model of cultural stereotypes*" (Fig. 1). This theoretical construct aims to explain gendered career choices by considering elements such as individual and institutional factors, gender culture and the influence of internalized cultural stereotypes (Gewinner, 2017). It integrates social-psychological, sociological and culture-based approaches into a basic framework for explaining career and academic choices.

We first describe the factors that explain gendered career choices at the micro-level. From a social-psychological perspective, we suggest that cognitive abilities and perceived self-efficacy significantly shape career choices, along with individual factors such as intelligence, interests and future aspirations. From a sociological perspective, we accentuate structural and institutional factors such as social status and access to education as key determinants of career choices.

Encompassing the macro-level, we add a sociocultural dimension from a culturally rooted perspective. We argue that gender stereotypes do influence career decisions. To address this, we use the concept of "gender culture" and, from it, "gender stereotypes." To define gender culture, we draw on Connell (1987) and Pfau-Effinger (1999). They argue that gender culture encompasses institutionalized expectations about gender, gender roles, relationships, values

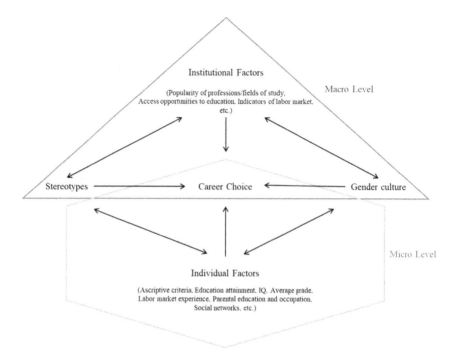

Fig. 1. Model of Cultural Stereotypes.

and ideals. These expectations, learned in the socialization process, persist and evolve over time, shaping behavior within social institutions.

Gender stereotypes, which arise from and are fundamental to the reproduction of a gender culture, limit individuals by suggesting that their characteristics are limited to those of their associated groups. These stereotypes arise from a mix of social, biological and psychological factors that are shaped by social and cultural contexts. Thus, we use Bem's (1981, 1983) "gender schema theory" to underscore the impact of stereotypes on developmental, academic and career choices. This theory posits that children assimilate behaviors and information associated with gender, allowing them to categorize information into masculine or feminine categories and influence their behavior accordingly. Our model emphasizes the importance of stereotypes in this developmental process and suggests that career perceptions are constrained by institutional limitations, access opportunities, economic cycles and labor market conditions.

Bringing together these disciplinary and micro-macro perspectives, we argue that cultural factors significantly influence perceptions, which in turn influence individual behavior. Our theoretical model helps researchers identify factors that influence gender-typical career choices, as well as academic choices or life plans as precursors to these career choices, highlighting the link between gender ideologies and early career related pathways.

Validation

Since the theoretical model of cultural stereotypes provides space for understanding career choices by incorporating individual background notions, it is able to address gendered career choices, particularly related to STEM. This is important because women remain persistently underrepresented not only in these fields of study but also in associated professions, which directly impacts gendered income differences (Statista Research Department, 2024). Moreover, gender typical career decisions affect the STEM areas, with men more likely to be engaged with technical professions and women more likely to be revealed in care work, service and related areas (Bächmann et al., 2024).

To empirically validate the theoretical model, a quantitative online survey was administered to around 20,000 students at a large research university in Germany, of which 1,516 (56.8% female, 41.8% male) completed the questionnaire (Gewinner & Esser, 2020). The investigation focussed on study and career choices of students, both in bachelor and master programs across the breadth of fields of study offered at the institution. The purpose of the survey was not only to test the model of cultural stereotypes but also to understand the career choices of young people. The questionnaire comprised a total of 81 questions relating to various aspects of studies, time at school and future prospects of the students, information resources about possible careers, family and peers, media use as well as socio-demographic data. One of the most important parts of the survey addressed individual values. Overall, the study concentrated on career and subsequent educational decisions in a retrospective manner and prospective further career aspirations.

Separate logistic regression models for men and women revealed gender differences in STEM choices. Traditional gender ideology significantly impacted men's career choices, aligning with previous research indicating a tendency for men to pursue STEM fields. For women, noncompliance with traditional, male breadwinner gender ideologies contributed to STEM subject choice. Overall, the findings show that latent mechanisms of individual ideal conceptions are crucial for gendered career choices but need to be carefully embedded in the broader context of socialization and socio-economic factors. Although the data relate to one university, they provide empirical support for the proposed culture-rooted theoretical model, demonstrating its ability to explain the complex interplay of individual, social and cultural factors influencing gendered career choices. The successful validation of the model highlights its potential as a valuable methodological tool for future research on gendered career trajectories in higher education, especially applied in further, diverse settings.

CONCLUSION AND IMPLICATIONS

Theoretical Implications

This study extends the existing theoretical landscape in higher education research by incorporating a culture-rooted perspective, considering latent mechanisms of socio-cultural factors and providing empirical evidence to support the nuanced influence of gender ideology and stereotypes on career choices in a specific educational context. We propose the theoretical "*model of cultural stereotypes*" that offers a more refined and contextually informed understanding of gendered career choices and can be applied within both quantitative and qualitative methodologies. Traditional theories of career choice, grounded primarily in psychological and sociological paradigms, have often focused only on individual factors and overlooked the cultural and institutional dimensions that shape individual decisions. The proposed model seeks to address this oversight by integrating social psychological, sociological and cultural approaches into a unified framework. This integration, we argue, provides a more nuanced understanding of gendered career choices among college students and offers a more holistic lens through which scholars can analyze and interpret the complexities of career decision-making. It enables researchers and practitioners to better identify and address the factors that contribute to gender disparities in STEM fields and career paths.

The "model of cultural stereotypes" challenges the implicit assumptions inherent in many existing theories, particularly those rooted in a positivist tradition. Traditional theories often assume a linear and normative career trajectory, overlooking the multiple realities that individuals face in an ever-changing professional landscape. Our model embraces the fluidity and complexity of career trajectories, recognizing the influence of societal expectations, gender culture and stereotypes in shaping individuals' career paths.

In sum, the theoretical implications of the model extend beyond the boundaries of conventional career choice theories in higher education research. By incorporating cultural-rooted dimensions, it enriches our theoretical toolkit by providing a more comprehensive framework that is responsive to the complexities of contemporary social dynamics. By engaging with this model, researchers are encouraged to explore the intersections between individual cognitive processes, institutional structures and cultural influences, thereby contributing to a more nuanced understanding of gendered career choices in higher education.

Methodological Implications

In addition to advancing theoretical perspectives on gendered career choices, the model of cultural stereotypes introduces novel methodological considerations that can enhance the rigor and depth of future research in this area. The model urges researchers to move beyond simplistic categorizations and delve into the complexities of gendered career choices. Recognizing the multifaceted nature of gender ideologies, the model urges scholars to adopt intersectional analyses that consider how various factors, such as race, ethnicity and socioeconomic status, intersect with gender to influence career choices. This methodological shift calls for more inclusive sampling strategies to ensure that diverse voices are represented in studies of gendered career trajectories.

To fully understand the impact of cultural, religious and gender differences on career choices, the model advocates a cross-cultural approach. Comparative studies across different societies and cultural contexts can reveal differences in how gender culture and stereotypes manifest themselves. Using qualitative methods such as in-depth interviews and focus group discussions, researchers can explore the lived experiences of individuals, providing a more contextualized understanding of the complex interplay between culture and career choices.

The career decision-making process is dynamic and unfolds over time. Our model suggests that researchers use longitudinal study designs to capture the evolving nature of gendered career choices. By tracking individuals' experiences and choices at multiple points in their educational and occupational trajectories, researchers can gain insight into the long-term effects of cultural stereotypes on career trajectories. This approach allows for a more nuanced examination of how individuals negotiate and navigate societal expectations over time.

We emphasize that career choices are often made on the basis of generalized or stereotyped perceptions, contributing to high dropout rates or persistent gender segregation in the workforce. Our theoretical model aims to provide insights into discrepancies in career choices among different groups (e.g. migrant populations) while analyzing cultural, religious and gender differences. Gendered career choices are influenced by factors operating at multiple levels: individual, interpersonal, institutional and cultural. The model encourages researchers to use multilevel analyses that consider these interrelated influences simultaneously. Advanced statistical techniques, such as hierarchical linear modeling or structural equation modeling, can unravel the complex interplay between micro- and macro-factors and provide a more comprehensive understanding of the mechanisms at play.

In conclusion, the methodological implications of the "model of cultural stereotypes" underscore the need for a diversified and nuanced approach to the study of gendered career choices. By integrating qualitative and quantitative methods, embracing intersectionality, adopting cross-cultural perspectives, and incorporating longitudinal designs, researchers can enrich their methodologies and contribute to a more holistic understanding of the complex dynamics surrounding career decisions in higher education.

Practical Implications and Challenges

Recognizing that career choices often depend on generalized or stereotypical perceptions, the model of cultural stereotypes calls for a re-evaluation of educational and career explanation approaches. The model highlights the impact of stereotypes on career choices, contributing to high dropout rates and persistent gender segregation in the workforce. Practical strategies to address these challenges include early interventions at the educational level. In advocating for early intervention, it's important to critically examine existing education systems and their responsiveness to change. Institutions may face bureaucratic hurdles, budget constraints or cultural resistance that impede the seamless implementation of programs aimed at challenging gender stereotypes. Addressing these challenges requires a pragmatic and adaptive approach that recognizes the potential limitations of immediate and widespread change.

The model advocates for a holistic understanding of career choices that goes beyond individual characteristics to consider external societal influences and stereotypes. The practical implementation of holistic guidance requires close collaboration between educational institutions and industry partners. The practical implications of the cultural stereotypes model underscore the importance of targeted, step by step interventions to address gendered career choices. By challenging stereotypes, promoting inclusivity and adopting culturally sensitive, intersectional and holistic approaches, educators and policymakers can contribute to a more equitable and diverse landscape in higher education and the workforce. However, critical reflection on its application is crucial to further assess its real-world impact, address potential challenges and ensure ethical and effective implementation in research strategies.

Regardless of the promising explanatory power of the model, it should be extensively tested in various contexts to fully capture its potential and identify possible weaknesses. As to the limitations of the proposed framework, one should keep in mind that from the methodological perspective, it is challenging to fully separate the macro- and the micro-levels of observation. This also applies to the interaction effect of the variables as explanatory factors within the model, since they have not been studied so far. A further highly demanding methodological step pertains to measuring the stereotypes and individual beliefs. Since an ample number of studies follow different operationalization logic and measurements, it might be helpful to agree on a standardized procedure in this regard.

REFERENCES

Achatz, J. (2008). Die Integration von Frauen in Arbeitsmärkten und Organisationen. *Geschlechterdifferenzen—Geschlechterdifferenzierungen: Ein Überblick über gesellschaftliche Entwicklungen und theoretische Positionen*, 105–138.

Aeschlimann, B., Herzog, W., & Makarova, E. (2016). How to foster students' motivation in mathematics and science classes and promote students' STEM career choice. A study in Swiss high schools. *International Journal of Educational Research, 79*, 31–41.

Alm, S., & Bäckman, O. (2015). Openness to gender atypical occupations in youth: Do peer groups and school classes matter?. *The Journal of Early Adolescence, 35*(1), 97–119.

Bächmann, A.-C., Kleinert, C., & Schels, B. (2024). *Ost wie West arbeiten Frauen und Männer häufig in unterschiedlichen Berufen* (Vol. 3). IAB-Kurzbericht. https://doi.org/10.48720/IAB.KB.2403

Bandura, A. (1986). *Social foundations of thought and action: A social cognitive theory*. Prentice-Hall.

Bem, S. L. (1981). Gender schema theory: A cognitive account of sex typing. *Psychological Review, 88*(4), 354.

Bem, S. L. (1983). Gender schema theory and its implications for child development: Raising gender-aschematic children in a gender-schematic society. *Signs: Journal of Women in Culture and Society, 8*(4), 598–616.

Blau, P. M., & Duncan, O. D. (1967). *The American occupational structure*. John Wiley & Sons Inc.

Bothfeld, S., Klammer, U., Klenner, C, Leiber, S., Thiel, A., & Ziegler, A. (2005). *WSI-FrauenDatenReport 2005. Handbuch zur wirtschaftlichen und sozialen Situation von Frauen*. Edition Sigma.

Buchmann, M., & Kriesi, I. (2012). Geschlechtstypische Berufswahl: Begabungszuschreibungen, Aspirationen und Institutionen. *Soziologische Bildungsforschung*, 256–280.

Chaxel, A. S. (2015). How do stereotypes influence choice?. *Psychological Science, 26*(5), 641–645.

Cheryan, S., Master, A., & Meltzoff, A. N. (2015). Cultural stereotypes as gatekeepers: Increasing girls' interest in computer science and engineering by diversifying stereotypes. *Frontiers in Psychology, 6*, 123074.

Cochran, D. B., Wang, E. W., Stevenson, S. J., Johnson, L. E., & Crews, C. (2011). Adolescent occupational aspirations: Test of Gottfredson's theory of circumscription and compromise. *The Career Development Quarterly, 59*(5), 412–427.

Code, J. (2020). Agency for learning: Intention, motivation, self-efficacy and self-regulation. *Frontiers in Genetics, 5*, 19.

Connell, R. W. (1987). *Gender and power*. Polity Press.

Correll, S. J., Benard, S., & Paik, I. (2007). Getting a job: Is there a motherhood penalty?. *American Journal of Sociology, 112*(5), 1297–1338.

Dasgupta, N., Scircle, M. M., & Hunsinger, M. (2015). Female peers in small work groups enhance women's motivation, verbal participation, and career aspirations in engineering. *Proceedings of the National Academy of Sciences, 112*(16), 4988–4993.

Davis, S. N., & Greenstein, T. N. (2009). Gender ideology: Components, predictors, and consequences. *Annual Review of Sociology, 35*, 87–105.

Deemer, E. D., Thoman, D. B., Chase, J. P., & Smith, J. L. (2014). Feeling the threat: Stereotype threat as a contextual barrier to women's science career choice intentions. *Journal of Career Development, 41*(2), 141–158.

Dicke, A.-L., Safavian, N., & Eccles, J. S. (2019). Traditional gender role beliefs and career attainment in STEM: A gendered story?. *Frontiers in Psychology, 10*, 1053. https://doi.org/10.3389/fpsyg.2019.01053

Dogan, U. (2015). Student engagement, academic self-efficacy, and academic motivation as predictors of academic performance. *The Anthropologist, 20*(3), 553–561.

Drake, C. E., Primeaux, S., & Thomas, J. (2018). Comparing implicit gender stereotypes between women and men with the implicit relational assessment procedure. *Gender Issues, 35*, 3–20.

Driesel-Lange, K., & Hany, E. (2005). *Berufsorientierung am Ende des Gymnasiums: Die Qual der Wahl. Schriften zur Berufsorientierungsforschung*. University of Erfurt.

Eagly, A. H., & Carli, L. L. (2007). *Through the labyrinth: The truth about how women become leaders*. Harvard Business School Press.

Eagly, A. H., & Wood, W. (2012). Social role theory. *Handbook of Theories of Social Psychology, 2*, 458–476.

Eccles, J. (2007). Where are all the women? Gender differences in participation in physical science and engineering. In S. J. Ceci & W. M. William (Eds.), *Why aren't more women in science? Top researchers debate the evidence*. American Psychological Association.

Eccles, J. S., Adler, T. F., Futterman, R., Goff, S. B., Kaczala, C. M., Meece, J. L., & Midgley, C. (1983). Expectancies, values, and academic behaviors. In J. T. Spence (Ed.), *Achievement and achievement motivation* (pp. 75–146). W. H. Freeman.

England, P. (2010). The gender revolution: Uneven and stalled. *Gender & Society, 24*(2), 149–166.

Erikson, R., & Goldthorpe, J. H. (1992). Individual or family? Results from two approaches to class assignment. *Acta Sociologica, 35*(2), 95–105.

Ertl, B., Luttenberger, S., & Paechter, M. (2014). Stereotype als Einflussfaktoren auf die Motivation und die Einschätzung der eigenen Fähigkeiten bei Studentinnen in MINT-Fächern. *Gruppendynamik und Organisationsberatung, 45*(4), 419–440.

Friedrich, A., Flunger, B., Nagengast, B., Jonkmann, K., & Trautwein, U. (2015). Pygmalion effects in the classroom: Teacher expectancy effects on students' math achievement. *Contemporary Educational Psychology, 41*, 1–12.

Funk, L., & Wentzel, W. (2014). *Mädchen auf dem Weg ins Erwerbsleben: Wünsche, Werte, Berufsbilder: Forschungsergebnisse zum Girls' Day–Mädchen-Zukunftstag 2013*. Verlag Barbara Budrich.

Gadassi, R., & Gati, I. (2009). The effect of gender stereotypes on explicit and implicit career preferences. *The Counseling Psychologist, 37*(6), 902–922.

Gauntlett, D. (2008). *Media, gender and identity: An introduction*. Routledge.

Gewinner, I. (2016). School leavers and their career choices – Transition or path dependency in Russia?. *Acta Universitatis Sapientae. Social Analysis, 6*(1), 31–45.

Gewinner, I. (2017). *Gendered career choices and stereotypes: A theoretical approach*. Discourses on gender and sexual inequality (Advances in gender research, Vol. 23, pp. 71–89). Emerald Publishing Limited.

Gewinner, I. & Esser, M. (2020). *Studienfachwahl an der Leibniz Universität Hannover. Befunde und Handlungsimplikationen*. Institutionelles Repositorium der LUH. https://doi.org/10.15488/9758

Gewinner, I., & Esser, M. (2021). *Geschlechtsspezifische Studienfachwahl und kulturell bedingte (geschlechts)stereotypische Einstellungen*. Career Service Papers (HRK).

Gianettoni, L., Carvalho Arruda, C., Gauthier, J.-A., Gross, D. & Joye, D. (2015). Berufswünsche der Jugendlichen in der Schweiz: Stereotype Rollenbilder und die Vereinbarkeit von Familie und Beruf. *Social Change in Switzerland*, (3). https://doi.org/10.22019/SC-2015-00006

Gottfredson, L. S. (1981). Circumscription and compromise: A developmental theory of occupational aspirations. *Journal of Counseling Psychology, 28*(6), 545.

Hadjar, A., & Becker, R. (2017). Erwartete und unerwartete Folgen der Bildungsexpansion in Deutschland. *Lehrbuch der Bildungssoziologie*, 211–232.

Haller, M., & Hoellinger, F. (1994). Female employment and the change of gender roles: The conflictual relationship between participation and attitudes in international comparison. *International Sociology, 9*(1), 87–112.

Hecken, A. E. (2006). *Bildungsexpansion und Frauenerwerbstätigkeit*. VS Verlag für Sozialwissenschaften.

Heilman, M. (2015). Gender stereotypes: Impediments to women's career progress. In I. Welpe, P. Brosi, L. Ritzenhöfer, & T. Schwarzmüller (Eds.), *Auswahl von Männern und Frauen als Führungskräfte* (pp. 73–84). Springer Gabler. https://doi.org/10.1007/978-3-658-09469-0_7

Helbig, M. (2012a). *Sind Mädchen besser? Der Wandel geschlechtsspezifischen Bildungserfolgs in Deutschland* (Vol. 959). Campus Verlag.

Helbig, M. (2012b). Warum bekommen Jungen schlechtere Schulnoten als Mädchen? Ein sozialpsychologischer Erklärungsansatz. *Zeitschrift für Bildungsforschung, 1*(2), 41–54.

Hesketh, B., Elmslie, S., & Kaldor, W. (1990). Career compromise: An alternative account to Gottfredson's theory. *Journal of Counseling Psychology, 37*(1), 49.

Hochschild, A. R. (1989). The economy of gratitude. *The sociology of emotions: Original essays and research papers, 9*, 95–113.

Holland, J. L. (1959). A theory of vocational choice. *Journal of Counseling Psychology, 6*(1), 35.

Holland Iantosca, M., & Lemke, M. (2022). The glass escalator in school counselling: Gender and leadership aspirations. *Gender and Education, 34*(7), 852–868.

Jaoul-Grammare, M. (2023). Gendered professions, prestigious professions: When stereotypes condition career choices. *European Journal of Education*, 1–26.

Jones, L. K., & Hite, R. L. (2021). A global comparison of the circumscription and compromise theory of career development in science career aspirations. *School Science & Mathematics, 121*(7), 381–394.

Junk, K. E., & Armstrong, P. I. (2010). Stability of career aspirations: A longitudinal test of Gottfredson's theory. *Journal of Career Development, 37*(3), 579–598.

Kay, M., Matuszek, C., & Munson, S. A. (2015, April). Unequal representation and gender stereotypes in image search results for occupations. In *Proceedings of the 33rd annual ACM conference on human factors in computing systems* (pp. 3819–3828).

Kessels, U. (2015). Zur Kompatibilität von Geschlechtsidentität, MINT-Fächern und schulischem Engagement: Warum wählen Mädchen seltener Physik und machen häufiger Abitur als Jungen. *Heterogenität und Diversität-Vielfalt der Voraussetzungen im naturwissenschaftlichen Unterricht*, 19–30.

Konstantinovsky, D. L., & Popova, E. S. (2015). Youth, the labor market, and the expansion of higher education. *Sociological Research, 11*, 37–48.

Lent, R. W., Brown, S. D., & Hackett, G. (1994). Toward a unifying social cognitive theory of career and academic interest, choice, and performance. *Journal of Vocational Behavior, 45*(1), 79–122.

Lobodzinska, B. (1996). Women's employment or return to "family values" in Central-Eastern Europe. *Journal of Comparative Family Studies, 27*(3), 519–544.

Lorenz, G., Gentrup, S., Kristen, C., Stanat, P., & Kogan, I. (2016). Stereotype bei Lehrkräften? Eine Untersuchung systematisch verzerrter Lehrererwartungen. *Kölner Zeitschrift für Soziologie und Sozialpsychologie*, *68*(1), 89–111.

Lörz, M., & Schindler, S. (2011). Bildungsexpansion und soziale Ungleichheit: Zunahme, Abnahme oder Persistenz ungleicher Chancenverhältnisse–eine Frage der Perspektive?/Educational Expansion and Social Inequality: Increase, Decline or Persistence of Unequal Opportunities. A Matter of Perspective?. *Zeitschrift für Soziologie*, *40*(6), 458–477.

Maaz, K., Baumert, J., & Trautwein, U. (2010). *Genese sozialer Ungleichheit im institutionellen Kontext der Schule: Wo entsteht und vergrößert sich soziale Ungleichheit?*. VS Verlag für Sozialwissenschaften.

Makarova, E., & Herzog, W. (2013). Hidden school dropout among immigrant students: A cross-sectional study. *Intercultural Education*, *24*(6), 559–572.

Makarova, E., & Herzog, W. (2014). Geschlechtsuntypische Berufswahlen bei jungen Frauen: Muss das Vorbild weiblich sein?. *Zeitschrift für Soziologie der Erziehung und Sozialisation*, *34*(1), 38–54.

Makarova, E., & Herzog, W. (2015). Trapped in the gender stereotype? The image of science among secondary school students and teachers. *Equality, Diversity and Inclusion: An International Journal*, *34*(2), 106–123.

Murdoch, J., Groleau, A., Ménard, L., Comoe, É., Blanchard, C., Larose, S., Doray, P., Diallo, B., & Haouili, N. (2010). *Professional aspirations: How do they influence the choice of a non-traditional field of study?* (Projet Transitions, Research Paper 10). Centre interuniversitaire de recherche sur la science et la technologie (CIRST). http://www.cirst.uqam.ca/transitions

Musgrave, P. W. (1967). Towards a sociological theory of occupational choice. *The Sociological Review*, *15*(1), 33–46.

Musgrave, P. W. (1970). Towards a Sociology of the Curriculum. *Paedagogica Europaea*, 37–49.

Musgrave, P. W. (2017). *The sociology of education*. Routledge.

Parsons, F. (1909). *Choosing a vocation*. Brousson Press.

Pfau-Effinger, B. (1999). The modernization of family and motherhood in Western Europe. In R. Crompton (Ed.), *Restructuring gender relations and employment: The decline of the male breadwinner* (pp. 60–80). Oxford University Press.

Ratschinski, G. (2009). *Selbstkonzept und Berufswahl. Eine Uberprufung der Berufswahltheorie von Gottfredson an Sekundarschulern*. Waxmann.

Retelsdorf, J., Schwartz, K., & Asbrock, F. (2015). "Michael can't read!"—Teachers' gender stereotypes and boys' reading self-concept. *Journal of Educational Psychology*, *107*, 186–194. https://doi.org/10.1037/a0037107

Reuben, E., Sapienza, P., & Zingales, L. (2014). How stereotypes impair women's careers in science. *Proceedings of the National Academy of Sciences*, *111*(12), 4403–4408.

Schunk, D. H. (1995). Self-efficacy, motivation, and performance. *Journal of Applied Sport Psychology*, *7*(2), 112–137.

Seron, C., Silbey, S. S., Cech, E., & Rubineau, B. (2016). Persistence is cultural: Professional socialization and the reproduction of sex segregation. *Work and Occupations*, *43*(2), 178–214.

Shen, F. C. (2015). The role of internalized stereotyping, parental pressure, and parental support on Asian Americans' choice of college major. *Journal of Multicultural Counseling and Development*, *43*(1), 58–73.

Shen-Miller, D., & Smiler, A. P. (2015). Men in female-dominated vocations: A rationale for academic study and introduction to the special issue. *Sex Roles*, *72*(7–8), 269–276. https://doi.org/10.1007/s11199-015-0471-3

Shin, Y. J., Lee, E. S., & Seo, Y. (2019). Does traditional stereotyping of career as male affect college women's, but not college men's, career decision self-efficacy and ultimately their career adaptability?. *Sex Roles*, *81*, 74–86.

Shrout, P. E., & Rodgers, J. L. (2018). Psychology, science, and knowledge construction: Broadening perspectives from the replication crisis. *Annual Review of Psychology*, *69*, 487–510.

Shu, Y., Hu, Q., Xu, F., & Bian, L. (2022). Gender stereotypes are racialized: A cross-cultural investigation of gender stereotypes about intellectual talents. *Developmental Psychology*, *58*(7), 1345.

Statista Research Department (2024). *Durchschnittliches Bruttoeinstiegsgehalt für Hochschulabsolventen nach Studienrichtung in Deutschland im Jahr 2018.* https://de.statista.com/statistik/daten/studie/183075/umfrage/einstiegsgehälter-fuerhochschulabsolventen-nach-studienrichtung/. Accessed on May 2, 2024.

Tokar, D. M., & Jome, L. M. (1998). Masculinity, vocational interests, and career choice traditionality: Evidence for a fully mediated model. *Journal of Counseling Psychology, 45*(4), 424.

Trauth, E. M., Cain, C. C., Joshi, K. D., Kvasny, L., & Booth, K. M. (2016). The influence of gender-ethnic intersectionality on gender stereotypes about IT skills and knowledge. *ACM SIGMIS – Data Base: The DATABASE for Advances in Information Systems, 47*(3), 9–39.

Wetterer, A. (2002). *Arbeitsteilung und Geschlechterkonstruktion. Gender at Work in theoretischer und historischer Perspektive.* UVK.

Wigfield, A., & Eccles, J. S. (1992). The development of achievement task values: A theoretical analysis. *Developmental Review, 12*(3), 265–310.

Wigfield, A., & Eccles, J. S. (2000). Expectancy–value theory of achievement motivation. *Contemporary Educational Psychology, 25*(1), 68–81.

Williamson, E. G. (1939). *How to counsel students: A manual of techniques for clinical counselors.* McGraw-Hill Book Company.

Xie, Y., & Shauman, K. A. (2003). *Women in science.* Harvard University Press.

Zafar, B. (2013). College major choice and the gender gap. *Journal of Human Resources, 48*(3), 545–595.

Zola, N., Yusuf, A. M., & Firman, F. (2022). Konsep social cognitive career theory. *JRTI (Jurnal Riset Tindakan Indonesia), 7*(1), 24–28.

HABITUS(CON)FIGURATION IN HIGHER EDUCATION: DIFFRACTING BOURDIEU THROUGH POSTHUMANISM

Nathalie Ann Köbli

University of Vienna, Austria

ABSTRACT

This chapter reimagines Pierre Bourdieu's concept of habitus through posthumanist theory, using the method of diffractive analysis. It explores how both human and nonhuman things (con)figure habitus by decentering humans as the main point of reference. First, an introduction is given to Bourdieu's theoretical concept of the habitus and its relevance for higher education research. This is then diffracted through the posthumanist ideas of (con)figuration, becoming with and nonhuman entities such as matter, companion species and technology. Finally, the resulting posthumanist concept of habitus(con)figuration is characterized by an attention to the agency of nonhuman matter and the processuality of the emergence of habitus. Applying this concept to students' experiences of social class shifts the way these are approached theoretically in higher education research, placing greater emphasis on non-linear entanglements. The chapter concludes with a set of questions that can be applied to empirical work when considering working with the concept of habitus(con)figuration.

Keywords: Posthumanism; Bourdieu; habitus(con)figuration; becoming with; nonhuman entities

INTRODUCTION

Processes, flows, in-between-status have to be taken into serious account, that is, into conceptual representation. Braidotti (2002, p. 63)

Pierre Bourdieu's (1979) theoretical framework of habitus is one of the leading concepts for theorizing how social class influences students' experiences in higher education. Since its definition in the 1970s, it has been reconceptualized by, for example, feminist theory (Adkins & Skeggs, 2004; McLeod, 2005; Moi, 1991), critical whiteness theory (Ahmed, 2007; Skeggs, 2004) and intersectional perspectives (Puwar, 2004). However, these reconceptualizations seem to place a strong focus on human relations and interactions as well as a dialectical relationship between humans and environments. In order to explore how classed experiences in higher education are produced by a myriad of material, spatial, human and non-human entanglements I propose a shift towards a posthumanist definition of habitus.

Posthumanism can be understood as a critical analytic tool to challenge anthropocentric notions of *the human* and to examine how subject positions are co-produced by nonhuman entities. The posthuman condition is located between the Sixth Extinction – the dying out of species – and the Fourth Industrial Revolution – the emergence of advanced technologies (Braidotti, 2019, p. 2). Braidotti (2019) argues that humanity cannot be thought without considering how these circumstances shape what it means to be human. For example, humanity can only exist and be understood in relation to rapid climate change in the 21st century in the sense that it affects everyday life and, by extension, human agency and identity. This is also the case with the increasing presence of new technologies. A recent example is the introduction of easily accessible artificial intelligence systems, such as ChatGPT, which fundamentally affect the properties that can be attributed to humans, as they can now be journalists, researchers and writers without respective training. Thus, in the posthuman condition, humans can only be thought in relation to the changing environments in which they are materially embedded.

This is in contrast to Bourdieu's understanding of humanity, in which *Anthropos* remains the main point of reference in describing social reality. Although in his theoretical framework individuals acquire their patterns of thinking, feeling and acting, i.e. their habitus, on the basis of their social and material environment, little attention is paid to the agential nature of nonhuman matter and how it shapes the habitus. Focusing on this from a posthumanist perspective changes the understanding of habitus by assuming that habitus is co-produced and constantly (con)figured with material, spatial, human and non-human entities. By focusing on the (con)figurations of habitus, the individual as a rational agent responsible for their successes and failures in higher education is decentered. This is particularly important in the face of increasing individualization in neoliberal times, where students are held accountable for their performances in higher education (Franceschelli et al., 2016). A posthumanist understanding of habitus in higher education can thus help counteract these forces.

This chapter will start with a brief introduction to both Bourdieu's concept of habitus and the theory of posthumanism. Then the focus will be on diffracting Bourdieu's theory of habitus through the concepts of (con)figuration, becoming with and non-human entities to arrive at a posthumanist reconceptualization of habitus(con)figuration. The aim of a posthuman definition of habitus(con)figuration is to offer a framework through which classed experiences in higher education can be rethought from a non-anthropocentric, new materialist and process-ontological point of view.

BOURDIEU'S THEORY OF THE HABITUS IN HIGHER EDUCATION RESEARCH

Bourdieu uses the Aristotelian concept of *hexis* as position/attitude and Thomas de Aquinas' translation of the term as *habitus* to refer to patterns of acting, thinking and perceiving. However, in contrast to Aristotle and Thomas de Aquinas, Bourdieu develops a relational understanding of habitus (Fröhlich & Rehbein, 2014, pp. 110–111). Accordingly, habitus is informed action, perception and thought that is formed in relation to social and material environments (Bourdieu, 1979; Fröhlich & Rehbein, 2014). Individuals are positioned in social fields according to the availability of their economic capital (money), cultural capital (education), social capital (networks) and symbolic capital (reputation). Positions within fields thus become central to the formation of specific patterns of acting, thinking and perceiving (Bourdieu, 1977). Tensions arise when these habitual patterns are no longer affirmed in a social field, as is the case with social mobility.

Bourdieu himself, born the son of a farmer, felt a kind of cleft habitus later in his life, as he describes towards the end of his academic career (Bennett, 2007; Bourdieu, 1996, 2007; Friedman, 2016). Ultimately, these tensions can produce individuals caught between two habitus, whom Bourdieu calls *transfuges* (Bourdieu, 1996; Friedman, 2016). Thus, in situations where transition between fields occur, habitus is described as something that stops becoming and is split in two – habitus A in one field/the past and habitus B in another field/the present.

This dialectical understanding of habitus persists in higher education research to this day. There is a large focus on failed and successful habitus adaptation (Bremer & Lange-Vester, 2014; Byrom & Lightfoot, 2013; Friedman, 2016; Reay, 2021; Reay et al., 2010). The assumption is that a primary habitus (from home) is in conflict with the institutional habitus (from the university). Research on this ranges from examining the habitus disjuncture of working-class students in higher education (Alheit, 2005; Franceschelli et al., 2016; Johansson & Jones, 2019; Kramer, 2013; Lee & Kramer, 2013; Reay, 2021; Reay et al., 2010) to describing strategies for adaptation (Abrahams & Ingram, 2013; Chen, 2022; Keane, 2023) and exploring reasons for academic failure with regard to habitus misfit (Byrom & Lightfoot, 2013; Lehmann, 2007; Nairz-Wirth et al., 2017; Quinn, 2004). For example, in their study, Nairz-Wirth et al. (2017) report that studying at an Austrian higher education institution was described as having barriers that were so difficult to overcome for non-traditional students that it caused "physical, mental and social" (p. 20) stress, resulting in dropout. The authors attribute this to the unsuccessful interaction between student habitus and the institutional habitus.

These approaches employ a dialectical relationality in thinking about habitus. They assume that a student with a habitus (that has certain characteristics) encounters the university (a field that has certain characteristics and a habitus with certain characteristics). This dialectical interaction can lead to the splitting of the student's original habitus (habitus A) or its transformation into another habitus (habitus B). The dialectical relationship between these two habitus can lead to conflict (transfuges). The assumption is that habitus and university are independent entities that can be characterized prior to their encounter. Posthumanist theory challenges this by thinking instead in terms of intra-action and rhizomic relationality.

POSTHUMANISM IN HIGHER EDUCATION RESEARCH

> What does it mean to say that subjects are relational? Firstly, that the agency commonly reserved for subjects is not the exclusive prerogative of *Anthropos*. Secondly, that it is not linked to classical notions of transcendental reason. Thirdly, that it is de-linked from a dialectical view of consciousness based on the opposition of self and others and their struggle for recognition. The knowing subject is not Man, or *Anthropos* alone, but a more complex assemblage that undoes the boundaries between inside and outside the self, by emphasising processes and flows. Braidotti (2019, pp. 45–46)

Posthumanism is a process-ontological theory that understands reality as processes that are in constant intra-action (as opposed to *inter*action, where entities are already assigned properties) and differentiation (Barad, 2007; Braidotti, 2019; Fox & Alldred, 2015; Schadler, 2016; Williams, 2018). It is assumed that there are no material or immaterial entities that initiate processes, but that namable entities emerge through processes of differentiation (Schadler, 2016). This is an ontological point because it defines what human and nonhuman entities *are* and how they acquire their properties. In posthumanism, the properties of entities are not defined prior to processes of differentiation but emerge as a result of them. This is in contrast to atomism, for example, which assumes that entities, or atoms, are pre-existing elements with pre-existing properties that enable material and immaterial processes (Schadler, 2016). Thus, intra-action describes how human and nonhuman entities are attributed properties through the processes of differentiation rather than through their mere existence (Barad, 2007).

When Rosi Braidotti (2019), a key posthumanist thinker, defines the knowing subject as a complex assemblage beyond man or Anthropos, she is referring to the human as the main point of reference for humanist knowledge production. This knowing subject is decentered by posthumanism by focusing on complex assemblages (and their processes of intra-action) that attribute properties to human and nonhuman entities. Posthumanism's understanding of *being human* goes beyond the capacities attributed to the human body and intellect (like the ability to think) by humanist ontologies. Rather, the focus is on how human beings *become* (human beings) with human and nonhuman entities, and how their properties, such as the ability to think, emerge through intra-action with other entities. Such an ontological shift from humanism to posthumanism influences which aspects are taken into account when conducting educational research. For example, if we assume that human properties (such as thinking) are not just attributed to the human body and intellect but are intra-related with a myriad of human and non-human things, we must also consider the role that non-human *matter* plays in this.

That is why posthumanism is closely related to new materialism. While posthumanism focuses on understanding subjectivity beyond human cognition (Braidotti, 2019), new materialism is more closely dedicated to examining how nonhuman matter co-produces phenomena (Barad, 2003, 2007; Bennett, 2018). Drawing also on Deleuzo-Guattarian philosophy and process-ontology, new materialism is engaged in exploring the importance of matter for understanding social reality (Bennett, 2010). This is accompanied by a strong emphasis on environmental perspectives, where human experience cannot be separated from the nonhuman matter that influences it. An important figure here is Jane Bennett (2010), who shows how, for example, food as nonhuman matter affects human experience so fundamentally that it cannot be ignored in describing social reality. Without placing human experience at the center of the inquiry, she emphasizes that nonhuman matter is not something passive that serves as a backdrop for human cognition and interaction but rather plays an active role in human experience.

In doing so, both posthumanism and new materialism emphasize that entities that are perceived as separate from each other are connected by a myriad of entanglements (Barad, 2007). Thus, the properties of human and nonhuman entities that emerge in processes of intra-action are *transversally connected* to many other, human and nonhuman, entities. Transversality means understanding human and nonhuman entities "across multiple axes" (Braidotti, 2019, p. 40) where all elements of an assemblage are linked to each other (transversally) and thus lack independence (Schadler, 2016). In this way, human actions, such as thinking, cannot be understood independently of nonhuman influences, such as food, because they are transversally linked in the attribution of properties to entities (the thinking human and the nutritious food) (Bennett, 2010). Thus, the relevance of humans as meaning-making machines is reduced (Deleuze & Guattari, 1983). Such a theoretical lens influences how research is conducted in higher education.

Applying posthumanist theory to higher education research means to assume that education is a complex process of becoming with human and nonhuman entities (Ceder, 2018). Chappell et al. (2023) illustrate this by redesigning higher education teaching and learning through posthumanism. In their study, the authors respond to the effects of the neoliberalization of higher education, as well as positivist and interpretivist ways of doing research, by de-centering human cognition in the design of teaching and learning approaches. This is done by engaging in materially embodied ways of knowing that challenge the assumption that only the human mind can understand and *know*. The authors suggest that, in addition to scholarly reading, teaching and learning, higher education should include explicitly embodied, felt experience (e.g. in the form of dance or performance) when engaging with socially relevant issues such as, for example, sexuality. For this to happen, spaces must be created for creative pedagogy where human and nonhuman intra-actions are acknowledged as the driving force of teaching and learning (Chappell et al., 2023).

Such acknowledgement can be also found in Taylor and Gannon's (2018) diffractive analysis of academic life. In their analysis, they map the human and nonhuman relations in which they are entangled in everyday academic life to "resist slippage into data logic and usual habits of sense-making" (p. 469). Their experimental intervention results in a collection of photographs and poems about "the intensive, affective and sensorial entanglements that attend contemporary academic life 'everywhere and all the time'" (p. 484). In doing so, the posthumanist lens helps to acknowledge the intra-action of human and nonhuman agents in producing phenomena that "glow" in the data – something that Chappell et al. (2023, p. 2,073) also emphasize. Another example of how diffractive analysis can enrich higher education research can be found in Sakr (2020). She draws upon the Deleuzian concepts of becoming, assemblage and affect to "deepen pedagogic reflection" (p. 141) in the student feedback of undergraduate students.

Drawing upon these examples of enacting posthumanist theory in higher education, I will diffract Bourdieu's theory of the habitus through the posthumanist concepts of (con)figuration, becoming with and nonhuman entities in order to start understanding habitus *somewhere else* (Stengers, 2011; Taylor & Gannon, 2018).

DIFFRACTING HABITUS: A POSTHUMANIST UNDERSTANDING OF HABITUS(CON)FIGURATION

Karen Barad (2007) refers to diffraction as both a physical phenomenon and a method in the social sciences that makes patterns of difference visible. Contrary to reflection, which is the mirroring of sameness, diffraction focuses on "differences that our knowledge-making practices make and the effects they have on the world" (p. 72). Applying this method to reading aims at reading texts through one another in order to draw new and unexpected conclusions (Barad, 2007; Geerts & Van der Tuin, 2021). Diffraction "differs from the standard practice of doing a review of the literature, [as it] is opposed to cutting into two" (Murris & Bozalek, 2019), meaning that the boundaries between theory, reading, understanding and the researcher are recreated in the process of the theory work. Barad illustrates this by repeatedly rereading texts and theories, focusing specifically on, for example, every single punctuation mark or the sound of their voice when reading out loud. Knowing theory through various channels (such as other forms of theory, sound or hyperfocus on specific text elements) rather than just based on the representation of words and sentences thus creates new, relational knowledge that sees theory as a toolbox rather than tools (Deleuze & Foucault, 1977).

I would like to deepen what Burnard and Stahl (2024) have already begun: namely, the coupling of Bourdieu's theoretical framework with process ontological theory. By bringing Bourdieu's notion of the habitus into relation with posthumanism, new knowledge is created about how habitus is (con)figured with human and nonhuman entities, how this results in classed experiences in higher education and the questions that are asked in higher education research.

(Con)Figuration

(Con)figurations are "critical tools to account for... materially embedded and embodied locations and power relations" (Braidotti, 2011, p. 12). They are not a metaphor but "a living map, a transformative account of the self" (Braidotti, 2011, p. 10), in posthumanist terms, cartographies of becoming (Braidotti, 2002). Imagine a map, like the Marauder's Map in Harry Potter, that constantly transforms itself as the landscape, it is meant to represent changes. The things that appear on the map are "kinds sutured together" (Barad, 2015, p. 401) into a patchwork – a (con)figuration. Here, the prefix "(con)" emphasizes the many different human and nonhuman *kinds* that make up figurations and that, when sutured together, represent a whole, namable entity – in this case, habitus.

Reading Bourdieu's theory of habitus through the posthumanist concept of (con)figuration means acknowledging that habitus is never inherent to the individual but is constantly (con)figured with human and nonhuman agents in processes of becoming. And while Bourdieu also emphasizes the noninherent and relational nature of habitus (Bourdieu, 1998; Fröhlich & Rehbein, 2014) and aims to overcome the dualism of the individual and society (Bourdieu, 1990a; Jenkins, 1992), he still describes the emergence and reproduction of habitus as dialectical (Bourdieu, 1977; Jenkins, 1992).

> One has to return to practice, the site of the dialectic of the *opus operatum* and the *modus operandi*; of the objectified products and the incorporated products of historical practice; of structures and *habitus*. Bourdieu (1990b, p. 52)

This is where Bourdieu's understanding of relationality differs from a posthumanist one. While Bourdieu's dialectic understanding of habitus is defined as relational as well, posthumanism has a different understanding of relationality. Posthumanism views relationality as anti-dialectic as dialectical thinking provides the basis for the distinction between "self and others and their struggle for recognition" (Braidotti, 2019, p. 45). Instead, relationality is conceptualized as rhizomic assemblages in posthumanism. Thus, (con)figurations draw "a cartography of [non-dialectical and rhizomic] power relations" (Braidotti, 2003, p. 54) from a posthumanist point of view. When we then consider that patterns of thinking, feeling and acting that are learned in social contexts shape students' experiences in higher education (Bourdieu, 2007; Reay, 2021), the way we approach the study of such power relations that lead to classed experiences changes. The consequences of such a shift from dialectic relationality to rhizomic relationality can be illustrated by the notion of a "divided" habitus.

Bourdieu describes habitus as "divided" or "torn" (1999, pp. 510–511) when an individual's patterns of thinking, feeling and acting cannot be performed in a social field because the dominant patterns of thinking, feeling and acting within that field are significantly different. In empirical studies, this is expressed, for example by working-class students, as feeling like two people (Keane, 2023, p. 13), being between two worlds – the old world of social origin and the new world of higher education – (Friedman, 2016, p. 138) and feeling that they do not fit into either (Lee & Kramer, 2013, p. 29). Within Bourdieu's dialectical relationality, we can make sense of the division of habitus by assuming that the original habitus (formed within a social background) is challenged by something foreign (the new social field), which changes the properties of the original habitus and leads to conflictual and classed experiences in higher education.

Within a posthumanist framework of habitus(con)figuration, however, there is never an original habitus to be changed, divided or transformed. What is understood as the original habitus, the habitus against which later versions are compared, is also "constantly changing and redefining" (Braidotti, 2002, p. 39). This constant change means that a divided habitus is not a property of the original habitus that has been altered by a new field but instead is a specific (con)figuration produced by human and nonhuman entities in intra-action. Thus, change, division and transformation are immanent to the becoming of habitus(con)figurations with human and nonhuman entities. There is no original, primary habitus, because what can be perceived and called habitus has always been in constant (con)figuration. By entering and being in higher education, the entities of such (con)configurations change and new (con)configurations of habitus are created, some of which might be experienced as division. Thus, patterns of acting, thinking and feeling always have the potential to be experienced as "divided." If habitus *is* experienced as such in higher education, posthumanist educational researchers need not ask what happens to the students' original habitus, but what power relations and their elements or entities of such processes of (con)figuration are so pivotal that habitus is (con)figured as feeling divided.

In sum, there are two crucial ways in which such a posthumanist view of habitus changes research in higher education. First, it can no longer be assumed that there is an original habitus that is transformed in a way that leads to classed experiences by entering higher education. Instead, habitus(con)figuration is an ongoing process that, under certain circumstances, produces classed experiences in higher education (e.g. feeling caught between worlds). So, the question becomes: what elements of habitus(con)figurations are responsible for the phenomena of classed experiences? If habitus is in a constant process of (con)figuration, but has not always produced classed experiences, then what is it about becoming with higher education that *does* produce classed experiences? Herein lies the second major shift in focus towards habitus(con)figuration. In asking about the elements or entities that (con)figure habitus in higher education in a particular way (for example, as being divided/not belonging/between two worlds), nonhuman entities such as animals, plants, space and materiality need to be included in our focus. How are habitus(con)figurations transversally connected with human and nonhuman entities? And how do they co-(con)figure particular properties of habitus? Since in posthumanist theory subjects and subjective experiences emerge through becoming with human and nonhuman agents (instead of being inherently such) (Barad, 2007; Braidotti, 2002), in a next step it is necessary to better understand the role of *becoming with* in the posthumanist definition of habitus(con)figuration.

Becoming With

Let's return to the image of the Marauder's Map in Harry Potter as an example of (con)figuration. What causes the constant transformation of the map? In order to approach this question, the aforementioned description of (con)figurations as cartographies of becoming is explored (Braidotti, 2002).

The concept of becoming is central to posthumanist theory. Based on Deleuze's poststructuralist considerations on ontology (Deleuze & Guattari, 1983), becoming describes the nondualistic and nondialectical formation of human and nonhuman properties. More specifically, becoming is alternative to the concept of *being*, which assumes that human and nonhuman things have inherent properties that are somewhat stable over time and form the basis of their agency. Contrary to this, Barad states that properties and agencies are not products of an essence (being) but rather an activity (becoming). This process–ontological perspective views humans as "neither pure cause nor pure effect but part of the world in its open-ended becoming" (Barad, 2003, p. 821). Haraway (2008) expands this notion by emphasizing that becoming is an act of co-production of companion species, thus becoming *with* human and nonhuman agents. Subjects, then, do not exist, but rather become (Schadler, 2013) with human and nonhuman agents. Consequently, (con)figurations do not map existing things; they map processes of becoming.

Thinking about habitus with the concept of becoming calls into question the origin of the emergence of habitus. Within a posthumanist concept of habitus(con)figuration, it cannot be assumed that there is a point at which habitus emerges and begins. With this, posthumanism challenges the assumption of linearity that is proposed by Bourdieu's "limited understanding of history as little more than the cumulation of one thing following another" (Jenkins, 1992, p. 60). Although Bourdieu theorizes past experiences as being active in the present, which points towards a process-oriented approach, he nevertheless states that the habitus is "practical hypotheses based on past experience" (Bourdieu, 1990b, p. 54). Here, the term *based on* refers to a linear development that starts at some point in time and space. The assumption of habitus as the *cumulation* of history with *fixed boundaries of time and space* – that, as closed units influence the present – is challenged by the concept of becoming with.

In posthumanist theory, boundaries are (con)figured in processes of becoming with (Barad, 2007; Braidotti, 2002). This supports the point made above that habitus is in constant (con)figuration, which is why the past only *matters* to the extent that it is (con)figured in processes of becoming. The past is not the basis for cumulation or a blueprint for action, but a potential that can be (con)figured in a myriad of ways in processes of becoming with. In this way, the past and the boundaries of time and space are constantly renegotiated and redefined (Barad, 2007). To illustrate, how the notion of becoming with changes our focus in higher education research, Sakr's (2020) study of student feedback is discussed below.

In their study, Sakr (2020) and her colleague Burghardt examined student feedback and pedagogic reflection in higher education through a Deleuzian approach. Given that university teachers are often defensive to student feedback, which defeats its purpose, the author used the concept of becoming as "a radical departure from how we often think about the student experience" (p. 136). Instead of gathering student feedback in a written format, the research team collected 31 drawings which expressed feedback to an undergraduate module. They then proceeded to map emerging themes in the drawings. They aimed at mapping processes that were not causally identifiable "with a beginning, middle and end [but] open to multiple possibilities that simultaneously emerge and are part of a wider and more curious sense-making process" (p. 142). In accordance with the Deleuzian concept of becoming, the authors abandoned causal and linear notions of time and space:

> We tend to think about the university as a particular place – a physical (or possibly digital) entity with boundaries. As a result, we position what happens within the university as distinct from what happens outside of the university. Similarly, we think about the typical 3- or 4-year degree as somehow separate both from what came before and what will come after. Thus, time and place are used to create boundaries between students' experience and all other facets of their life experience. (p. 136)

Understanding the feedback drawings through the concept of becoming meant that the possible interpretations of student experiences went beyond dualistic descriptions such as good/bad or relevant/irrelevant and opened up more embodied aspects "such as their hunger, fatigue and the feeling of being 'weighed down' during academic study" (p. 142). This approach fostered connectedness and intersubjectivity which lead to less defensive interpretations by university teachers. The authors show that student experience in higher education is becoming with a myriad of human and nonhuman entities without being confined by the boundaries of university time and space. This abandonment of causality and linearity, which comes with enacting educational research with the concept of becoming, marks a clear break with Bourdieu's theory of habitus being *based on* past experience. In Sakr's (2020) study, past experiences and history may be (con)figured in processes of becoming in such a way that they significantly shape students' experiences in higher education, but they are not based on them.

Accordingly, a posthumanist concept of habitus(con)figuration needs to embrace the "messiness of student experience" (Sakr, 2020, p. 141). This approach may be unsatisfactory because of its unpredictability. However, it also allows for a more nuanced exploration of how classed experiences are produced in higher education, abandoning the notion that "history is experienced as the taken-for-granted, axiomatic necessity of objective reality [and is therefore] the foundation of the habitus" (Jenkins, 1992, p. 49) and instead acknowledging that the foundations of habitus are "constantly changing and redefining" (Braidotti, 2002, p. 39) in processes of becoming with. In the next section, the nonhuman entities with which habitus is becoming with are explored in more detail.

Non-human Entities

> When an I acts, it does not exercise exclusively human powers, but includes those of its food, micro-organisms, minerals, artefacts, sounds, bio-and other technologies, and so on. Bennett (2018, p. 448)

In posthumanism, agency does not lie in human cognitive capacity but is produced by assemblages in which humans are entangled. To understand this better, the concepts of assemblage and entanglement need to be described in more detail. In Deleuzo Guattarian philosophy, assemblages consist of "elements (or multiplicities) of several [human and non-human] kinds" (Deleuze & Guattari, 1988, p. 36), between which connections are established. The linking of elements – which are then entangled – ultimately produces agency (which is not limited to human agency, but that of the whole assemblage). In this context, entanglement is to be understood as the lack of a separate, innate essence of a single element. It is only through connection with the other elements that each element of an assemblage can *do* something (Barad, 2007). Herein lies the importance to take nonhuman entities into account when researching habitus(con)figurations in higher education. Human activity is never *just human* – it is transversally linked to a myriad of elements within assemblages that produce its agency. Thus, when classed patterns of thinking, feeling and acting are displayed and observed, this activity could only have come about through entanglement with non-human entities.

Bourdieu's theory of habitus emphasizes nonhuman entities that contribute to patterns of thinking, feeling and acting. He refers to these nonhuman influences, such as architecture, nature and space, as parts of the *fields* that interact dialectically with humans (Bourdieu, 2005). For example, Waterson's (2005) research employing Bourdieu's theory of habitus shows how human interaction with local landscapes in eastern Indonesia produces specific patterns of thinking, feeling and acting among members of the Toraja religion. It is assumed that this interaction takes place *between* human beings and animals, plants, architecture and inanimate matter. This marks a central difference to the relation in which human and nonhuman entities are understood in posthumanism. As mentioned earlier, in posthumanism *inter*action is replaced by the notion of *intra*-action (Barad, 2007). Thus, *humans* and *fields* emerge as the result of human and nonhuman intra-action rather than being closed systems with activity between them. Nonhuman agents do not need to be mediated by humans in order to be entangled with them and (con)figure habitus. The main agential nonhuman elements in posthuman theory – matter, companion species and nature-cultures, as well as technology – will now be discussed.

Matter is agential. It has the *thing-power* to move and to be moved. Bennett (2010) describes thing power as attending to the *it* as an actant, "since things do in fact affect other bodies, enhancing or weakening their power" (p. 3). Imagine drinking a glass of water. In Cartesian oppositional thinking, this scenario involves the oppositions of object (glass and water)/subject (human) and active (human)/passive (glass and water). However, Bennett argues that things can be powerful agents as they modify "the human [and non-human] matter with which it comes into contact" (p. 44). Therefore, to say that inanimate matter is agential is not to say that "non-human objects have agency in the strong sense: a glass of water doesn't have intentions or a will" (Bennett, 2018, p. 448). Rather, it means that neither a person nor a glass of water has agency when considered in isolation. The agency that can be exercised in drinking a glass of water is produced in the assemblage that produces that activity.

Other significant nonhuman entities are companion species – animals that we share spaces with. According to Haraway (2008, p. 17), belonging to the same species is defined as "the ability to interbreed reproductively." As humans are not the only species inhabiting the world, human subject positions can only be considered in relation to companion species. Haraway's point here is to think about what companion species might think, feel, do and make available to humans as they "make each other up in the flesh. Significantly other to each other, in specific difference" (p. 16). Thus, *becoming with* always means considering the web of companion species entangled in these processes.

Often discussed along with this is the becoming with nature. In a conventional humanist conception, this includes trees, plants, bacteria and so on. In posthumanism, however, these nonhuman agents are not seen as "natural" or in opposition to human-made "culture," coining the term nature-culture continuum (Braidotti, 2013). For example, there are no "laws of nature" about what trees are and what they do. Instead, the idea of trees emerges in the intra-action of human and nonhuman agents. Humans are no more involved in shaping *culture* than they are in shaping *nature*. The concept of the nature-culture continuum aims to overcome the idea of human exceptionalism in Cartesian thought in order to promote species equality and a "more compassionate [and responsible] aspect of subjectivity" (Braidotti, 2013, p. 86). Animals, plants and the environment are thus not passive backdrops to human life but are entangled with everyday activities across multiple axes (Braidotti, 2019, p. 40).

Technology is also given great importance as a nonhuman entity in posthumanist theory. A posthumanist notion of technology centers "the specific properties of the technological objects themselves, aiming at developing new forms of agency" (Braidotti, 2019, p. 59). This does not mean that technology is supposed to *advance* humanity (that is the hope of trans-humanism). Instead, posthumanism aims to inquire technology's role in knowledge production "by pointing to its involvement in processes of becoming [with]" (Hoel, 2018, p. 421). In social research, for example, this means that no findings can be viewed independently from the technological agents that were involved in creating them. I could not have written this diffractive analysis of habitus without my laptop, extra display, keyboard, computer mouse, Zotero, Wi-Fi and so on. A posthumanist understanding of research as an assemblage (Fox & Alldred, 2017) would acknowledge that this book chapter is not the merit of an independent *I* but a (con)figuration of human and nonhuman entities.

To sum up, nonhuman agents such as matter, companion species, nature-cultures and technology are not in dialectical interaction with humans, but rather (con)figure what humans are and what they can do. Thus, even if habitus is something that is perceived as a human expression of classed patterns of thinking, acting and feeling, it is transversally connected to nonhuman elements of assemblages. When employing the posthumanist concept of habitus(con)figuration in higher education, research needs to (also) focus on the nonhuman entities involved in such processes of (con)figuration.

In what follows, I summarize the posthumanist reconceptualization of habitus(con)figuration and discuss how this raises new questions for higher education research.

CONCLUSION

Bourdieu's theory of habitus is one of the most widely used theories in researching classed experiences in higher education. However, its lack of focus on processuality and the role of nonhuman entities require a posthumanist reconceptualization which decenters the human and emphasizes intraspecies and intramaterial connectedness. This means adopting a process-ontological, anti-dialectical and new materialist perspective in describing habitus(con)figuration by diffracting the theory of habitus through the posthumanist concepts of (con)figurations, becoming with and nonhuman entities. The goal of diffraction is not to combine or add theories but to read theories through each other. The resulting diffraction pattern, which I will summarize, is the basis for researching habitus(con)figuration in higher education.

To assume that habitus is not an entity that begins at some point and remains stable over periods of time, but a constant process of (con)figuration composed of components woven together, emphasizes the myriad of human and nonhuman entities that are involved in producing what we can identify as a human habitus(con)figurations can be understood as dynamic maps that "account for... materially embedded and embodied locations and power relations" (Braidotti, 2011, p. 12). What does this mean for the study of habitus(con)figuration in higher education? First, it means that classed patterns of thinking, feeling and acting are not *brought in by students from home*, but are (con)figured in higher education settings as such. The experiences, memories and patterns that students bring with them are, of course, relevant, but not central. This puts an increased emphasis on the settings in which habitus is (con)figured, as the human student is decentralized as the main point of reference for habitus. With this decentralization comes an increased focus on nonhuman entities such as animals, plants, space and inanimate matter. Thus, habitus is (con)figured as a specific nameable entity in becoming with human and nonhuman things.

Becoming with marks a central concept in the posthumanist description of habitus(con)figuration, as it challenges the assumption that habitus emerges at a point in time and is built and transformed on this basis. The assumption of foundations is discarded altogether, focusing instead on the ways in which the boundaries of time and space are constantly renegotiated and redefined in processes of becoming with (Barad, 2007). In posthumanist theory, the past is not a blueprint for action, or even the basis for potential action, but simply a potential within processes of (con)figuration. Thus, habitus *is* not but *becomes with* human and nonhuman things. Such a process-ontological perspective on habitus(con) figuration brings back into focus the settings in which habitus is (con)figured as a specific nameable entity. In researching habitus(con)figuration in higher education, one would focus less on analyzing and interpreting students' family histories, but rather on mapping how and what family histories become with higher education settings (which involve humans, animals, plants, space and inanimate matter) and how this leads to specific habitus(con)figurations.

Higher education environments are assemblages of human and nonhuman entities. In Bourdieu's theory of habitus, there has been a proportionately greater emphasis on humans and their role in defining habitus. However, a posthumanist understanding of habitus(con)figuration suggests that human agency and activity are transversally linked to non-human entities. In this way, habitus is (con)figured through the entanglement of human and nonhuman things, which requires a focus on matter, companion species and technology in the study of habitus(con)figuration in higher education. Matter, even if inanimate, is agential in the sense that it has the power to "affect other bodies, enhancing or weakening their power" (Bennett, 2010, p. 3). Companion species are also significant in defining human subject positions, as Haraway (2008) points out. And considering the Fourth Industrial Revolution, with the increasing incorporation of artificial intelligence into everyday practices, technology cannot be ignored as an important nonhuman entity in (con)figuring habitus in higher education (Braidotti, 2019).

However, there are also limitations to the use of posthumanist concepts, such as habitus(con)figuration, in higher education research. The process-ontological foundation of posthumanism requires that the complex entanglements of social settings be taken into account in research. By focussing on how human and non-human entities intra-act in the production of specific (con)figurations of habitus, researchers must account for a myriad of entities rather than being able to focus only on human experiences. This results in descriptions that make it more difficult to draw boundaries between human and non-human influences than it is in Bourdieu's theoretical framework. For example, Bourdieusian theory can clearly draw boundaries between types of capital (social, economic, symbolic and cultural) and where individuals are located depending on their respective capital assets in social fields. There are (pre-existing) spatial, temporal, human and non-human boundaries that make such a clear analysis possible. Thinking with posthumanism, however, such a reduction of complexity is neither possible nor welcome. This can lead to additional resources, such as time, being needed to account for the complexity of habitus(con)figurations. In addition, posthumanism and new materialism use their own words to better describe their ontological orientation. This language can be difficult to grasp and work with, especially when communicating research results to audiences unfamiliar with the vocabulary. It is therefore necessary to take these limitations into account when implementing a posthumanist perspective in higher education research.

This chapter serves as a suggestion of how a posthumanist reading of Bourdieu's concept of the habitus might open up new questions and ways of thinking with habitus in higher education research that do not take humans as the main point of reference. In line with Taguchi and St. Pierre's (2017) postqualitative approach of *concept as method*, the concept of habitus(con)figuration offers "a way where concepts - acts of thought - are practices that reorient thinking" (Taguchi & St. Pierre, 2017, p. 643), and thus become methods that guide educational inquiry. Thinking with habitus(con)figuration in higher education research thus leads to new questions about the research interest, the choice of methodology and methods, the data analysis, and the presentation of results from a posthumanist, new materialist and process-ontological point of view. These questions aim to approach the emergence and (re)production of classed patterns of action, feeling and perception as the products of human and nonhuman intra-action. They focus on how such patterns are produced, maintained and disrupted within specific settings (involving human and nonhuman entities) in higher education.

I would like to end this chapter with a set of questions that should be asked when researching habitus(con)figuration from a posthumanist perspective.

- When and where are classed patterns of action, feeling and perception (habitus) displayed in higher education? When and where is habitus becoming with higher education?
- When and where is habitus not becoming with higher education (any longer)?
- What are the temporal and spatial boundaries of higher education?
- What are the temporal and spatial boundaries of habitus?
- What are human and nonhuman entities that habitus is (con)figured with in higher education?
- How is habitus displayed/observed? What other, nonhuman entities are part of this display/observation?
- What kind of nonhuman entities, such as matter, companion species and technology, affect human and nonhuman bodies in processes of habitus(con)figuration?
- How is *the human* produced as the main point of reference for habitus?
- How can habitus(con)figurations be traced and presented visually/audibly/sensorially/with words?

REFERENCES

Ahmed, S. (2007). A phenomenology of whiteness. *Feminist Theory*, *8*(2), 149–168. https://doi.org/10.1177/1464700107078139

Abrahams, J., & Ingram, N. (2013). The chameleon habitus: Exploring local student's negotiations of multiple fields. *Sociological Research Online*, *18*(4), 1–14. https://doi.org/10.5153/sro.3189

Adkins, L., & Skeggs, B. (2004). *Feminism after Bourdieu*. Blackwell Publishing.

Alheit, P. (2005). "Passungsprobleme": Zur Diskrepanz von Institution und Biographie – Am Beispiel des Übergangs sogenannter "nicht-traditioneller" Studenten ins Universitätssystem. In H. Arnold (Ed.), *Sozialpädagogische Beschäftigungsförderung: Lebensbewältigung und Kompetenzentwicklung im Jugend- und jungen Erwachsenenalter* (pp. 159–172). Juventa.

Barad, K. (2003). Posthumanist performativity: Toward an understanding of how matter comes to matter. *Signs: Journal of Women in Culture and Society*, *28*(3), 801–831. https://doi.org/10.1086/345321

Barad, K. (2007). *Meeting the universe halfway: Quantum physics and the entanglement of matter and meaning*. Duke University Press.

Barad, K. (2015). TransMaterialities. *GLQ: A Journal of Lesbian and Gay Studies*, *21*(2–3), 387–422. https://doi.org/10.1215/10642684-2843239

Bennett, T. (2007). Habitus clivé: Aesthetics and politics in the work of Pierre Bourdieu. *New Literary History*, *38*(1), 201–228. https://doi.org/10.1353/nlh.2007.0013

Bennett, J. (2010). *Vibrant matter: A political ecology of things*. Duke University Press.

Bennett, J. (2018). Vibrant matter. In R. Braidotti & M. Hlavajova (Eds.), *Posthuman glossary*. Bloomsbury Academic.
Bourdieu, P. (1977). *Outline of a theory of practice*. Cambridge University Press.
Bourdieu, P. (1979). *Die feinen Unterschiede: Kritik der gesellschaftlichen Urteilskraft* (26. Auflage). Suhrkamp.
Bourdieu, P. (1990a). *In other words. Essays towards a reflexive sociology*. Stanford University Press.
Bourdieu, P. (1990b). *The logic of practice*. Stanford University Press.
Bourdieu, P. (1996). *The state nobility: Elite schools in the field of power* (1. publ.). Stanford University Press.
Bourdieu, P. (1998). *Practical reason*. Stanford University Press.
Bourdieu, P. (1999). *The weight of the world. Social suffering in contemporary society*. Polity Press.
Bourdieu, P. (2005). Habitus. In J. Hillier & E. Rooksby (Eds.), *Habitus: A sense of place* (2nd ed., pp. 43–52). Routledge.
Bourdieu, P. (2007). *Sketch for a self-analysis*. University Of Chicago Press.
Braidotti, R. (2002). *Metamorphoses: Towards a materialist theory of becoming*. Polity Press.
Braidotti, R. (2003). Becoming woman: Or sexual difference revisited. *Theory, Culture & Society*, *20*(3), 43–64. https://doi.org/10.1177/02632764030203004
Braidotti, R. (2011). *Nomadic subjects: Embodiment and sexual difference in contemporary feminist theory* (2nd ed.). Columbia University Press.
Braidotti, R. (2013). *The posthuman*. Polity Press.
Braidotti, R. (2019). *Posthuman knowledge*. Polity.
Bremer, H., & Lange-Vester, A. (Eds.) (2014), *Soziale Milieus und Wandel der Sozialstruktur: Die gesellschaftlichen Herausforderungen und die Strategien der sozialen Gruppen*. VS Verlag für Sozialwissenschaften. https://doi.org/10.1007/978-3-531-19947-4
Burnard, P., & Stahl, G. (2024). Coupling Bourdieu and Barad: Exploring the vitality of cross-cutting conceptual meetings. In G. Stahl, G. M. Mu, P. Ayling, & E. B. Weininger (Eds.), *The Bloomsbury handbook of Bourdieu and educational research* (1st ed., pp. 47–59). Bloomsbury Publishing Plc. https://doi.org/10.5040/9781350349193
Byrom, T., & Lightfoot, N. (2013). Interrupted trajectories: The impact of academic failure on the social mobility of working-class students. *British Journal of Sociology of Education*, *34*(5–6), 812–828. https://doi.org/10.1080/01425692.2013.816042
Ceder, S. (2018). *Towards a posthuman theory of educational relationality* (1st ed.). Routledge.
Chappell, K., Natanel, K., & Wren, H. (2023). Letting the ghosts in: Re-designing HE teaching and learning through posthumanism. *Teaching in Higher Education*, *28*(8), 2066–2088. https://doi.org/10.1080/13562517.2021.1952563
Chen, J. (2022). Clothing and identity: Chinese rural students' embodied transformations in the urban university. *Journal of Sociology*, *58*(3), 379–394. https://doi.org/10.1177/14407833211038613
Deleuze, G., & Foucault, M. (1977). Intellectuals and power. In M. Foucault (Ed.), *Language, counter-memory, practice: selected essays and interviews* (pp. 205–217). Cornell University Press.
Deleuze, G., & Guattari, F. (1983). *Anti-Oedipus: Capitalism and schizophrenia*. University of Minnesota Press.
Deleuze, G., & Guattari, F. (1988). *A thousand plateaus: Capitalism and schizophrenia* (Vol. 1). Athlone Pr.
Fox, N. J., & Alldred, P. (2015). New materialist social inquiry: Designs, methods and the research-assemblage. *International Journal of Social Research Methodology*, *18*(4), 399–414. https://doi.org/10.1080/13645579.2014.921458
Fox, N. J., & Alldred, P. (2017). *Sociology and the new materialism: Theory, research, action* (1st ed.). Sage.
Franceschelli, M., Evans, K., & Schoon, I. (2016). 'A fish out of water?' The therapeutic narratives of class change. *Current Sociology*, *64*(3), 353–372. https://doi.org/10.1177/0011392115595064
Friedman, S. (2016). Habitus clivé and the emotional imprint of social mobility. *The Sociological Review*, *64*(1), 129–147. https://doi.org/10.1111/1467-954X.12280
Fröhlich, G., & Rehbein, B. (2014). Bourdieu-Handbuch: Leben—Werk—Wirkung. In *Bourdieu-Handbuch* (Sonderausgabe). J. B. Metzler'sche Verlagsbuchhandlung & Carl Ernst Poeschel GmbH.
Geerts, E., & Van der Tuin, I. (2021). Almanac: Diffraction & reading diffractively. *Matter: Journal of New Materialist Research*, *2*(1), 173–177. https://doi.org/10.1344/jnmr.v2i1.33380

Haraway, D. J. (2008). *When species meet*. University of Minnesota Press.
Hoel, A. S. (2018). Technicity. In R. Braidotti & M. Hlavajova (Eds.), *Posthuman glossary* (pp. 421–423). Bloomsbury Academic.
Jenkins, R. (1992). *Pierre Bourdieu. Key sociologists*. Routledge.
Johansson, M., & Jones, S. (2019). Interlopers in class: A duoethnography of working-class women academics. *Gender Work Organization*, *26*, 1527–1545. https://doi.org/10.1111/gwao.12398
Keane, E. (2023). Chameleoning to fit in? Working class student teachers in Ireland performing differential social class identities in their placement schools. *Educational Review*, 1–20. https://doi.org/10.1080/00131911.2023.2185592
Kramer, R.-T. (2013). Habitus(-wandel)« im Spiegel von »Krise« und »Bewährung. *Zeitschrift für Qualitative Forschung*, *14*(1), 13–32. https://doi.org/10.3224/zqf.v14i1.15450
Lee, E. M., & Kramer, R. (2013). Out with the old, in with the new? Habitus and social mobility at selective colleges. *Sociology of Education*, *86*(1), 18–35. https://doi.org/10.1177/0038040712445519
Lehmann, W. (2007). "I just didn't feel like I fit in": The role of habitus in university dropout decisions. *Canadian Journal of Higher Education*, *37*(2), 89–110. https://doi.org/10.47678/cjhe.v37i2.542
McLeod, J. (2005). Feminists re-reading Bourdieu: Old debates and new questions about gender habitus and gender change. *Theory and Research in Education*, *3*(1), 11–30. https://doi.org/10.1177/1477878505049832
Moi, T. (1991). Appropriating Bourdieu: Feminist theory and Pierre Bourdieu's sociology of culture. *New Literary History*, *22*(4), 1017. https://doi.org/10.2307/469077
Murris, K., & Bozalek, V. (2019). Diffracting diffractive readings of texts as methodology: Some propositions. *Educational Philosophy and Theory*, *51*(14), 1504–1517. https://doi.org/10.1080/00131857.2019.1570843
Nairz-Wirth, E., Feldmann, K., & Spiegl, J. (2017). Habitus conflicts and experiences of symbolic violence as obstacles for non-traditional students. *European Educational Research Journal*, *16*(1), 12–29. https://doi.org/10.1177/1474904116673644
Puwar, N. (2004). *Space invaders: Race, gender and bodies out of place*. Berg.
Quinn, J. (2004). Understanding working-class "drop-out" from higher education through a sociocultural lens: Cultural narratives and local contexts. *International Studies in Sociology of Education*, *14*(1), 57–74. https://doi.org/10.1080/09620210400200119
Reay, D. (2021). The working classes and higher education: Meritocratic fallacies of upward mobility in the United Kingdom. *European Journal of Education*, *56*(1), 53–64. https://doi.org/10.1111/ejed.12438
Reay, D., Crozier, G., & Clayton, J. (2010). 'Fitting in' or 'standing out': Working-class students in UK higher education. *British Educational Research Journal*, *36*(1), 107–124.
Sakr, M. (2020). Deleuzian approaches to researching student experience in higher education. In J. Huisman & M. Tight (Eds.), *Theory and method in higher education research* (pp. 131–145). Emerald Publishing Limited. https://doi.org/10.1108/S2056-375220200000006009
Schadler, C. (2013). *Vater, Mutter, Kind werden: Eine posthumanistische Ethnographie der Schwangerschaft*. Transcript.
Schadler, C. (2016). New Materialism und Allgemeine Systemtheorie. Eine kritische Parallellektüre. In K. Möller & J. Siri (Eds.), *Systemtheorie und Gesellschaftskritik* (pp. 133–150). Transcript Verlag.
Skeggs, B. (2004). *Class, self, culture*. Routledge.
Stengers, I. (2011). *Thinking with Whitehead: A free and wild creation of concepts*. Harvard University Press.
Taguchi, H. L., & St. Pierre, E. A. (2017). Using concept as method in educational and social science inquiry. *Qualitative Inquiry*, *23*(9), 643–648. https://doi.org/10.1177/1077800417732634
Taylor, C. A., & Gannon, S. (2018). Doing time and motion diffractively: Academic life everywhere and all the time. *International Journal of Qualitative Studies in Education*, *31*(6), 465–486. https://doi.org/10.1080/09518398.2017.1422286
Waterson, R. (2005). Enduring landscape, changing habitus: The Sa'dan Toraja of Sulawesi, Indonesia. In J. Hillier & E. Rooksby (Ed.), *Habitus: A sense of place* (2nd ed., pp. 334–354). Routledge.
Williams, J. (2018). Process ontologies. In R. Braidotti & M. Hlavajova (Eds.), *Posthuman glossary*. Bloomsbury Publishing.

DISCONTINUING, FADING OUT OR JUST SIMPLY LEAVING? THE IMPORTANCE OF MEASURING STUDENT DEPARTURE BEHAVIOUR IN DIFFERENT WAYS

Elisabeth Hovdhaugen[a] and Monia Anzivino[b]

[a]Nordic Institute for Studies of Innovation, Research and Education, Norway
[b]University of Trento, Italy

ABSTRACT

This chapter discusses student departure, students leaving their programme before degree completion, and how that phenomenon can be measured in different contexts. Hence, the chapter is largely methodological and uses Norway and Italy as contrasting cases to illustrate different kinds of measurements and how this involves the conceptualisation of dropout or student departure. From the different meanings the concept of dropout takes on, the authors identify different definitions and ways of operationalising it, which also depend on the theoretical perspective and the resulting research questions. Moreover, by using the country case studies, the authors show how context-specific educational system traits, as well as country policy characteristics, are intertwined with the methodological definition of the concept of dropout in higher education.

Keywords: Dropout in higher education; measurement; Norway; Italy; educational policy

INTRODUCTION

Student departure, students leaving their programme before degree completion, is an issue which has received increased attention in the past decades (Vossensteyn et al., 2015). Reports indicate that this is a critical issue in many countries (see for example Quinn, 2013; Schnepf, 2017; Organisation for Economic Cooperation and Development (OECD), 2019), and in some contexts, student departure is comparatively large.

There are many ways of recording student departure, and it has historically been done in a multitude of ways. A common misconception is to assume that the dropout rate is just the opposite of the completion rate, which is a too simplistic way of understanding the phenomenon. The reason for this is that such a definition assumes that all students who do not complete within the estimated time to degree have dropped out of higher education. Older versions of the OECD's 'Education at a Glance' reports use this measure (see for example OECD, 1998, 2004, 2007). Today, the OECD have discontinued using this simplistic understanding and focus more on completion rates. However, over time the OECD has also tried out various other concepts related to departure, such as 'survival rates' or students who 'fail to successfully complete the program they enter' (OECD, 2009, p. 69). This overview of just the ways OECD has defined students who leave prior to degree completion indicates that there are many ways of defining the concept of student departure or dropout.

The aim of this contribution is primarily related to methods in higher education, by defining concepts and discussing how definitions are related to data sources and analyses. The chapter will problematise the definitions of student departure, or dropout which is the concept we mainly will use, as well as show the advantages of using several data sources to map and document the phenomenon.

Dropping out has several negative consequences, both for the individual, the institution and society at large. At the social level, it represents a waste of public and private resources, and it hampers the development of human capital, important for the job market, which in turn may hinder economic and social development (Bound & Turner, 2011; OECD, 2023, p. 108). At the individual level, it has negative consequences because it may result in lower-qualified jobs, increasing social inequalities, low self-esteem and a reduced ability to understand the complex issues of contemporary society (see for example Aina et al., 2022; Chies et al., 2014; Hovdhaugen, 2009). Finally, at the institutional level, students dropping out is a problem for universities because it impacts their resource situation, especially if institutional funding is in any way linked to the proportion of students graduating or graduating on time. Additionally, high levels of student departure may also have a negative impact on institutional reputation and thus potentially on the future recruitment of students (see for example Al Hassani & Wilkins, 2022; Tinto, 1975).

Given its relevance, it is essential to understand the size of the phenomenon of student departure. However, its magnitude depends partly on how it is measured and partly on how it is defined. Indeed, in the empirical literature, higher education dropout rates are highly variable because they are often measured differently and based on data from different sources.

THE MULTIPLE MEANINGS OF THE DROPOUT CONCEPT: DEFINITION AND MEASUREMENT

There are many ways of recording student departure, and it has historically been done in a multitude of ways. The notion of 'student departure' was termed by Tinto in his book *Leaving College* as a means to cover different forms – and then different meanings – of students leaving their degree prior to degree completion. The word 'dropout', indeed, would have a negative connotation, as this labels the individual as a failure, even though this is rarely how the individuals see themselves (see Tinto, 1993, p. 3). Also, the term 'failure' may sometimes be used as synonymous with dropout, as well as 'non-completion', 'abandonment', 'desertion' and 'disaffiliation'. These are all words that describe the students' dropping out as an involuntary process, a suffered experience. With a less negative connotation, the term 'withdrawal' implies rather a choice, as a form of intended event. Hence, by using different words to describe the process of leaving higher education prior to degree completion one may also move to different kinds of understandings of the process, both more positive and more negative ones. Tight (2020) points out that the ideas of student retention and engagement are linked and are concepts which build on each other.

All the previous terms indicate an action from the side of the individual, that is the meaning is focused on the student's perspective. Differently, the terms 'attrition' and 'retention' reveals an institutional perspective, where also the university's role is also called into question. The institutional perspective is often adopted by American studies (see for example Bean & Metzner, 1985; Pascarella & Terenzini, 1991, 2005; Tinto, 1982, 1987) to talk about student departure and its analysis. The reason for this is threefold: (1) that student departure often is seen from an institutional perspective in the US, following Tinto's (1993) argument that what happens at the institution is important, (2) that American higher education institutions have a vested interest in keeping students they have accepted for the full degree as they generate revenue through tuition fees, and (3) that many studies use data from one or few institutions, as there is no national registry data covering all higher education institutions in the USA.

In addition to the distinctions between positive and negative connotations subtended by the different terms and between individual and institutional perspectives, the phenomenon of student departure can also be analysed by distinguishing *when* the interruption occurs (in what level of the study or when in the course), the reversibility of the interruption (if students can return or not) and the motivations for leaving, as Tinto (1975, 1993) pointed out.

Students can leave the university system altogether, or they can change from one higher education institution to another (with or without maybe remaining in the same disciplinary area), or they can switch between different types of degree or fields of study (Hovdhaugen, 2009; Tinto, 1993). Commonly, students leaving their degree programme before completion leave during the first year; however, there are also instances of students leaving at another, later stage of their student career, sometimes as late as having finished all examinations without completing the final dissertation and thus not eligible to receive the certificate for completion.

The different temporality of leaving could be related to the motivations leading to dropout from university, as well as the possibility to reverse the abandonment. There may be different reasons for leaving early and late, as there are different reasons linked to the type of departure. In the first case, early leaving may be linked to the study programme being too academically demanding or the choice of study field being wrong, while students leaving late may do so due to a good job offer. Correspondingly, Hovdhaugen and Aamodt (2009) point out that there are different types of reasons for transferring to a different study programme and for leaving higher education altogether (dropping out).

These distinctions define several types of dropout and different perspectives of the issue. Which of these are appropriate for studying student departure in a particular setting or country is related to the theoretical approach, the research questions and the aims of the study and the available data. In the next section, we will examine briefly the main theoretical approaches and the different definitions that derive from them.

DIFFERENT THEORETICAL APPROACHES TO STUDENT DEPARTURE

In addition to being linked to research question and aims of the study, the chosen theoretical approach can also influence how dropout is defined and measured. Over the last few decades, scholars from different disciplinary fields have developed three main theoretical models to study the dropout from higher education: one derived from sociology, another from a psychological perspective and, finally, an economic understanding of the phenomenon.

The sociological models focus on the importance of social and academic integration, the relationship between the student and their environment, particularly the institution the student is attending. Dropout is interpreted as a longitudinal process where students' commitment and goals (Tinto, 1975, 1993), students' habitus and the link between that and the habitus of the institution (Reay et al., 2001; Thomas, 2002) and their social conditions (Bean, 1980) interact with the academic institution structure and organisation and its practices, norms and values.

There are also psychological theories focusing on the relevance of social and academic integration for intention to drop out as, but these theories emphasise the role of students' psychological characteristics such as self-efficacy, attributions, expectations and motivations to determine their grade of academic integration (see for example Brooman & Darwent, 2014; Morelli et al., 2023). These characteristics may influence the student's interaction with the institution through a psychological process that, if successful, results in positive internal attribution and motivation, leading to integration and institutional fit.

Finally, economic theories consider dropout as the result of a process where students calculate costs and benefits of their current study and alternatives they may have (both at university and possible job offers), making it a rational choice (Becker & Hecken, 2009). In this case, students weigh the expected financial returns from education and the financial costs, opportunity costs and expected educational success, taking into account their financial situation and academic performance. If the costs are greater than the benefit, the rational decision for the student would be to leave. Hence, this is more of a rational choice approach to the process of dropping out.

To sum up, the different theoretical views of student departure do lead to slightly different kinds of analyses and thus possibly also to different ways of measuring and studying dropout. For instance, the view of dropout as a process, as exemplified in sociological ways of understanding dropout, implies a longitudinal perspective that needs to access data (registry or survey data) on the same individuals repeatedly for many years. For studies of the interaction between student and institution using the psychological perspective, survey data at micro-level is required. This type of data can capture student's attitudes, experiences and motivations through psychological scales. Both these perspectives can be covered using various forms of qualitative data. Finally, for studies using an economic rational choice approach, only information regarding the student is strictly necessary.

DIFFERENT DATA SOURCES, DIFFERENT OPERATIONALISATION, AND DIFFERENT MEASURES

When working with dropout data it is important to also pay attention to the type of data sources used, as the phenomenon cannot be measured the same way when the researcher use survey data and administrative data. These are both two primary data sources, which will require different definitions of the phenomenon. When using survey data, respondents most commonly define themselves as dropouts or students who have left their degree prematurely. In registry data on the other hand, the researcher usually has to define who has dropped out and who should still be counted as a student.

Hence, the point of departure is different in the two types of data, and this may also have implications for over- or under-estimation of the phenomenon. In survey data, it may be that students do not define themselves as dropouts, even though they have left their degree before completion, leading to the underestimation of dropout. In administrative data the opposite might be a problem, that researchers define students as dropouts even if they are not, because they fulfil some initial criteria set. For example, will students go in and out of the administrative data, if they for example have a gap year, or if they are sick for a longer period. Thus, it becomes a question if this then should be defined as dropout or not (given that the student eventually returns and continues their higher education). This illustrates the inherent challenge in using administrative data to define dropout that it is a risk of overestimating the share dropping out.

In order to create comparable measures from data in administrative registers, at the national level is it common to estimate aggregate indicators, such as the share of students who return to take the second year of their bachelor's degree, or the share or students who are retained though the full programme. These indicators are labelled as 'aggregate' as they may not be estimated based on micro-data, but rather a computation of the number of students starting the second year as a share of students starting in the first year. These may be based directly on large data bases where students are registered and can be tracked though their educational career (as in the Norwegian case) or aggregate data, whereby it is possible to calculate first-year dropout by looking at the ratio between those enroled in the second year and those who matriculated the first year (which is the usual way to calculate this in Italy).

TWO CASE STUDIES – AN ILLUSTRATION OF TYPES OF DROPOUTS IN DIFFERENT SYSTEMS

The types of dropouts relevant in a particular higher education system are linked to a range of system features, as well as the policy and practice in that country. Thomas and Hovdhaugen (2014) point to several aspects being relevant: access to higher education, as in the share of students who start higher education, as well as how restricted or competitive access is, the structure of the system (if there are several types of institutions or several tiers of institutions), if there is only one or more routes to access higher education, and the level of flexibility in the system. They conclude by stating 'structure and organisation of HE [higher education], especially the extent to which it is possible to transfer between institutions affects the level of completion and non-completion' (Thomas & Hovdhaugen, 2014, p. 464), which directly points to how system flexibility affects if dropout rates are high or not.

In order to illustrate how dropout has been and can be measured, we will present two case studies, Norway and Italy, where we show the systems' features in connection with the implemented policies and the data used in studies on students leaving university. The two countries face similar challenges regarding timely completion in higher education, as both countries have had slow study progression and relatively high dropout rates (compared to other OECD countries) for decades. There are educational system features which might be driving dropout rates, such as system flexibility, costs to students in the higher education system, and the current labour market situation. In Norway, the low cost of enrolment allows students to 'try out higher education' and also to use the flexibility inherent in the possibility to transfer credits from one institution to another (Thomas & Hovdhaugen, 2014). In Italy, when unemployment rates increase, the university can function as a form of 'parking lot', where students who could have entered the labour market but who are unlikely to find a job right away, and thus are likely to be unemployed, can keep busy as students while waiting for an open position. This is facilitated by the relatively low cost of staying at university. This is then a way for students who have completed their degree to avoid unemployment (Hovdhaugen & Stensaker, 2018).

However, there are also quite large differences between the two countries. Norway, a small Nordic country with about 5.5 million inhabitants, has a higher education system with around 300,000 students and 48.1% of adults with a tertiary level education (OECD, 2023). The higher education system is formally binary (Kyvik, 2009), consists of ten public universities, six public specialised university institutions (focusing in one area, such as music or architecture) and five public university colleges, spread all over the country. There are also some private institutions in Norway, but in terms of student numbers they only constitute around 15% of the system. In this paper, we will focus on students at public institutions in Norway.

Italy is more than 10 times as big as Norway in terms of population, 59 million people, with around 1.8 million students in higher education and only 20.3% of adults with a tertiary level education (OECD, 2023). The higher education system consists of a range of institutions, with 68 public universities as the largest single institutional type, including four polytechnics and three specialised universities. In addition to public universities, there are 20 private universities providing in-person education and 11 online universities that are required to do in-person examinations but where all the teaching is done online. The share of private providers in higher education is limited (Trivellato et al., 2016), and in this study, we only focus on public institutions.

A Case Study From Norway

As a policy issue, dropout in higher education has become more important over time, from the 1990s onwards. In the early 1990s Norwegian higher education experienced a large increase in student numbers (Aamodt, 1995). This increase in students also enhanced the focus on student completion and dropout and spurred the first few studies on the topic. However, it seems as if, in the first studies done on the issue, dropout was not the primary focus of the project, but rather first-year students and their experiences (see Berg, 1992; Egge, 1992; Eikeland & Ogden, 1988). As this group of students are more likely to leave higher education, dropout was an issue that emerged through these studies, which all were surveys. Hence, in all these studies dropout was more of a byproduct of a larger research question or as a potential outcome for the subjects studied.

As student numbers in Norway rose during the 1990s and it became possible to use data from administrative registers to research students' movement in and out of higher education, studies using this kind of data emerged. Aamodt (2001) focuses on dropout and completion in the entire system, differentiating primarily between types of institutions and levels of dropout by gender and region. The main findings of the study are that university students tend to leave more often than students in university colleges, that men are more likely to leave without a degree than women, and that there are some observable field of study differences. However, due to data limitations it was not possible to do more in depth investigations into these differences. In a continuation of the project, Aamodt (2002) focused exclusively on students at Norway's then largest institution, the University of Oslo, as this was one of the institutions with the lowest levels of completion.

During the same time period, there was a general idea in society that higher education was inefficient, and students spent too much time finishing their degrees. As a consequence of this a commission was set down, which delivered their report on changes to the system in May 2000 (NOU, 2000:14). As this commission's work overlapped with the start of the Bologna process (Bologna Declaration, 1999), a consequence was that the Bologna ideas were adopted and the three-year undergraduate + two-year master's degree scheme was suggested. This change of degree structure was implemented in practice from autumn semester 2003, as the 'Quality' reform (St.meld no. 27, 2000–2001). This was a reform which involved a range of changes in higher education: in the funding structure, in teaching and follow-up of students, as well as in governance of institutions.

Comparisons of student departure rates in undergraduate university education before and after implementation of the reform show that the reform had no practical effect on dropout, but it did reduce the rates of students switching from one institution to another (Hovdhaugen, 2011). Another study, looking at statistical patterns of withdrawal at universities and university colleges also did not find any change in dropout. This study points to two possible explanations. The first is that dropout is largely due to external factors, such as motivation to study and academic preparedness, or that students take on a job rather than continue studying to degree completion. Consequently, the institutions cannot really impact their dropout rates. The second possible explanation is that registration of students has changed, and after the reform, students would be taken off the lists as a student if they are not active and 'produce' credits. Hence, before the reform, an individual could choose to be registered as a student for as long as they wanted to, while after the reform students who did not take any credits in a year lost their right to be registered as students in that programme (Aamodt & Hovdhaugen, 2011, p. 8). This implies that students who are delayed in their studies may lose their spot in the study programme, and if the student wants to start studying again, they have to reapply and get admitted again.

When the new study programmes were introduced, application to higher education also changed. At university, students used to only apply to a particular school (such as the Faculty of Humanities or Faculty of Social Sciences) prior to the reform, but after the reform they applied to a specific study programme (e.g. History, Sociology or Political Science). Hence, the number of available options to apply to (number of study programmes) increased heavily, and students also needed to choose their major before applying (as the programme usually was linked to the field of study the student majored in). The new programme structure also opened up creating closer learning communities between students (Tinto, 2000, 2003, pp. 1–8), which in turn is assumed to contribute to students staying enroled. But with the admission tied to the programme rather than the schools, students were now supposed to progress though their programme by completing their courses. Another new feature of the system after the reform was that institutions could remove a student's right to study in a programme if they did not take any credits, which in practice meant that students who pause or fail too much have to leave the programme and reapply (and get admitted) in order to be able to complete the degree.

However, the dropout rates in general university education stayed the same, while fewer students switched from one institution/programme to another (Hovdhaugen, 2011). Hence, from an institutional perspective the rate of students leaving reduced, as fewer students switched from institution to institution. From an individual perspective students might to a greater extent have experienced a more direct route towards degree completion. However, this may not have directly observable in effects on graduation rates, as the flexibility of the system is the same as before the implementation of the reform. Flexibility in the Norwegian higher education system is mainly linked to the possibility to transfer credits between institutions and programmes. This implies the even if a student 'restarts' in a new programme, it might be possible to integrate previously taken courses in the new programme and thus not cause the student to become delayed (Thomas & Hovdhaugen, 2014).

Switching programmes is very closely linked to field of study, as it is more common in general degrees in humanities and social sciences than in short professional degrees, such as nursing, social work and pre-school teaching. Several studies show that students in short professional degrees, with a clearly defined labour market, are less inclined to change programme. In these groups of students generally dropout rates are low, but the few who leave the programme leave higher education altogether rather than making a new choice (Aamodt & Hovdhaugen, 2011; Helland & Hovdhaugen, 2022).

When it comes to studies of student departure in Norway, there have largely been two types, both quantitative: studies using survey data and studies using data from public registries. The first studies, done in the 1990s and early 2000s, were often based on only one institution, either using survey or administrative data. In recent years, administrative data have become more accessible and as this enables a full higher education system coverage, where all students at all types of institutions are present in the data. Most of the recent studies of student departure in Norway are done using registry data (see Hovdhaugen, 2011, 2015; Helland & Hovdhaugen, 2022, Hundebo, 2023).

The two data sources, survey data and registry data may give diverging results, as Hovdhaugen (2009) found the dropout rate to be 16–18% four years after study start in a retrospective survey study, while in registry data for the same period dropout rates were found to be around 30% (Hovdhaugen, 2011). The reason for this difference is likely that while the rate based on survey may suffer from non-response and those who left early on in their studies not being motivated to participate, the registry data study may over-rate dropout as there may be students who do return to higher education after the period of observation (four years) is over. Hence, this challenge is linked to definitions and the timespan the study covers.

Access to higher education is also an issue which is at least partly linked to flexibility in the higher education system. Access to higher education in Norway is almost solely based on grades from upper secondary education (Sandsør et al., 2022), and students have to have completed with a higher education entrance certificate in order to be eligible to apply to any study programme. The application process is centralised and done digitally, and students rank their options (as a combination of study programme and institution), implying that if they do not get admitted to their first choice, they are in the competition for their second or third choice (applicants can list a total of 10 choices).

Most programmes only require the general certificate for admission, but some programmes, such as medicine, engineering and science programmes, require students to have taken particular subjects, in advanced mathematics and science, to be eligible to participate in the competition for a spot in the study programme. These types of programmes are generally more competitive to get access to, while the majority of programmes in Norwegian higher education have low or no grade requirements for access. This means that most applicants can get a spot in higher education, particularly if they are willing to study outside any of the three major cities/universities (Oslo, Bergen and Trondheim).

A Case Study From Italy

The Italian higher education system has undergone several reforms in recent decades, several of which were at least partially aimed at increasing the number of graduates among young adults. However, although these reforms have led to some improvements in indicators of study success, the Italian system is still characterised by a poor capacity to produce graduates, high levels of dropout, and chronic graduation delays (Aina et al., 2018; Benvenuto et al., 2012). According to the OECD (2008), Italy had one of the highest dropout rates (55%), and according to the 2022 edition, only 21% of students in a bachelor's programme graduate by the end of the estimated time-to-degree, with 32% not graduated and no longer enroled in higher education after the estimated time of the bachelor programme plus three years (OECD, 2022).

The graduation rates and the proportion of students completing within estimated time-to-degree improved in the years immediately after the introduction of the two study cycles (bachelor's degree of three years and the master's degree of two years duration, known as '3+2 reform') (Di Pietro & Cutillo, 2008), but later studies have shown a new growth in dropout rates after a few years in the last cohort analysed (Argentin & Triventi, 2011). The National Agency for the Evaluation of the University and Research System (ANVUR) has reported that dropout rates between the first and the second year have decreased in programmes in both cycles for quite some time, until 2019/2020, when it was about 12% for three-year programme. Then it increased again, to reach the 2011level, about 15% for three-year programmes. The departure from university in the years following the first year of study is also sizeable. The most updated data show that 'within the estimated time-to-degree, approximately one in five students drop out of university studies and after six years this ratio rises to one in four' (ANVUR, 2023, p. 43).

Following the suggestions made by Thomas and Hovdhaugen (2014) about which aspects of the educational system could be relevant to the dynamic of non-completion rates, we examine some features of the Italian system.

Since the educational reforms in 1969, access to higher education has been open to all students graduating from a five-year academic, technical or vocational programme in upper secondary education. However, graduates from technical and vocational programmes enrol less frequently than graduates from academic programmes and are also more likely to drop out. For some university programmes, access is selective based on grades and admission test scores. Selection tests are used in degree programmes with more applicants than the possible number of entries. For the degree programmes in Medicine and Surgery, Veterinary, Health professions and Primary Education, the test is national, and the maximum number of students entering the programmes each year is decided by the Ministry. For other degree programmes, the selection test is local, and in other cases, there is no selective test required for admission. However, there is a guidance test specifically designed to prevent study from being unsuccessful. This test can be helpful to individuals who are unsure if they have the minimum level of knowledge required for success in the degree programme, and the test will direct them to additional classes to gain the required skills.

Italian tuition fees are based on the family's level of income. Fees are relatively low (but are higher than in the Nordic countries, see OECD, 2021), and they vary significantly by geographical area as well as by fields of study (Contini et al., 2018). The presence of the preferred degree course in one's town mainly determines the cost of living for the student, as many students choose to live with their family while studying. In Italy, all regions have at least one university, and in the most populous ones, there are many universities that student-commuters can easily reach (Ballarino, 2015). Thus, students can choose to stay with their family and live in a more rural area with lower living costs.

In Italy, it is possible to change degree programme within the same university or to transfer to another university. The acknowledgement of acquired credits and examinations is possible if the content of the two programmes is similar. Students can withdraw from one programme and enrol in another or transfer their academic achievements to another university, asking for complete or partial recognition of their previous studies. Changes between the first and second year are about 15% and about half transfer to another university (ANVUR, 2018). Pauses during studies are also possible (explicitly by a formal interruption of studies or implicitly by not paying the fees), and students can continue after the pause. For instance, in the event of the birth of a child, it is possible to formally suspend studies temporarily.

However, students can be 'timed out' of the system if the student does not pass any examination (or achieve a certain number of credits) for several consecutive years. The time before a student would be timed out used to be eight consecutive years, until the 1999 reform. Today, the conditions for being timed out vary across study programme and university. A time out cannot occur if the student has passed all the examinations but has not completed the final thesis, which is required for graduation. In this case, the student cannot lose his/her study place and can come back and finish the degree anytime, even after many years.

These system characteristics can explain why a large proportion of students spend more time than estimated to complete their degree and therefore finish late. Universities have tried to combat this by instituting higher fees for students who do not complete their university examinations within a set time period, thereby aiming at reducing the proportion of students who are timed out from university studies.

In addition to student departure as a potential financial and reputational challenge for institutions, the Italian higher education rules can have implications for the operationalization and measurement of the dropout phenomenon. Since students can be enrolled at the university for many years without passing an examination, this may make who should be considered a dropout challenging to define. Should students who are registered but have no study progression be considered students or dropouts? And should the students who have passed all the examinations, apart from their final thesis, and thus postponed graduation (perhaps indefinitely) be considered dropouts?

In conceptual terms, timing out students who have no study progression is an extreme: without a direct action of leaving from the side of the student, they are 'banned' from completion. This is like letting one's study career perish. However, before the formal time out, students can stay many years in a 'condition in-between', enroled but inactive, and in some universities, students may never be timed out by paying their fees and failing an examination every three/four/five years. Hence, they can have student status that lasts a lifetime. As the rules for time out vary across institutions, it becomes difficult to reach an agreement on a convincing measure of dropout at the national level.

On the other hand, at the institutional level it is possible to distinguish between different types of leaving, as this is registered in the administrative data at institutional level. Thus, the institutional data contains information on whether the student leaving was an explicit withdrawal or an implicit abandonment (due to the non-renewal of enrolment). Programme changes within the same university as well as changes to another institution are registered, making it possible to track transfers to and from other universities. This opens two possible ways of using the data, either by using administrative data to, for example, study differences between different kinds of student departure, or by using the administrative information as a basis for a survey.

Italian scholars have used institutional data from individual universities to study dropout. Zago et al. (2014) used data from University of Padua to investigate student success in university studies. They used administrative data and an event history approach to distinguish university results in programme changes, study-delay, dropout and graduation. They merged the administrative data with a survey on psychological aspects related to the university experience in order to investigate factors associated with study success. Anzivino and Rostan (2018) used longitudinal administrative data from the University of Pavia and an event-history approach to investigate the different types of dropout and factors associated with dropout. They distinguished dropout in four categories: (1) implicit dropout (the non-renewal of enrolment), (2) explicit dropout (the withdrawal from a programme), (3) transfer to another university, and (4) time-out. By merging administrative data with survey data on reasons for leaving the institution they formulated a dropout typology, which was based on different dimensions of motivations for leaving, highlighting how implicit dropout and time-out have similar motivational profiles, and explicit dropout is partly motivated by the same reasons for abandonment of the transfer to another institution.

DISCUSSION AND CONCLUSION

This aim of this chapter has been to discuss the many meanings of dropout, how this relates to the educational context, and the importance of measuring the phenomenon in an appropriate way. We have shown how definitions, theoretical approaches, the operationalisation and different kinds of data can impact on the possibilities to study the phenomenon and its variations.

The concept of dropout or student departure has multiple meanings. The problem of dropout in higher education can be investigated from a narrow point of view as the individual leaving their university studies without graduating or from a large one, as an educational dispersion which includes suspension, withdrawal, delay, change of programme and/or institution. Most commonly, dropout at university refers to the failure to complete the degree programme and thus leaving before graduation.

The theoretical perspective – and the research questions derived from it – implies the choice between different definitions and operationalisation. This process, however, cannot be separated from, on the one hand, the nature and quality of the available data sources; and, on the other hand, from the educational system within which the measurement takes place, where the data are collected and where also exogenous factors may play a role in determining the extent and the causes of the dropout phenomenon, and the possibilities to study and measure its several expressions.

The two case studies have shown how policies change, and the different characteristics of the higher education systems can affect the way dropout is considered and measured, providing examples of the implications of the specific context on the study of dropout.

In both countries, the flexibility of the system – allowing students to change programme and institution without losing credits and examinations – favours students' persistence, enabling them to reshape an initial wrong choice of programme. From the methodological point of view, to measure dropout in a narrow sense, this could imply considering time to degree as a more flexible way to measure completion rather than focussing on the estimated time-to-degree of the study programme. Even if the systems are flexible, the transfer experience could mean that the student requires more time to complete than a student following the regular path.

In Norway, transfers, or students switching from one institution/programme to another, are the most common type of student departure (Hovdhaugen, 2009), far more common than dropout. This implies that student departure probably is a more urgent matter for institutions, since student leave the programme they started, but less of a problem for individuals and society.

In Italy, the large autonomy of the university institutions makes it possible to have different rules for when students are timed out, such as the different number of years of inactivity or other conditions set for time out. To measure this form of dropout at a supra-institutional level, then, it is necessary to take into account this characteristic and to fix an adequate observation time. These differing conditions for time-out at institutions also leaves open the conceptual issue about how to consider who has actually completed. A relevant example here is how to handle students who have finished the examinations but not graduated, and students who occasionally try, failing, to pass one examination avoiding the definitive time out.

The case studies have shown that Norway and Italy face similar challenges in higher education in terms of slow progression and high dropout rates, as their higher education systems grow, in line with the development suggested by Trow (1973, 2006). But, as the case studies displayed, there are also significant differences, starting with the graduation rate among the adult population, which is much higher in Norway than in Italy.

In any higher education system, is it important to be able to measure student departure or dropout in a proper way. This calls for a thorough investigation of exactly what the pattern of departure looks like in the particular country, both in terms of how high the rates are, what kind of student departure we are talking about and when it occurs. However, in order to be able to get good estimates of dropout, and useful indicators or feedback for institutions, there is a need for system-wide data on students leaving their institution prior to degree completion. These kind of data open up studies of the bigger picture of dropout and departure. Measuring and qualifying different kinds of departure, however, is much more difficult without micro-level data.

Thus, in settings where these kind of data are difficult to obtain, institutional data may also be a valuable source of data for the individual institution (even though this kind of data does not always make it possible to distinguish between different kinds of dropout/departure, such as in Norway). But at the same time, it is better to have some data covering students' pathways through a higher education system, as all forms of knowledge will enhance our understanding of what drives completion and dropout in that particular higher education system.

REFERENCES

Aamodt, P. O. (1995). Floods, bottlenecks and backwaters: An analysis of expansion in higher education in Norway. *Higher Education*, *30*(1), 63–80.

Aamodt, P. O. (2001). *Studiegjennomføring og studiefrafall: En statistisk oversikt*. NIFU Report 14/2001. NIFU.

Aamodt, P. O. (2002). *Studiemobilitet til og fra Universitetet i Oslo*. NIFU Report 10/2002. NIFU.

Aamodt, P. O., & Hovdhaugen, E. (2011). *Frafall og gjennomføring i lavere grads studier før og etter kvalitetsreformen. En sammenlikning mellom begynnerkullene fra 1999, 2003 og 2005*. NIFU Report 38/2011. NIFU.

Aina, C., Baici, E., Casalone, G., & Pastore, F. (2018). *The economics of university dropouts and delayed graduation: A survey*. IZA Discussion Paper, No. 11421. Institute for Labor Economics.

Aina, C., Baici, E., Casalone, G., & Pastore, F. (2022). The determinants of university dropout: A review of the socio-economic literature. *Socio-Economic Planning Sciences*, *79*, 101102. https://doi.org/10.1016/j.seps.2021.101102

Al Hassani, A. A., & Wilkins, S. (2022). Student retention in higher education: The influences of organizational identification and institution reputation on student satisfaction and behaviors. *International Journal of Educational Management*, *36*(6), 1046–1064.

ANVUR. (2018). *Rapporto sul sistema della formazione superiore e della ricerca*. ANVUR.

ANVUR. (2023). *Sintesi. Rapporto sul sistema della formazione superiore e della ricerca*. ANVUR.

Anzivino, M., & Rostan, M. (2018).*Indagine sulla scelta di cambiare o interrompere il corso di studi*. University of Pavia, Research Report.

Argentin, G., & Triventi, M. (2011). Social inequality in higher education and labour market in a period of institutional reforms: Italy, 1992–2007. *Higher Education*, *61*, 309–323.

Ballarino, G. (2015). Higher education, between conservatism and permanent reform. In U. Ascoli & E. Pavolini (Eds.), *The Italian welfare state in a European perspective: A comparative analysis* (pp. 207–234). Bristol University Press.

Becker, R., & Hecken, A. E. (2009). Higher education or vocational training? An empirical test of the rational action model of educational choices suggested by Breen and Goldthorpe and Esser. *Acta Sociologica*, *52*(1), 25–45.

Bean, J. P. (1980). Dropouts and turnover: The synthesis and test of a causal model of student attrition. *Research in Higher Education*, *12*(2), 155–187.

Bean, J. P., & Metzner, B. S. (1985). A conceptual model of nontraditional undergraduate student attrition. *Review of Educational Research*, *55*(4), 485–540.

Benvenuto, G., Decataldo, A., & Fasanella, A. (2012). *C'era una volta l'università? Analisi longitudinale delle carriere degli studenti prima e dopo la "grande riforma"*. Bonnano Editore.

Berg, L. (Ed.) (1992), *Begynnerstudenten*. Rapport 8/1992. NAVFs utredningsinstitutt.

Bologna Declaration. (1999). *Towards the European higher education area*. Conference of Minsters responsible for Higher Education in 29 European countries. Bologna, Italy.

Bound, J., & Turner, S. (2011). Dropouts and diplomas: The divergence in collegiate outcomes. In E. Hanushek, S. Machin, & L. Woessmann (Eds.), *Handbook of the economics of education* (Vol. 4). Elsevier.

Brooman, S., & Darwent, S. (2014). Measuring the beginning: A quantitative study of the transition to higher education. *Studies in Higher Education*, *39*(9), 1523–1541. https://doi.org/10.1080/03075079.2013.801428

Chies, L., Graziosi, G., & Pauli, F. (2014). Job opportunities and academic dropout: The case of the University of Trieste. *Procedia Economics and Finance*, *17*, 63–70.

Contini, D., Cugnata, F., & Scagni, A. (2018). Social selection in higher education. Enrolment, dropout and timely degree attainment in Italy. *Higher Education*, *75*, 785–808.

Di Pietro, G., & Cutillo, A. (2008). Degree flexibility and university drop-out: The Italian experience. *Economics of Education Review*, *27*(5), 546–555.

Egge, M. (1992). Frafall blant begynnerstudentene. In L. Berg (Ed.), *Begynnerstudenten*. Report 8/1992. NAVFs utredningsinstitutt.

Eikeland, O.-J., & Ogden, T. (1988). *Begynnerstudenter i sitt første semester ved Universitetet i Bergen*. Universitetet i Bergen.

Helland, H., & Hovdhaugen, E. (2022). Degree completion in short professional courses: Does family background matter?. *Journal of Further and Higher Education*, *46*(5), 680–694.

Hovdhaugen, E. (2009). Transfer and dropout: Different forms of student departure in Norway. *Studies in Higher Education*, *34*(1), 1–17.

Hovdhaugen, E. (2011). Do structured study programmes lead to lower rates of dropout and student transfer from university?. *Irish Educational Studies*, *30*(2), 237–251.

Hovdhaugen, E. (2015). Working while studying: The impact of term time employment on dropout rates. *Journal of Education and Work*, *28*(6), 631–651.

Hovdhaugen, E., & Aamodt, P. O. (2009). Learning environment: Relevant or not to students' decision to leave university?. *Quality in Higher Education*, *15*(2), 177–189.

Hovdhaugen, E., & Stensaker, B. (2018). Variation in student success across Europe: Exploring the relevance of system-level explanations. *International Journal of Chinese Education*, *7*(2), 229–245.

Hundebo, P. O. (2023). Degree completion among students with an immigrant background in short-cycle welfare-oriented professional education. *Tertiary Education and Management*, *29*(1), 41–61.

Kyvik, S. (2009). *The dynamics of change in higher education: Expansion and contraction in an organisational field*. Springer.

Morelli, M., Chirumbolo, A., Baiocco, R., & Cattelino, E. (2023). Self-regulated learning self-efficacy, motivation, and intention to drop-out: The moderating role of friendships at university. *Current Psychology, 42*, 15589–15599. https://doi.org/10.1007/s12144-022-02834-4
OECD. (1998). *Education at a glance 1998*. Organisation for Economic Co-operation and Development.
OECD. (2004). *Education at a glance 2004*. Organisation for Economic Co-operation and Development.
OECD. (2007). *Education at a glance 2007*. Organisation for Economic Co-operation and Development.
OECD. (2008). *Education at a glance 2008*. Organisation for Economic Co-operation and Development.
OECD. (2009). *Education at a glance 2009*. Organisation for Economic Co-operation and Development.
OECD. (2019). *Education at a glance 2019*. Organisation for Economic Co-operation and Development.
OECD. (2021). *Education at a glance 2021*. Organisation for Economic Co-operation and Development.
OECD. (2022). *Education at a glance 2022*. Organisation for Economic Co-operation and Development.
OECD. (2023). *Education at a glance 2023: OECD Indicators*. Organisation for Economic Co-operation and Development.
Pascarella, E. T., & Terenzini, P. T. (1991). *How college affects students. Findings and insights from twenty years of research*. Jossey-Bass.
Pascarella, E. T., & Terenzini, P. T. (2005). *How college affects students. A third decade of research*. Jossey-Bass.
Quinn, J. (2013, October). *Drop-out and completion in higher education in Europe among students from under-represented groups*. NESET-Report. European Commission.
Reay, D., Davies, J., David, M., & Ball, S. J. (2001). Choices of degree or degrees of choice? Class, 'race' and the higher education choice process. *Sociology, 35*(4), 855–874.
Sandsør, A. M. J., Hovdhaugen, E., & Bøckmann, E. (2022). Age as a merit in admission decisions for higher education. *Higher Education, 83*, 379–394.
Schnepf, S. V. (2017). How do tertiary dropouts fare in the labour market? A comparison between EU countries. *Higher Education Quarterly, 71*(1), 75–96.
Thomas, L. (2002). Student retention in higher education: The role of institutional habitus. *Journal of Educational Policy, 17*(4), 423–442.
Thomas, L., & Hovdhaugen, E. (2014). Complexities and challenges of researching student completion and non-completion of HE programmes in Europe: A comparative analysis between England and Norway. *European Journal of Education, 49*(4), 457–470.
Tight, M. (2020). Student retention and engagement in higher education. *Journal of Further and Higher Education, 44*(5), 689–704.
Tinto, V. (1975). Dropout from higher education: A synthesis of recent research. *Review of Educational Research, 45*(1), 89–125.
Tinto, V. (1982). Limits to theory and practice in student attrition. *Journal of Higher Education, 53*(6), 687–700.
Tinto, V. (1987). *Leaving college: Rethinking the causes and cures of student attrition*. University of Chicago Press.
Tinto, V. (1993). *Leaving college: Rethinking the causes and cures of student attrition* (2nd ed.). University of Chicago Press.
Tinto, V. (2000). Linking learning and leaving: Exploring the role of the college classroom student departure. In J. M. Braxton (Ed.), *Reworking the student departure puzzle* (pp. 81–94). Vanderbilt University Press.
Tinto, V. (2003). *Learning better together: The impact of learning communities on student success*. Higher Education Monograph Series, 2003-1 (pp. 1–8), Syracuse University.
Trivellato, P., Triventi, M., & Traini, C. (2016). Private higher education in Italy (Ch. 3, 29–52). In M. Shah & C. S. Nair (Eds.), *A global perspective on private higher education*. Chandos Publishing.
Trow, M. (1973). *Problems in the transition from elite to mass higher education*. Report for Carnegie Commission on Higher Education. Carnegie Commission on Higher Education.

Trow, M. (2006). Reflections on the transition from elite to mass to universal access: Forms and phases of higher education in modern societies since WWII. In J. J. F. Forest & P. G. Altbach (Eds.), *International handbook of higher education* (Vol. 1, pp. 243–280). Springer.

Vossensteyn, H., Stensaker, B., Kottman, A., Hovdhaugen, E., Jongbloed, B., Wollscheid, S., Kaiser, F., Cremonini, L., Thomas, L., & Unger, M. (2015). *Dropout and completion in higher education in Europe.* European Commission.

Zago, G., Giraldi, A., Clerici, R. (2014). *Successo e insuccessonegli studi universitari. Dati, interpretazioni e proposte dall'ateneo di Padova.* Il Mulino.

NORWEGIAN PUBLIC DOCUMENTS

NOU 2000:14. (2000). *Frihet med ansvar – Om høgre utdanning og forskning i Norge.* Mjøs-utvalget. https://www.regjeringen.no/no/dokumenter/nou-2000-14/id142780/

St.meld no. 27 (2000–2001). *Gjør din plikt – Krev din rett. Kvalitetsreform av høyere utdanning.* [Do your duty – Demand your rights] Whitepaper submitted on March 9, 2001. https://www.regjeringen.no/no/dokumenter/stmeld-nr-27-2000-2001-/id194247/

BEYOND THE ORIGINAL: EXPLORING REPLICATION RESEARCH IN HIGHER EDUCATION

Karlijn Soppe[a] and Jeroen Huisman[b]

[a]*Utrecht University, The Netherlands*
[b]*Ghent University, Belgium*

ABSTRACT

In this chapter, the authors outline what replication research is and explain why this could be a helpful tool to support the trustworthiness and credibility of (earlier) research findings. Replication research has received increased attention in the light of the so-called 'replication crisis': a series of studies in psychology failed to reproduce the findings from previous studies. In higher education, replication research is relatively rare, and researchers should be aware of various challenges. The authors take stock of studies on higher education – most of these in the area of teaching and learning – that have used a replication design. Somewhat surprisingly, many studies in our field are not sufficiently clear about what exactly has been replicated and in some cases the term replication was misused. We conclude that replication research can be useful, but researchers carefully need to consider whether their approach indeed contributes to increased trustworthiness and credibility of earlier findings.

Keywords: Higher education; replication; credibility; methodological rigour; trustworthiness

INTRODUCTION

Science is characterized by an ongoing quest for reliable knowledge and effective practices. In this dynamic context, the significance of replication research is becoming increasingly prominent, serving as a crucial pillar for strengthening the credibility and generalizability of scientific discoveries. In replication research, researchers attempt to replicate the methods and procedures of original studies as closely as possible to determine whether the original findings can be confirmed in a new context, with different samples, or using alternative methodologies. The goal of replication research is to verify the robustness of scientific findings, detect potential errors or biases in original studies and thus enhance the credibility and trustworthiness of scientific knowledge. Replication research plays a critical role in validating and building upon existing research findings. Interestingly, while replication research has received widespread attention in many fields and disciplines, especially in the social and behavioural sciences, it has largely escaped the attention of higher education researchers. Of course, not all research lends itself easily for replication, but there are many quantitative studies in our field (Ferrão, 2020; Tight, 2013; Wells et al., 2015) and many of these adhere to a positivistic or post-positivistic perspective. Nevertheless, replication studies appear to be far from common (Freese & Peterson, 2017).

This chapter aims to contribute to the methodological rigour and cumulative knowledge-building in the field of higher education research, ultimately fostering a more robust foundation for evidence-based practices and informed decision-making in higher education. We first pay attention to the so-called 'replication crisis': a general concern about research practices, primarily in psychological research, where many scientific results could not be reproduced. The attention to this crisis is necessary to fully comprehend the current approaches to replication in the context of concerns about academic misconduct. Thereafter, we will carry out a scoping review to gain an understanding of the use of replication in higher education research. Before closing the chapter with several suggestions for the use of replication in our field, we will identify some possible pitfalls and challenges.

THE REPLICATION CRISIS AND ITS IMPACT

At the beginning of the 21st century, the scientific community found itself in a heated debate regarding the reproducibility of findings in many areas of research (Frias-Navarro et al., 2019). This debate, nowadays most commonly known as 'the replication crisis', gained traction within the field of psychology with influential contributions in both the scientific literature and popular news outlets (see e.g. Earp & Trafimow, 2015; Pashler & Wagenmakers, 2012). Soon evidence emerged of psychologists showing academic misconduct, including adherence to questionable research practices (QRPs) and outright fraud (e.g. John et al., 2012; Simmons et al., 2011; Stroebe et al., 2012). The most impactful was an article by Brian Nosek et al. (Open Science Collaboration, 2015), who replicated 100 experimental and correlational studies published in psychology journals. They found that only one-third of the replicated studies had significant results, while this was 97% for the original articles. The authors (2015, p. 943) concluded that 'A large portion of replications produced weaker evidence for the original findings despite using materials provided by the original authors'.

The non-reproducibility of original findings can originate from conscious, intentional actions of researchers as well as more subtle but still unethical behaviour. In his book *Research Ethics in the Social Sciences*, Bos (2020) distinguishes between deadly sins and daily sins. Deadly sins are those actions that are clearly fraudulent and punishable by severe penalties. Clear examples are *fabrication* (e.g. Derksen, 2021), which entails making up data, and *plagiarism*, the presentation of work or ideas from others, without fully acknowledging their work. Whereas the occurrence of deadly sins in published work is fairly uncommon and difficult to prevent (i.e. it would take a lot of time of editors and reviewers to detect it), most unethical scientific practice is much more subtle, more commonplace and even harder to prevent.

These so-called daily sins are somewhere between conscious and unconscious behaviour and are commonly referred to as QRPs. Although viewed as more tolerable by the scientific community than plagiarism and fabrication (Bos, 2020), QRPs pose a serious concern regarding the credibility of scientific research (Banks et al., 2016; John et al., 2012). QRPs are defined as 'design, analytic or reporting practices that have been questioned because of the potential for the practice to be employed with the purpose of presenting biased evidence in favour of an assertion' (Banks et al., 2016, p. 3). Several meta-analyses have shown that QRPs are more common than research misconduct (i.e. fabrication and plagiarism) and that researchers are more inclined to report about the misconduct and QRPs committed by others than when asked about their own scientific practices (Fanelli, 2009; Pupovac & Fanelli, 2015; Xie et al., 2021).

While not as egregious as outright research misconduct, QRPs involve actions that may bias results, inflate the significance of findings, or undermine the transparency and rigour of the research process. They are seen as violations of the American Psychological Association (APA, a leading scientific and professional organization of psychological researchers, educators and clinicians) ethics principles of integrity, fidelity and responsibility of the researcher. QRPs are often placed in a context of publication pressure. Researchers need to publish to further their career, but journals tend to favour articles that show significant results (Condon et al., 2017). As a result, scientific studies that fail to produce significant results tend to end up in a desk drawer, which is often referred to as the file-drawer problem. Because these non-significant results are undesirable for publication, the file-drawer problem in return causes publication bias. QRPs are strongly linked to testing hypotheses against the null-hypothesis (null hypothesis significance testing; NHST) and include practices like p-hacking (incorrectly rounding p-values to make effects seem significant or manipulating data until p is lower than alpha), HARKing (hypothesizing after the results are known/presenting post hoc hypotheses as if they were developed a priori) and testing all sorts of relations until significant effects are found, which is sometimes referred to as data fishing (Banks et al., 2016; Bos, 2020).

Two studies are particularly noteworthy in relation to the prevalence of QRPs. Masicampo and Lalande (2012) collected the reported p-values from three high-level psychological journals and compared their distribution. When considering the file-drawer problem and the publication bias that results from it, one would expect to see a steady decline in reports with larger p-values. However, they found a peculiar peak of p-values just below 0.05, offering proof for large scale p-hacking. John et al. (2012) found that QRPs are commonplace. They conducted a survey of over 2,000 psychologists with incentives for honesty and showed that most respondents admitted to taking part in QRPs. While QRPs can bias results, inflate significance and undermine the transparency and rigour of research, they may not always involve deliberate intent to deceive or falsify data. Instead, QRPs may also arise from perceived pressures to publish positive results, confirmation biases or methodological decisions made with insufficient consideration of their potential impact on research outcomes. Nowadays, these cases are often referred to as sloppy science.

When QRPs veer into deliberately manipulating data, results or other aspects of research to mislead others or present false conclusions it is referred to as falsifying. Examples of falsifying are data trimming, massaging, altering, misrepresenting information or not reporting certain information at all (Bos, 2020). Falsifying is seen by some as the conscious form of QRPs, while others classify it as outright fraud (i.e. a deadly sin), or take the stance that data fabrication is a subcategory of falsifying. There is consensus, however, that falsifying concerns deliberate behaviour challenging research ethics like honesty and due diligence.

In large driven by the replication crisis, several solutions to battle scientific misconduct and, especially, QRPs have become more prevalent over the last decade. The most severe measure that can be taken is the retraction of articles by authors that are suspected of research misconduct. The problem with retraction is that it happens after misconduct has been proven and hence it severely damages the reputation of both the accused author and their colleagues. Where such reputation damage might be justifiable regarding the researcher who commits the scientific misconduct (see for example the cases of Diederik Stapel or Andrew Wakefield), co-authors on fraudulent papers and particularly PhD students (who may not yet be fully aware of the ins and outs of academic misconduct) often face considerable scrutiny or even severe reputation damage. Moreover, the time between publication and retraction is often long, leading to a large body of research building on fraudulent findings. This in itself can cause severe damage to the reputation of science in general.

Another, less severe, solution that takes place after research has been published is post-publication peer review (PPPR), one of the forms of open peer review (Ford, 2013). Unlike traditional pre-publication peer review, PPPR occurs – partially or fully – after a journal has published the article. Post-publication peer review operates through various mechanisms, primarily facilitated by online platforms and academic forums. Researchers, upon encountering a published work, can offer critiques, comments or additional insights directly on the platform hosting the research article. These comments often undergo moderation to ensure relevance and civility. Some platforms employ rating systems where readers can vote on the quality or significance of comments, helping to surface the most insightful contributions. Additionally, authors may engage in discussions with reviewers to address concerns or provide clarifications. Moreover, scholars can publish formal responses or rebuttals to published works in academic journals, initiating a dialogue that contributes to the refinement of ideas and findings.

PPPR is less severe and swifter than retraction, which might tackle issues of reputation damage for researchers and science in general. However, PPPR is also associated with some concerns regarding the swiftness of disseminating results

(O'Sullivan et al., 2021). Some researchers are concerned that a shift towards PPPR will cause the publication of bad research designs resulting in poor quality outcomes. Others, however, point at the potential of PPPR to instigate meaningful discussions and a shift towards more transparency. That said, changing the peer review process as a stand-alone intervention will not solve the problem of misconduct and QRPs. PPPR is just one aspect of a larger movement towards open science, which is the combination of open scientific knowledge, open dialogues, open infrastructures and open engagement of societal actors. Open science practices include, but are not limited to, pre-registration of studies; making data FAIR (findable, accessible, interoperable and reusable) and publishing open access. Researchers can, for example, use the Open Science Framework (OSF, www.osf.io) to manage their projects, share data, collaborate with others, pre-register studies and make their research workflows more transparent. Each of these practices deal with certain aspects of the research process and can thus potentially contribute to overcoming QRPs. For example, pre-registration – the practice of outlining research plans, including hypotheses and methods, and making those available to others – severely limits possibilities of p-hacking and as a result contributes to less publication bias.

Conducting replications as a standard component of the research cycle has also been suggested as a possible solution to the replication crisis. First, and foremost, replication studies can help distinguish between genuine scientific discoveries and false positives. If a finding consistently fails to replicate across multiple independent studies, it raises doubts about its validity and suggests that the original result may have been due to chance, bias or other factors. Second, replication studies allow researchers to assess the robustness of research findings across different contexts, populations and methods. By uncovering methodological flaws or biases in the original studies that may have contributed to non-replication, researchers can improve the reliability and credibility of (their) research findings.

Another function of establishing replication research as standard practice is to promote ethical behaviour. Replication studies promote transparency and openness in science by making research methods, data and analyses more accessible to the scientific community. This transparency facilitates critical evaluation and verification of research findings. Moreover, the replication crisis has spurred efforts to promote reproducible research practices. These practices help mitigate publication bias, selective reporting and other factors that contribute to non-replicability.

In sum, replication studies initially were promoted and carried out to increase the credibility and trustworthiness of research findings (in a positivist or post-positivist tradition). More recently, replication is suggested as one of the solutions to combat academic misconduct. Despite the change from a positive approach (can we confirm findings?) to a somewhat more critical approach (can we trust these findings?), the basic principles of conducting replication research have not changed.

WHAT IS REPLICATION RESEARCH?

Replication research refers to the process of independently recreating previous research findings to assess their reliability, validity and generalizability. Clear definitions of replication are often lacking, possibly because the meaning of the word seems obvious (Schmidt, 2009). As a result, the word replication is used to mean different things in various contexts. Moreover, researchers sometimes use different terminology to refer to virtually the same thing. What is generally agreed upon, however, is that replication research refers to the process of repeating the methods and procedures of original studies as closely as possible to determine the accuracy of the original findings. Often the aim is to identify whether original findings can be confirmed in a new context, with different samples, or using alternative methodologies. The goal of replication research is to verify the robustness of scientific findings, detect potential errors or biases in original studies, and enhance the credibility and trustworthiness of scientific knowledge. Replication research plays a critical role in validating and building upon existing research findings.

There are different types of replication studies. The most commonly distinguished types are 'direct' (or 'exact') replication and 'conceptual' replication (Hudson, 2021; Schmidt, 2009). A third type that is commonly used is called replication with extension, but other terminology such as partial replication and approximate replication can also be found. Different types of replication research serve different objectives of advancing scientific knowledge. In direct replications, researchers attempt to keep the replication study as identical to the original study as possible, especially with regard to the procedures, concepts and measurement of those concepts. Schmidt (2009) defines this as the repetition of a procedure. Direct replication allows for establishing the reliability of the original findings. Reliability of findings is of particular importance in situations where study outcomes may lead to policy recommendations (e.g. Crandall & Sherman, 2016) or have an impact on practice (e.g. the efficacy of a particular medical treatment or a particular pedagogical method). However, direct replication designs are especially challenging for the social sciences because it can be difficult or impossible to duplicate conditions and methods in experimental situations that involve complex human behaviour. Moreover, direct replications are susceptible to systematic errors, i.e. flaws in the design of the study (Cai et al., 2018) that can threaten the internal validity.

These potential problems can be dealt with by conducting a so-called conceptual replication. In this kind of replication one re-uses the conceptual framework rather than the exact study. In other words, in a conceptual replication one tests whether the outcomes of an original study hold 'across a range of operationalizations of independent and dependent variables' (Crandall & Sherman, 2016, p. 95). Conceptual replications serve as a test of external validity, i.e. whether and to what extent findings of the original study can be generalized to different contexts. Schmidt (2009, p. 91) defines conceptual replication as 'Repetition of a test of a hypothesis or a result of earlier research work with different methods'. In conceptual replication, researchers are interested in whether the relation between concepts of the original study holds, even if measured differently, in a different sample or different context. Conceptual replications offer researchers the opportunity to deal with flaws in the design of the initial research. However, that does come at the expensive of the comparability of the original study and its replication.

Direct and conceptual replications can be full, replicating the entire original study, or partial, replicating part of an experiment or some of the concepts. Direct replications can be expanded with additional components such as an extra experimental condition or an extra concept (e.g. outcome variable) to further investigate or enhance the original findings. This is called replication with extension, and it is often considered a separate type of replication research. By combining replication with new data collection or additional analyses, researchers can deepen their understanding of the phenomenon under study and provide a more comprehensive assessment of its implications.

In reality, the lines between these theoretically distinguished types of replication research are not always that clear-cut. Moreover, different terminologies can be found in the literature, such as systematic replication, approximate replication and modified replication, which all seem to be similar to/versions of conceptual replication as it is described here. Furthermore, unclarity exists around the terms replicability and reproducibility. The reproduction of a study entails the use of both the same data and the same methods as the original study. In replication research either data, methods or both are different from the original study (Condon et al., 2017). A specific challenge is to what extent a different method can be used in the replication study. If, for instance, a qualitative study based on interviews is able to confirm findings from a quantitative study using a survey (same research question, similar/comparable population, etc.), it could be argued that this is a proper design for a conceptual replication. On the other hand, qualitative and quantitative research are based on different epistemologies, which implies that findings, almost by default, cannot be adequately compared. Hence, it is more common to, for example, use a survey to replicate a laboratory experiment.

When designing a replication study, one should first establish the aim of the replication. Direct replications are the most suitable method when the goal is to confirm original findings. When the objective is generalization, one should opt for a conceptual replication, and a replication with extension is the way to go when the aim is to confirm original findings and expand the conceptual model at the same time. Thereafter, the methods, procedures and results of the original study should be thoroughly examined to understand its design and findings. Based on this assessment, a replication protocol can then be established which details the type of replication, sample (size), procedures, measures, data collection methods and (statistical) analyses. It is important to detail when a result is considered to be replicated prior to the data collection of the replication study. One can for example consider an effect replicated when it is significant in both the original study and the replication. Stricter criteria entail looking at effect size (e.g. same range) or considering an effect only replicated if the test-statistic is (almost) the same. After data collection and analysis, results can be written down in article format. In doing so, it is good practice to refer to the original study in great detail, paying special attention to similarities and differences between the original study and the replication. In the discussion, authors should reflect on whether the results of the original study are deemed replicated and how to explain that in terms of the type of replication and the replication protocol.

A SCOPING REVIEW OF REPLICATION IN HIGHER EDUCATION RESEARCH

Approach

In order to gain an understanding of the use of replication in higher education, we took the Web of Science (WoS) as the point of departure and used the words 'replication' and 'higher education' as search terms for all WoS fields and selected Education and Educational Research as the WoS category. We contemplated including psychology as a category, knowing there are many psychology studies using students in higher education as respondents and being aware of the replication crisis that loomed largely in that discipline but wanted a clear focus on our own field. Given the nature of our interdisciplinary field, psychological studies would be covered anyway in journals focusing on educational psychology (e.g. *Educational Psychologist*). We wanted to cast a broad net, hence used all WoS fields, realizing that after further scrutiny a fair number of papers would not be relevant.

Our initial search (January 2024) yielded 89 studies. Indeed, many papers used the word 'replication' different from our interests, e.g. papers dealing with replication in the more generic sense, such as papers addressing how higher education contributes to the replication of social patterns of inequality, or papers addressing the replication of Eurocentric definitions and approaches in teaching and learning in the global South. Interestingly, we found 21 papers addressing replication, but upon reading the papers, we discovered that while all the authors argued that replication of their study *would be* worthwhile, their study itself was actually not a replication study. Putting these papers – focussing on another meaning of 'replication' or only suggesting that a replication of the work would be worthwhile – aside, we were left with 32 papers that more or less seriously seemed to address replication.

General Findings

Not surprisingly, most replication studies could be found in the area of teaching and learning, with a fair number of studies on second language learning. The micro-level context of learning, teaching and assessment lends itself to replication rather than, for example, research on higher education policy or governance themes. Bearing in mind that replication is most often used in a positivist tradition, almost all studies were quantitative, using a survey as the instrument, many of these targeting students. Most studies were carried out in Anglo–Saxon countries, which is partly due to our search in WoS for English-language papers.

Three examples help to understand what the replication studies entailed. Klein et al. (2019) were interested in how first-year students in physics and economics understand graph slopes. They repeated an earlier study of Susac et al. (2018) that compared physics and psychology students. The intention of the authors was to test the generalizability of the influence of context on the understanding of graphs. In a table, the authors explain the key methodological similarities and differences of their study and the one carried out by Susac and colleagues. The authors themselves label their study as a partial direct replication. However, given their aim of generalizability and altering of the sample, a conceptual replication seems a better classification for this study.

Schweighart et al. (2021) focused on students' drug use (for examinations). Initially, they investigated a sample of social work students from one German university, but then extended the study to include students from other universities and also in other disciplines. They do not explain the type of replication, but clearly stipulate that they intend to find out whether the initial findings could be generalized, which strongly suggests a conceptual replication. They conclude that the findings are satisfactorily consistent with the findings of the initial investigation.

Lastly, Stracke et al. (2023) replicated Stracke's (2007) study on learners of a foreign language who dropped out. Interestingly, this was also one of the very few qualitative studies we found. The authors qualify their work as an approximate replication, which should be understood (we checked the source the authors referred to) as the introduction of one (or more) element(s) of the original study. In Schmidt's terminology, this would probably be a conceptual replication. Indeed, the context of their study was quite different, looking at students at a Vietnamese university learning English (vs a German university where students learnt French or Spanish in the 2007 study). The sample was very small (five students), but nevertheless, the authors claim that 'It is noteworthy that the lack of complementarity and integration of the blend components is one of the main reasons for students to leave the course in both the 2007 study and this current study' (Stracke et al., 2023, p. 190), which according to the authors confirms the value of replication. Due to the lack of details on the methodology of the earlier study, the authors are not sufficiently transparent on the strength of their claims. One can also argue that so much time has passed between the two studies (and hence that contexts are significantly different), which a claim of replication seems somewhat overstated. Yet the study would have been interesting, even without the claim of reproduction.

These three studies are examples that intended to replicate earlier findings and explained – to some extent – the similarities of their study to the study they replicated. Not all studies were clear on this. It is hard to put a number to it, but only a few of the higher education replication studies were living up to the replication protocol described earlier. For instance, Boatright-Horowitz and Arruda (2013, p. 256) investigated undergraduate psychology students' perceptions of grades. They carried out their research at one particular university and claim that '[t]wo subsequent replications of this study revealed comparable results' but fail to supply any details of the replication studies. McKinley et al. (2024) claim their study on multilingualism is a replication but do not offer sufficient details of the earlier study for a clear understanding of similarities and differences.

Repeated Replications

The oldest study we found was Terenzini et al. (1981). They used a 34-item 'integration' measure from one of their previous studies, using Tinto's model on student dropout, to discover whether the findings of that study could be replicated on a different campus. The study seems to be a casebook example of direct replication: 'Except where noted otherwise, the present study was virtually identical to Study 1 in overall design, population definition, sampling design and procedures, variables employed, and analytical procedures adopted.' (p. 111). The authors carefully explain how the campus of the follow-up study differs from the campus of the initial study and – based on the empirical findings – claim that the construct validity of Tinto's model was supported. Not all substantive results were replicated, but the authors offer convincing arguments why this may be the case: specific characteristics of the 1981 study population of respondents could explain the differences, while not necessarily undermining the overall validity of the model.

Not only would this study count as a solid case of a replication study, the (core) researchers involved are the only ones that have carried out a couple of replication studies. Several researchers have noted that many researchers in higher education only once publish a paper on higher education. Tight (2023, p. 206) claims that 'most published research studies are one-offs'. It is therefore not surprising that also the replication studies are one-offs, i.e. a particular study is replicated, but no other researchers – as far as we could judge – have replicated the same study. Pascarella and Terenzini are the exception, having published three replication studies. Loes et al. (2015) clearly stipulate to what extent their study is similar and different from the predecessor (Pascarella et al., 1996). However, Pascarella et al. (2011) are less clear on what and how they replicated. They include 'a multi-institutional replication and extension' in their title, but the term replication is only used a couple of times in the body of the text. Clearly, the study uses a model that also has guided their earlier research on student persistence and dropout. It is also clear that they extend their research by investigating students from other institutions than the Pascarella et al. (2008) study. But in terms of methods, they state 'we did not use structural equation modelling to estimate the validity of the overall model… Such omnibus tests of models based on Tinto's constructs have already been conducted with considerable frequency[…] Rather, we limited our analysis to estimating the various net effects of exposure to effective instruction on persistence' (p. 12). Based on the data analysis, the conclusion is that 'This [the underlying causal mechanism] is quite similar to the earlier findings of Pascarella et al.' (p. 16). This may be true, but the reader is left puzzled regarding the differences/similarities of the original study/studies and the current one.

Replication as a Rare Methodology

While replication studies are slightly more common in our field nowadays, we hesitate to speak of a trend. Our field has grown tremendously, so we would expect an increase anyway. Moreover, the relatively small number of replication studies overall puts limits to discovering clear patterns. This caveat also applies to the journals that publish replication studies. Although US-based journals are more inclined to publish quantitative studies than European-based journals (Tight, 2007), we could not discover a pattern of certain journals being more prone to publish replication studies than others. Our 32 studies were found in some 20 different journals. Interestingly, *Assessment and Evaluation in Higher Education* published six papers that more or less seriously engaged with replication. In all other journals, we could find only one or two replication studies. Sixteen studies repeated their own initial study. This has clear advantages, since researchers are assumed to have in-depth knowledge of their earlier work. On the other hand, we reiterate the challenges of 'proper' replication and researchers that have already published on a particular topic have vested interests. This is not to say that researchers that adhere to a focused research programme (like Pascarella and Terenzini on student persistence) are biased but just to argue that it has advantages if 'independent' researchers carry out replication studies (or team up with the initial researchers, see e.g., Loes et al., 2015). Above all, the researchers' neutrality should prevail.

To put the number of replication studies in context, we compare our explorative findings with a study on replication in educational studies. Perry et al. (2022) investigated replication in educational studies (also using WoS) in the period 2011–2020 and found 442 replication studies (i.e. about 1 out of 500 studies was a replication study), including direct and approximate replications. Their definition of approximate replication largely coincides with the term we use in this paper: replication with extension. This percentage (0.2%) is only slightly higher than what Makel and Plucker (2014) found for the period 2000–2010 (0.13%). The percentage for higher education, based on our exploration, is much lower. As a proxy, we looked how many WoS papers (on education) contained the keyword 'higher education'. Our 32 papers that somewhat seriously addressed replication, compared to the 686,000 papers on 'higher education', is then a tiny drop in the ocean.

Types of Replications[...] and is it Really a Replication?

About two-thirds of the studies we investigated could be labelled as conceptual replication. Most of these studies used the same instrument (e.g. a scale developed in other work) and applied that in a (slightly) different context. Interestingly, there are probably many other higher education studies that re-use models, scales or instruments, but authors would not necessarily qualify or present their work as a replication. Within the set of replication studies, we see many ambiguities. Some – see the examples in the subsection 'general findings' – seemed to have a clear explanation for the type of replication they aim at (direct vs conceptual replication). Foung and Kohnke (2022) are transparently explaining, in all steps of the research process, that their study is a direct replication. We use Vinson et al.'s (2014) study on career services at US colleges and universities as an example of a study showing the ambiguities around replication. The aim of the study is to replicate Reardon et al.'s (1979) study, but immediately after stating this, the authors follow up by claiming: 'We anticipated that our findings would reveal changes in the delivery of career services over time, and we wanted to explore several new topics not examined in the 1979 study.' (p. 203). Not only is it unclear whether the authors aim at a direct replication or a replication with extension, but the additional reflection of the authors also actually undermines the purpose of replication. It would have been more accurate if the authors had not presented their study as a replication study, but a repeated study with the – equally relevant – aim to analyze changes over time.

Lissi et al.'s (2023) study also shows such ambiguities. They claim their study – on reading comprehension of deaf students – is a replication study. But it looks like they only used the same method (think-aloud procedure) and same classification of reading comprehension strategies as the original study. The texts used were of a different type, the students were in a different country, the samples in both studies (five students) were very small and the researchers found that their students used different comprehension strategies. This should have led the authors to discuss the non-replicability of the findings, but they are silent on this. We get the impression that in this case the term replication study is inappropriately used: the authors – and rightly so – make use of existing insights and borrow a framework from an earlier study (as almost all studies build on previous work), but that does not make it a replication study.

Similarly, Li and Shek's (2020) study, evaluating a leadership course, is presented as a replication study. However, details of what is exactly replicated are lacking. Moreover, inasmuch as this may be a replication study, it is primarily an evaluation study analyzing whether the leadership course has been effective (according to the students). That is, the study would have been valuable anyway, even if it would not have confirmed findings of previous studies.

In other studies – beyond the 32 more or less 'proper' replication studies – we found considerable ambiguity or authors unconvincingly arguing that their study is a replication. Ledzińska et al. (2014), investigating cognitive styles of students, did a pilot study ($n = 11$) and a full study ($n = 37$). From a statistical perspective, we can comment on the very small samples, limiting the strength of the findings, but here our focus is on the presentation of the method as a replication study. The full study is presented as a replication. There is a replication element, for students with similar backgrounds were chosen for the full study. But the authors fail to explain how the pilot and full study relate to each other in the language of replication studies.

Bhattacharya (2019), researching pro-social behaviour of students, argues her study uses a replication methodology, but she is using the same sample and uses bootstrapping techniques to estimate the standard errors (and confidence intervals) of the parameters. This in itself is a valuable exercise, but it is not a replication study, for this would require a new dataset. The same goes for carrying out a pre- and post-treatment survey (e.g. Vehovar & Štrlekar, 2023). Here the intent is to discover whether, for example, students learnt something. In other words, it is built upon the premise of *changes* in the responses pre- and post-treatment. As such, this type of study does not lend itself for validating the findings of a prior piece of research and therefore cannot be labelled as a replication study.

Finally, some studies do argue their work is a replication study but offer no or too limited details to the reader to let them assess what is replicated and how. We already referred to the Boatright-Horowitz and Arruda (2013) study lacking any details. Dean et al. (2023, p. 244) argue: 'By using a replication approach, we are increasing our understanding of the phenomenon under investigation'. Reading other work of the authors, we discovered how their study relates to their other research, but it is impossible to deduce from their 2023 article what is replicated and what the key findings of the replications are.

REFLECTIONS

Replication research is not some sort of holy grail; it is one of the many methods that can contribute to more rigorous scientific practices and certainty of knowledge. Replicating a study once and finding the same (or similar) outcomes does not mean that the results are true. Studies of a statistical nature are always probabilistic, meaning that the replication study also runs the risk of type I/II errors, i.e. incorrectly accepting/rejecting hypotheses. Hence, the cautious framing of replicated results is necessary.

Replication is far from common in our field. Part of the explanation is that it is primarily used in quantitative research, so many researchers using qualitative methods may not even consider replication, for their aim is not necessarily the generalizability of findings. Another explanation may be that higher education researchers think that it is very difficult to directly replicate a study, given that higher education contexts may differ significantly across settings (within and across countries), or that they expect not to be able to publish a replication study (Condon et al., 2017). It is also important to note that the power of replication is dependent on other characteristics of the replication study. For example, if we assume that higher education researchers primarily use convenience sampling (which at least in the social sciences is common practice, even though the gold standard of random sampling should be preferred, see Zhao, 2021), this already puts limits to the relevance of replication. The low number of direct replication studies are in sync with these explanations.

That said, the examples presented in this chapter show that it is possible to carry out replication studies (see especially the Terenzini and Pascarella studies on student persistence and dropout) and that this adds to our understanding of the robustness, validity and generalizability of findings. Research on arguably 'universal' themes like retention, student well-being, learning strategies, etc. lend themselves easier for replication. It could also be argued that especially in times of quite significant changes in higher education and society at large, replication is becoming even more important. One may raise the question on how robust much research has been on student learning in the past three years, knowing that much of that research was carried out during the pandemic: would replication studies reveal the same consistent results? But replication requires an effort from the researchers to carefully delineate what type of replication is used, why and how. Whereas we presented examples of good practice (Foung & Kohnke, 2022; Klein et al., 2019), many replication studies on higher education fall short in offering the reader sufficient guidance on how their study is similar to/different from the replicated study. The trend towards open science may be a boost for the much-needed transparency.

At the same time, we get the impression that the term replication is often misused. Whether this is due to a lack of understanding on the side of the researchers or an attempt of the authors to try to boost the methodological rigour of their study is unclear. But it is clear that such approaches may put replication in a bad light or, at least, confuse scholars about what replication actually entails. We felt that quite a few of the studies we read were offering interesting insights and that their message would have been sufficiently strong or even stronger if the authors had not chosen to present their work as a replication study. Here clearly a role is to be played by reviewers and editors of higher education journals to be alert to inappropriate or counterproductive use of the term replication.

In all, replication research – although not much used in the field of higher education – is worthwhile. It is a relevant tool to increase the trustworthiness of findings, and this will help to build a stronger knowledge base in our field. This is not only relevant for researchers but also for those who make use of the knowledge: practitioners and policymakers. In addition, it is a useful tool in the context of transparent research processes and in combatting mistakes and academic misconduct. It does, however, require researchers to clearly stipulate what exactly they aim to replicate. Our exploration of the higher education literature shows that there are good examples but that there is definitely scope for improvement. Not only are there imperatives for authors submitting their work but likewise efforts from peer reviewers and journal editors.

REFERENCES

Banks, G. C., Rogelberg, S. G., Woznyj, H. M., Landis, R. S., & Rupp, D. E. (2016). Evidence on questionable research practices: The good, the bad, and the ugly. *Journal of Business and Psychology*, *31*, 323–338. https://doi.org/10.1007/s10869-016-9456-7

Bhattacharya, H. (2019). Do pro-social students care more for the environment? *International Journal of Sustainability in Higher Education*, *20*(4), 761–783. https://doi.org/10.1108/IJSHE-11-2018-0223

Boatright-Horowitz, S. L., & Arruda, C. (2013). College students' categorical perceptions of grades: It's simply 'good' vs. 'bad'. *Assessment & Evaluation in Higher Education*, *38*(3), 253–259. https://doi.org/10.1080/02602938.2011.618877

Bos, J. (2020). *Research ethics for students in the social sciences*. Springer Nature. https://doi.org/10.1007/978-3-030-48415-6

Cai, J., Morris, A., Hohensee, C., Hwang, S., Robison, V., & Hiebert, J. (2018). The role of replication studies in educational research. *Journal for Research in Mathematics Education*, *49*(1), 2–8. https://doi.org/10.5951/jresematheduc.49.1.0002

Condon, M. D., Graham, E. K., & Mroczek, D. K. (2017). On replication research. In *The Wiley-Blackwell encyclopedia of personality and individual differences: Vol. II. Research methods and assessment techniques*. John Wiley and Sons. https://doi.org/10.31234/osf.io/2fn5x

Crandall, C. S., & Sherman, J. W. (2016). On the scientific superiority of conceptual replications for scientific progress. *Journal of Experimental Social Psychology*, *66*, 93–99. https://doi.org/10.1016/j.jesp.2015.10.002

Dean, J., Roberts, P., & Perry, L. B. (2023). School equity, marketisation and access to the Australian senior secondary curriculum. *Educational Review*, *75*(2), 243–263. https://doi.org/10.1080/00131911.2021.1909537

Derksen, M. (2021). A menagerie of imposters and truth-tellers: Diederik Stapel and the crisis in psychology. In S. Woolgar, E. Vogel, D. Moates & C.-F. Helgesson (Eds.), *The imposter as social theory*. Bristol University Press. https://doi.org/10.51952/9781529213102.ch003

Earp, B. D., & Trafimow, D. (2015). Replication, falsification, and the crisis of confidence in social psychology. *Frontiers in Psychology*, *6*, 621. https://doi.org/10.3389/fpsyg.2015.00621

Fanelli, D. (2009). How many scientists fabricate and falsify research? A systematic review and metaanalysis of survey data. *PLoS One*, *4*(5), e5738. https://doi.org/10.1371/journal.pone.0005738

Ferrão, M. E. (2020). Statistical methods in recent higher education research. *Journal of College Student Development*, *61*(3), 366–371. https://doi.org/10.1353/csd.2020.0033

Ford, E. (2013). Defining and characterizing open peer review: A review of the literature. *Journal of Scholarly Publishing*, *44*(4), 311–326. https://doi.org/10.3138/jsp.44-4-001

Foung, D., & Kohnke, L. (2022). The development and validation of the Feedback in Learning Scale (FLS): A replication study. *Educational Research and Evaluation*, *27*(1–2), 164–187. https://doi.org/10.1080/13803611.2021.2022320

Freese, J., & Peterson, D. (2017). Replication in social science. *Annual Review of Sociology*, *43*, 147–165. https://doi.org/10.1146/annurev-soc-060116-053450

Frias-Navarro, D., Pascuell-Llobell, J., Pascual-Soler, M., Perezgonzalez, J., & Berrios-Riquelme, J. (2019). Replication crisis or an opportunity to improve scientific production? *European Journal of Education*, *29*, 618–631. https://doi.org/10.1111/ejed.12417

Hudson, R. (2021). Explicating exact versus conceptual replication. *Erkenntnis*, 1–22. https://doi.org/10.1007/s10670-021-00464-z

John, L. K., Loewenstein, G., & Prelec, D. (2012). Measuring the prevalence of questionable research practices with incentives for truth telling. *Psychological Science*, *23*(5), 524–532. https://doi.org/10.1177/0956797611430953

Klein, P., Küchemann, S., Brückner, S., Zlatkin-Troitschanskaia, O., & Kuhn, J. (2019). Student understanding of graph slope and area under a curve: A replication study comparing first-year physics and economics students. *Physical Review Physics Education Research*, *15*. https://doi.org/10.1103/PhysRevPhysEducRes.15.020116

Ledzińska, M., Batalla, J. M., & Stolarski, M. (2014). Cognitive styles could be implicitly assessed in the Internet environment: Reflection-impulsivity is manifested in individual manner of searching for information. *Journal of Baltic Science Education*, *13*(3), 133–145. https://doi.org/10.33225/jbse/14.13.133

Li, X., & Shek, D. T. L. (2020). Objective outcome evaluation of a leadership course utilising the positive youth development approach in Hong Kong. *Assessment & Evaluation in Higher Education*, *45*(5), 741–757. https://doi.org/10.1080/02602938.2019.1696944

Lissi, M. R., González, M., Escobar, V., Vergara, M., Villavicencio, C., & Sebastián, C. (2023). Reading comprehension strategies used by Chilean deaf adults. A think-aloud study. *Deafness & Education International*, *25*(3), 228–247. https://doi.org/10.1080/14643154.2023.2181513

Loes, C. N., Salisbury, M. H., & Pascarella, E. T. (2015). Student perceptions of effective instruction and the development of critical thinking: A replication and extension. *Higher Education*, *69*, 823–838. https://doi.org/10.1007/s10734-014-9807-0

Makel, M. C., & Plucker, J. A. (2014). Facts are more important than novelty: Replication in the education sciences. *Educational Researcher*, *43*(6), 304–316. https://doi.org/10.3102/0013189X14545513

Masicampo, E. J., & Lalande, D. R. (2012). A peculiar prevalence of p values just below .05. *Quarterly Journal of Experimental Psychology*, *65*(11), 2271–2279. http://doi.org/10.1080/17470218.2012.711335

McKinley, J., Sahan, K., Zhou, S., & Rose, H. (2024). Researching EMI policy and practice multilingually: Reflections from China and Turkey. *Language and Education*, *38*(1), 5–22. https://doi.org/10.1080/09500782.2023.2246954

Open Science Collaboration. (2015). Estimating the reproducibility of psychological science. *Science*, *349*(6251). https://doi.org/10.1126/science.aac4716

O'Sullivan, L., Ma, L., & Doran, P. (2021). An overview of post-publication peer review. *Scholarly Assessment Reports*, *3*(1). https://doi.org/10.29024/sar.26

Pascarella, E., Edison, M., Nora, A., Hagedorn, L., & Braxton, J. (1996). Effects of teacher organization/preparation and teacher skill/clarity on general cognitive skills in college. *Journal of College Student Development, 37*, 7–19.

Pascarella, E. T., Salisbury, M. H., & Blaich, C. (2011). Exposure to effective instruction and college student persistence: A multi-institutional replication and extension. *Journal of College Student Development, 52*(1), 4–19. https://doi.org/10.1080/00091383.2011.568898

Pascarella, E. T., Seifert, T. A., & Whitt, E. J. (2008). Effective instruction and college student persistence: Some new evidence. *New Directions for Teaching and Learning, 115*, 55–70. https://doi.org/10.1002/tl.325

Pashler, H., & Wagenmakers, E. J. (2012). Editors' introduction to the special section on replicability in psychological science a crisis of confidence? *Perspectives on Psychological Science, 7*, 528–530. https://doi.org/10.1177/1745691612465253

Perry, T., Morris, R., & Lea, R. (2022). A decade of replication study in education? A mapping review (2011–2020). *Educational Research and Evaluation, 27*(1–2), 12–34. https://doi.org/10.1080/13803611.2021.2022315

Pupovac, V., & Fanelli, D. (2015). Scientists admitting to plagiarism: A meta-analysis of surveys. *Science and Engineering Ethics, 21*(5), 1331–1352. https://doi.org/10.1007/s11948-014-9600-6

Reardon, R., Zunker, V., & Dyal, M. (1979). The status of career planning programs and career centers in colleges and universities. *The Vocational Guidance Quarterly, 28*, 154–159.

Schmidt, S. (2009). Shall we really do it again? The powerful concept of replication is neglected in the social sciences. *Review of General Psychology, 13*(2), 90–100. https://doi.org/10.1037/a0015108

Schweighart, R., Kruck, S., & Blanz, M. (2021). Taking drugs for exams: An investigation with social work students. *Social Work Education, 40*(6), 737–755. https://doi.org/10.1080/02615479.2020.1857352

Simmons, J. P., Nelson, L. D., & Simonsohn, U. (2011). False-positive psychology: Undisclosed flexibility in data collection and analysis allows presenting anything as significant. *Psychological Science, 22*(11), 1359–1366. https://doi.org/10.1177/0956797611417632

Stracke, E. (2007). A road to understanding: A qualitative study into why learners drop out of a blended language learning (BLL) environment. *ReCALL, 19*(1), 57–78. https://doi.org/10.1017/S0958344007000511

Stracke, E., Nguyen, G. H., & Nguyen, V. (2023). EFL learners dropping out of blended language learning classes: A replication of Stracke (2007). *ReCALL, 35*(2), 178–192. https://doi.org/10.1017/S0958344023000010

Stroebe, W., Postmes, T., & Spears, R. (2012). Scientific misconduct and the myth of self-correction in science. *Perspectives on Psychological Science, 7*(6), 670–688. https://doi.org/10.1177/1745691612460687

Susac, A., Bubic, A., Kazotti, E., Planinic, M., & Palmovic, M. (2018). Student understanding of graph slope and area under a graph: A comparison of physics and nonphysics students. *Physical Review Physics Education Research, 14*. https://doi.org/10.1103/PhysRevPhysEducRes.14.020109

Terenzini, P. T., Lorang, W. G., & Pascarella, E. T. (1981). Predicting freshman persistence and voluntary dropout decisions: A replication. *Research in Higher Education, 15*(2), 109–127.

Tight, M. (2007). Bridging the divide: A comparative analysis of articles in higher education journals published inside and outside North America. *Higher Education, 53*(2), 235–253. https://doi.org/10.1007/s10734-005-2429-9

Tight, M. (2013). Discipline and methodology in higher education research. *Higher Education Research and Development, 32*(1), 136–151. https://doi.org/10.1080/07294360.2012.750275

Tight, M. (2023). Positivity bias in higher education research. *Higher Education Quarterly, 77*, 201–214. https://doi.org/10.1111/hequ.12388

Vehovar, V., & Štrlekar, L. (2023). When to conduct student evaluation of teaching surveys: Before or after the final examination? *Assessment & Evaluation in Higher Education*. (online first). https://doi.org/10.1080/02602938.2023.2298771

Vinson, B. M., Reardon, R. C., & Bertoch, S. C. (2014). Career services at colleges and universities: A 30-year replication study. *Journal of College Student Development, 55*(2), 203–207. https://doi.org/10.1353/csd.2014.0018

Wells, R. S., Kolek, E. A., Williams, E. A., & Saunders, D. B. (2015). "How we know what we know": A systematic comparison of research methods employed in higher education journals, 1996-2000 v. 2006-2010. *Journal of Higher Education*, *86*(2), 171–198. https://doi.org/10.1080/00221546.2015.11777361

Xie, Y., Wang, K., & Kong, Y. (2021). Prevalence of research misconduct and questionable research practices: A systematic review and meta-analysis. *Science and Engineering Ethics*, *27*(4), 41. https://doi.org/10.1007/s11948-021-00314-9

Zhao, K. (2021). Sample representation in the social sciences. *Synthese*, *198*, 9097–9115. https://doi.org/10.1007/s11229-020-02621-3

AUTOETHNOGRAPHY IN HIGHER EDUCATION RESEARCH: A MARGINAL METHODOLOGY FOR THE MARGINALIZED?

Malcolm Tight

Lancaster University, UK

ABSTRACT

Autoethnography as a methodology has proved increasingly attractive to higher education researchers in recent years, particularly those in marginalized positions. This article examines the extant research literature, focusing on the origins and meaning of the approach, how it has been applied in practice and the issues and critiques that have been raised. It concludes that collaborative forms of autoethnography probably offer the best way forward.

Keywords: Autoethnography; higher education; higher education research; systematic review; collaborative research

INTRODUCTION

Autoethnography as a methodology has proved increasingly attractive to higher education researchers in recent years, particularly to those in marginalized positions. This article examines the extant research literature on autoethnography, focusing on the origins and meaning of the approach, how it has been applied in practice and the issues and critiques that have been raised, before reaching some conclusions.

Methodologically, the article makes use of the techniques of systematic review (Jesson et al., 2011; Tight, 2021; Torgerson, 2003), an approach that seeks to identify, analyze and synthesize all of the research that has been published on a particular topic – in this case, on the use of autoethnography in higher education research. In practice, of course, some limits have to be set on the scope of a systematic review, most notably in terms of the language of publication (in this case confined to English), the date of publication and the accessibility of published articles (all available articles, books and other publications identified were examined).

Databases – Google Scholar, Scopus and Web of Science – were searched using keywords – "autoethnography," "higher education," "university," "college" and related terms – to identify potentially relevant articles, books and reports that had been published on the topic. Those identified were then accessed (mostly through downloads) and examined and retained for further analysis if they proved to be relevant. The reference lists in the articles and reports were checked for other potentially relevant sources to follow up that had not been initially identified.

ORIGINS AND MEANING

It is obvious from its name that autoethnography is an offshoot or development from ethnography, the methodology which has long been practiced by anthropologists and some sociologists:

> Ethnography is the study of people in naturally occurring settings or 'fields' by means of methods which capture their social meanings and ordinary activities, involving the researcher participating directly in the setting, if not also the activities, in order to collect data in a systematic manner but without meaning being imposed upon them externally. Brewer (2000, p. 10)

The primary techniques involved in collecting ethnographic data are observations and interviews.

Autoethnography is a relatively recent development. In one of the earliest publications to use the term, Hayano (1979) defines it in the following way: "auto-ethnography is concerned with how anthropologists conduct and write ethnographies of their 'own people'" (p. 99). By this he means that, rather than studying some far away and exotic group or tribe, the focus is much more local. There are clear links here to narrative analysis (Bochner, 2012) and other forms of participatory research that emphasize the first person.

The understanding of autoethnography has, however, moved on since Hayano was writing. Contemporary definitions cast it as the study of personal experience:

> Autoethnography is an approach to research and writing that seeks to describe and systematically analyze (graphy) personal experience (auto) in order to understand cultural experience (ethno). This approach challenges canonical ways of doing research and representing others and treats research as a political, socially-just and socially-conscious act. A researcher uses tenets of autobiography and ethnography to do and write autoethnography. Thus, as a method, autoethnography is both process and product. Ellis et al. (2011, p. 1); see also Adams et al. (2022)

Though the focus on personal experience may be seen as being overly self-centred, autoethnographers seek to make it clear that they study themselves in relation to others and culture in general:

The term *autoethnography* has multiple meanings but largely refers to both the method and product of researching and writing about personal lived experiences and their relationship to culture[...] Autoethnographers research themselves in relation to others. Boylorn and Orbe (2021b, p. 4)

Alexander (2023, p. 2) places particular emphasis on the positive purpose of the approach: "Autoethnography is a culture-centered qualitative methodology that foregrounds individual voice to make articulations about cultural experience as a curative for what ails us." From this description, one can already detect reasons why those in marginalized positions might find the methodology attractive.

It is a characteristic of methodological approaches that they tend to fissure or fracture over time, with more recent proponents and practitioners putting forward new variants or specialisms. Thus, Anderson (2006) proposes analytic instead of evocative (i.e. the original approach) autoethnography:

The five key features of analytic autoethnography that I propose include (1) complete member researcher status, (2) analytic reflexivity, (3) narrative visibility of the researcher's self, (4) dialogue with informants beyond the self, and (5) commitment to theoretical analysis. (p. 378)

Ellis et al. (2011) recognize a range of variants of autoethnography: indigenous/native ethnographies, reflexive dyadic interviews, reflexive ethnographies, layered accounts, interactive interviews, community autoethnographies, co-constructed narratives and personal narratives.

More recently, critical autoethnography (Boylorn & Orbe, 2021a; Holman Jones, 2016) has come on the scene: "Critical autoethnography is concerned with culture and power, and it is also concerned with constructions and theorizations of cultural identities, intersectionality and social inequalities" (Boylorn & Orbe, 2021b, p. 6). The concern with the experience of the marginalized is again evident here.

The other major development has been collaborative autoethnography (Chang et al., 2013/2016, Cruz et al., 2020), where two or more autoethnographers work together on a piece of research:

We define CAE [collaborative autoethnography] as a qualitative research method in which researchers work in community to collect their autobiographical materials and to analyze and interpret their data collectively to gain a meaningful understanding of sociocultural phenomena reflected in their autobiographical data. (Chang et al., 2013/2016, pp. 23–24)

As Lapadat (2017, p. 589) argues, collaborative autoethnography has the potential to respond to some of the reservations expressed about single person autoethnography:

I suggest that collaborative autoethnography, a multivocal approach in which two or more researchers work together to share personal stories and interpret the pooled autoethnographic data, builds upon and extends the reach of autoethnography and addresses some of its methodological and ethical issues. In particular, collaborative autoethnography supports a shift from individual to collective agency, thereby offering a path toward personally engaging, nonexploitative, accessible research that makes a difference.

Other practitioners, working in pairs rather than larger groups, refer to duoethnography (Kidd & Finlayson, 2015; Snipes & LePeau, 2017).

Many other variants or specialisms have been suggested, including organizational autoethnography (Boyle & Parry, 2007; Doloriert & Sambrook, 2012), sensory autoethnography (Matas, 2019), autoethnographic vignettes (Humphreys, 2005), the combination of autoethnography with ethnography (O'Byrne, 2007), autonetnography (Howard, 2019), where the research is done online, and performance autoethnography (Denzin, 2003):

> Autoethnographic performance is the convergence of the 'autobiographic impulse' and the 'ethnographic moment' represented through movement and critical self-reflexive discourse in performance, articulating the intersections of peoples and culture through the innersanctions [sic] of the always migratory identity. (Spry, 2001, p. 706)

There are doubtless other variants that I have not yet come across.

APPLICATION AND PRACTICE

While autoethnography is undeniably a specialist methodology, it has quite a significant appeal. For example, in a search carried out on 12/3/24 using Scopus, 605 articles were identified with the words "autoethnograph*," "higher" and "education" in their titles, abstracts or keywords, and 47 of these had these three words in their titles, indicating a likely focus on the topic of interest. A similar search using "university" instead of "higher" and "education" identified 819 and 37 articles, respectively.

This appeal is also global. Admittedly, the majority of the (English language) published articles identified in the searches carried out for this research were authored by researchers based in the main English-speaking nations of Australia (Austin & Hickey, 2007; Boyle & Parry, 2007; Duncan, 2004; Edwards, 2017; Gander, 2024; Holman Jones, 2016; Vickers, 2007; Yoshida, 2024), Canada (Butz & Besio, 2004; Lapadat, 2017; O'Byrne, 2007; Wall, 2006, 2008), New Zealand (Godber & Atkins, 2021; Kidd & Finlayson, 2015; Maydell, 2010; Ruth et al., 2018; Tolich, 2010), the United Kingdom (Chapman-Clarke, 2016; Delamont, 2009; Deschner et al., 2020; Doloriert & Sambrook, 2012; Egeli, 2017; Learmonth & Humphreys, 2011; Lumsden, 2021; Matas, 2019; Moosavi, 2022; Sparkes, 2000; Struthers, 2014; Trahar, 2013; Walford, 2004, 2021) and, most notably of all, the United States (Alexander, 2023; Ashlee et al., 2017; Bhattacharya, 2018; Blum, 2018; Bochner, 2012; Boss et al., 2019; Castillo-Montoya et al., 2022; Chang et al., 2014; Cruz et al., 2020; Dreistadt, 2022; Elbelazi & Alharbi, 2020; Estes et al., 2018; Forber-Pratt, 2015; Hernandez et al., 2015; Higgins, 2023; Hobbs & Whitsett, 2023; Kim, 2020; Montiel et al., 2022; Ngunjiri & Hernandez, 2017; Ngunjiri et al., 2010; Pahom et al., 2023; Santiago et al., 2017; Snipes & LePeau, 2017; Sobre-Denton, 2012; Warren-Gordon & Jackson-Brown, 2022).

Yet, despite the predictable dominance of the main English-speaking countries, examples of autoethnographic research related to higher education were identified from countries as varied as Botswana (Pheko, 2018), Brazil (Almeida & Paranhos, 2023; Valentim, 2018), China (Peters et al., 2020; Qin et al., 2023), the Democratic Republic of Congo (Pindi, 2018), Denmark (Winkler, 2018), Finland (Nordbäck et al., 2022; Tienari, 2019), France (Almeida & Paranhos, 2023, Deschner et al., 2020), Hong Kong (Oleksiyenko, 2021), Israel (Tsalach, 2022), Japan (Gaitanidis & Shao-Kobayashi, 2022; Morikawa, 2023), Pakistan (Syed, 2022), Poland (Szwabowski & Wężniejewska, 2017), Russia (Paukova et al., 2019), South Africa (Davids, 2022; Le Roux, 2017; Richards, 2008), Spain (Odriozola, 2023), Sweden (Zawadzki & Jensen, 2020) and Turkey (Keleş, 2022). This list includes examples from all continents, though Europe and Asia are particularly well represented.

Some articles focused on particular disciplines or subject areas, such as accounting (Haynes, 2017), applied linguistics (Keleş, 2022), business/management (Karra & Phillips, 2008; Learmonth & Humphreys, 2011), counselling psychology (Egeli, 2017), geography (Butz & Besio, 2004), health (Richards, 2008), human resource development (Grenier, 2015), religion (Dreistadt, 2022; Elbelazi & Alharbi, 2020), sport (Sparkes, 2000) and teacher education (Austin & Hickey, 2007). With the notable exceptions of a lack of examples from science and engineering, this again demonstrates a considerable spread of interest.

It is a characteristic of autoethnographic research in higher education that the focus is most often on the marginalized or disadvantaged; the research approach seems to allow them more of a voice, with which they can document and fight back against the oppression they experience. Thus, many of the articles identified, particularly from the United States, were authored by Black or minority ethnic researchers and focused on issues particular to them (Alexander, 2023; Ashlee et al., 2017; Boss et al., 2019; Castillo-Montoya et al., 2022; Hernandez et al., 2015; Montiel et al., 2022; Moosavi, 2022; Ngunjiri & Hernandez, 2017; Santiago et al., 2017; Tsalach, 2022; Warren-Gordon & Jackson-Brown, 2022).

A similar number of articles focused on the position of women in higher education and/or took a feminist perspective on autoethnography (Ashlee et al., 2017; Boss et al., 2019, Deschner et al., 2020; Edwards, 2017, Hernandez et al., 2015; Montiel et al., 2022, Santiago et al., 2017; Warren-Gordon & Jackson-Brown, 2022). Edwards (2017, p. 621) displays a typical approach:

> In this paper, a woman with more than two decades experience as a full-time academic in the field of higher education relates her sense of loss and purposelessness when attempts to reach for a higher level position were consistently unsuccessful. Using autoethnography she relates her experiences of sexism in higher education, and the ways in which sexism turns into oppression through silencing. She proposes how her experiences point to the need for change, and she indicates that training to reduce gender bias has been proven to improve feelings of workplace fit for participants who collaborate with people who have addressed their gender bias.

Similarly, other articles have examined the experience of foreign-born academics (Hernandez et al., 2015; Kim, 2020; Vaishnav et al., 2023), those from sexual minorities (Alexander, 2023) or lower socio-economic groups (Tsalach, 2022), have taken a postcolonial approach (Toyosaki, 2018) or focused on resistance (Alexander, 2023; Almeida & Paranhos, 2023, Deschner et al., 2020), symbolic violence (Almeida & Paranhos, 2023), bullying (Higgins, 2023; Sobre-Denton, 2012; Vickers, 2007; Zawadzki & Jensen, 2020) or depression (Jago, 2002).

The approaches taken in these studies may be usefully illustrated by a number of examples. Thus, Hernandez et al. (2015, p. 533) analyze how they managed to survive and thrive as foreigners in US higher education:

> Based on experiences as graduate students and later as faculty and leaders, we trace the development of three empowering and transforming navigational strategies we utilized to survive and thrive at a US institution – exploiting multifocal lenses, reconfiguring identities, and engaging tempered radicalism. We discuss how the cultivation of a unique standpoint as outsiders/within can be a valuable resource for foreign-born women of color to advance active research agendas and to leverage their position in the academy.

Ruth et al. (2018, p. 154) employ autoethnography to give them voice to fight back against the neoliberal academy:

> Our proposition is that 'giving voice' in the manner in which we have done so is an affective means of 'talking back' against neo-liberal regimes of performativity which may also be effective as a form of localized resistance, strengthening our ability to cope with the anxiety such regimes provoke.

To give a third and final example, Ashlee et al. (2017, p. 101) describe using collaborative autoethnography for mutual support and survival:

> The origins of this collaboration were born out of necessity. Our so-called academic home, a rurally located, affluent, and predominantly white Midwest institution of higher learning, felt more like a prison. As woke womxn [sic] of colour graduate students, we sought each other out for survival. What initially began as informal chats and check-ins evolved into life-giving conversations of empathy, encouragement, and resilience. For our own wellness and wokeness, we banded together. By enduring the micro and macro-aggressions of living in the crosshairs of intersectional oppression, we formed a sista scholar familia.

Not all autoethnographic studies in higher education have focused on the marginalized; some, though the minority, have examined a diverse range of other topics, including the experience of administrators who also teach (Boss et al., 2019), leadership development (Chang et al., 2014; Ngunjiri & Hernandez, 2017), grade inflation (Blum, 2018) and the impact of Covid-19 (Godber & Atkins, 2021; Hobbs & Whitsett, 2023). Trahar (2013, p. 367) recounts how she used autoethnography to change and develop her teaching practices:

> Through personal reflections and conversations with her 'selves' on her teaching and on her supervisory relationships with doctoral researchers, the author strives to show how she reduced her reliance on familiar ideas and changed the shape of her teaching through questioning her 'selves', beliefs and values.

ISSUES AND CRITIQUE

Unsurprisingly, for a methodology that has now been practiced for a number of decades worldwide, autoethnography has raised a variety of issues and attracted significant critique.

Some of this critique has been rather dismissive. Thus, Delamont (2009), one of the best-known practitioners of ethnography, views autoethnography as a retreat:

> Ethnographic research is hard. It is physically tiring, intellectually taxing, demands a high level of engagement, and at every stage crises can arise. Precisely for those reasons it is worth persevering, capitalising on all the insights that can be drawn from reflexive writing about ethnography. Retreat into autoethnography is an abrogation of the honourable trade of the scholar. (p. 61)

Some practitioners of autoethnography have been told in no uncertain terms what their colleagues thought about the approach:

> some years ago, whilst walking with a colleague to the campus café for a mid-morning coffee, I mentioned to him that I was writing an article about my experiences, in my younger days, of being a high-level sports performer whose career was prematurely terminated by a serious injury and the impact this then had on my life. Without breaking his stride, he said, "Sounds like an academic *wank* to me". Sparkes (2022, p. 263)

Clearly, for some, taking a focus on the self, albeit in relation to the rest of the world, is too selfish, inward-looking and personal to be worthy of research. Autoethnographers themselves, as well as acknowledging the problems they have experienced regarding the acceptability of the method, also point out, in contrast to Delamont's view, its practical difficulties:

> The author's experience of writing an autoethnography about international adoption has shown her[...] that autoethnography can be a very difficult undertaking. In writing her autoethnography, she confronted anxiety-producing questions pertaining to representation, balance, and ethics. As well, she dealt with the acceptability of her autoethnography by informal and formal reviewers. Wall (2008, p. 38)

In a later article, Wall (2016) proposed a "moderate and balanced" approach as a way of responding to these issues: "I propose a moderate and balanced treatment of autoethnography that allows for innovation, imagination, and the representation of a range of voices in qualitative inquiry while also sustaining confidence in the quality, rigor, and usefulness of academic research" (p. 1).

This is not to downplay the potential risks of autoethnography. Having outlined these, Jackson and Mazzei (2008) suggest making a closer link to narrative forms of research as a possible solution:

> in an attempt to engage the crises of representation by transgressively blurring genres and writing against the disembodied voice of objectivism, autoethnographers run the risk of simply replacing one privileged center with another, making similarly narrow claims to truth, authority, and authenticity as objectivism: autoethnography has exchanged transcendency for transparency. To keep autoethnographic practices 'vigilant'... we explore ways in which experience and the narrative 'I' may be reconstituted in narrative research. (p. 299)

Karra and Phillips (2008) take a more positive stance, stressing the strengths of autoethnography as a form, perhaps the ultimate form, of insider research, while noting there is still a need to somehow maintain a critical distance:

> the strengths of this mode of research are considerable. Researching in your own cultural context eases the problems of access that plague researchers, reduces the resources required to conduct research, facilitates the development of trust and rapport, and reduces the problems of translation that are so prevalent in research that spans cultural boundaries. At the same time, the same factors that lead to these strengths also create a number of challenges. In particular, I have pointed to the problem of maintaining a critical distance, managing role conflicts, and the limits of serendipity. (p. 556)

Also taking a positive stance, Ellis (2009), while acknowledging that autoethnographic approaches can be improved, effectively argues that the critiques made of it are a demonstration of its impact and worth:

> Critiques from those hostile to autoethnography show that scholars with different goals, objectives, and perspectives find something of interest to push back against or something so irritating to them that they can't help but respond. Autoethnography is not being ignored; it has gained enough of a following that critics feel it is important to challenge it in order to hold onto the hegemony of their way of doing research... Critiques from those who share the goals of interpretive social science - some of whom have engaged in forms of autoethnographic writing - are more problematic. I am hopeful that those formulating these critiques ultimately have the goal of improving autoethnography and that these responses signal a maturation of this approach and a readiness to expand our horizons. If that is true, their critical responses should serve to make autoethnography more nuanced, evocative, and complex. (p. 373)

In the spirit of improving practice, Tolich (2010) addresses the ethical issues faced by autoethnographers and offers 10 foundational guidelines. Le Roux (2017) goes further in proposing five criteria to assess the rigour of autoethnographic research: subjectivity, self-reflexivity, resonance, credibility and contribution. She concludes that

> Checklists[...] cannot substitute for informed judgement. Any appraisal of autoethnographies should be subject to individual judgement based on insight and experience. Competent researchers and appraisers of research must acquire not only the ability to use and understand the application of various research skills but also the acumen to judge when some kinds of research are likely to prove more productive and germane than others. Recognizing the need to appraise research against evaluative guidelines wins respect and gains acceptability for the research process and product. (p. 204)

Walford (2021) firmly positions autoethnography within ethnography in arguing that "worthwhile auto-ethnography, of whatever type, should meet the criteria set for worthwhile ethnography as such" (p. 31).

DISCUSSION

Autoethnography has come a long way in the few decades since it emerged from ethnography. While still regarded with suspicion in some methodological quarters – something it is not alone in; after all, the entirety of qualitative research is still viewed with distaste by some quantitative researchers – autoethnography has expanded, diversified and caught the attention of many qualitative researchers, particularly those in marginalized positions.

Autoethnography might best be regarded as one of a group of method/ologies that emphasize the self or the personal. These would include auto/biographical studies, participant observation, narrative forms of analysis and the focus on voice, insider research and reflection (Costley et al., 2010; DeWalt & DeWalt, 2011; Mertova & Webster, 2020). Overwhelmingly qualitative in their approach, these method/ologies each emphasize the importance of analyzing personal data in a broader social context.

Two of the points made earlier in this article deserve some further discussion:

- why autoethnography, as a marginal methodology, so attracts the interest of the marginalized and
- whether the trend towards collaborative autoethnography is strengthening or weakening the methodology.

A Marginal Methodology for the Marginalized?

Autoethnography may be regarded as a marginal methodology. While it has undoubtedly been increasing in popularity, it is still only employed by a small minority of higher education researchers (and social researchers in general). As we have seen, it has attracted staunch criticism from both within the qualitative research field and beyond it.

Why, then, does autoethnography seem to appeal particularly to researchers who are themselves in marginalized positions: e.g. ethnic minorities, women and those from lower social classes? It might be expected that researchers from such backgrounds would be especially keen to demonstrate their methodological rigour. On the contrary, however, many seize on autoethnography. Why might this be the case? I can think of two related reasons though there may be others.

First, employing autoethnography allows them to emphasize their marginality and difference. As a methodology much derided by the mainstream, autoethnography is available to the marginalized to call their own. It may then be used to draw attention to their marginality and to argue that the majority position needs to change.

Second, the emphasis placed by autoethnography on the individual's experience, set within the broader context of the society and polity, speaks to the marginalized. This is their experience, which the methodology enables them to express in a powerful way. More conventional qualitative or quantitative methods would not allow the same degree of prominence to be given to their story.

Autoethnography, therefore, is a highly attractive methodology for those researching in marginalized positions, both in higher education and elsewhere though it need not be the only methodology they use (Pearce, 2020).

Collaborative Autoethnography: Strength or Weakness?

Seen from that perspective, the trend towards more collaborative – rather than individual – forms of autoethnography might seem to be a retrograde step or a weakness. Granted, this might cause the critics of autoethnography to moderate their objections as the degree of collaboration, and thus the "sample size," grew. Yet, the loss of the highlighted individual experience could be a significant one.

Much depends, however, on how collaborative autoethnography is practiced. If the researchers involved are of like mind, and from the same or similar marginalized positions, their shared story (as in the examples given earlier in this chapter) could have added power. Their collaborative research could forcefully combine individual elements with the overall shared experience. The sharing of their experience and research approach should, at the same time, provide needed support and bolster their commitment.

CONCLUSION

Autoethnography has developed from ethnography over the last few decades, emphasizing the experience of the individual within the broader social and cultural context. It has appealed in particular – both in higher education research and in social research more broadly – to researchers in marginalized positions, serving as a methodology to highlight and fight back against that marginality. Many detailed and critical autoethnographies, focusing on the issues faced by marginalized individuals and their contexts, have been produced in this way.

Autoethnography has also been the subject of significant critique from those who view the focus on the individual as both self-indulgent and unconvincing as a research strategy. Collaborative forms of autoethnography, however, offer a promising way forward, which should strengthen both methodological acceptability and the transferability of their findings.

REFERENCES

Adams, T., Holman Jones, S., & Ellis, C. (2022). Introduction – Making sense and taking action: Creating a caring community of autoethnographers. In T. Adams, S. Holman Jones, & C. Ellis (Eds.), *Handbook of autoethnography* (2nd ed., pp. 1–19). Routledge.

Alexander, B. (2023). Onboarding, orientation and mentoring as *culture-crafting* processes: A rac(e)y autoethnography of resistance in higher education administration. *Qualitative Inquiry*. https://doi.org/10.1177/10778004221144072

Almeida, D. de, & Paranhos, W. (2023). Erased bodies in the university space: Autoethnography as a form of visibility. *Journal for Critical Education Policy Studies*, *20*(3), 311–344.

Anderson, L. (2006). Analytic autoethnography. *Journal of Contemporary Ethnography*, *35*(4), 373–395.

Ashlee, A., Zamora, B., & Karikari, S. (2017). We are woke: A collaborative critical autoethnography of three "womxn" of color graduate students in higher education. *International Journal of Multicultural Education*, *19*(1), 89–104.

Austin, J., & Hickey, A. (2007). Autoethnography and teacher development. *International Journal of Interdisciplinary Social Sciences*, *2*, 9 p.

Bhattacharya, K. (2018). Coloring memories and imaginations of 'home': Crafting a de/colonizing autoethnography. *Cultural Studies ↔ Critical Methodologies, 18*(1), 9–15.

Blum, D. (2018). Experiences of grade inflation at an online university in the United States: An autoethnography. *Qualitative Report, 23*(7), 1583–1612.

Bochner, A. (2012). On first-person narrative scholarship: Autoethnography as acts of meaning. *Narrative Inquiry, 22*(1), 155–164.

Boss, G., Karunaratne, N., Huang, C., Beavers, A., Pegram-Floyd, V., & Tullos, K. (2019). "It's a double-edged sword": A collaborative autoethnography of women of color higher education and student affairs administrators who teach in the college classroom. *Journal of Women and Gender in Higher Education, 12*(2), 166–185.

Boyle, M., & Parry, K. (2007). Telling the whole story: The case for organizational autoethnography. *Culture and Organization, 13*(3), 185–190.

Boylorn, R., & Orbe, M. (2021a). *Critical autoethnography: Intersecting cultural identities in everyday life* (2nd ed.). Routledge.

Boylorn, R., & Orbe, M. (2021b). Introduction: Critical autoethnography as method of choice/choosing critical autoethnography. In R. Boylorn & M. Orbe (Eds.), *Critical autoethnography: intersecting cultural identities in everyday life* (2nd ed., pp. 1–18). Routledge.

Brewer, J. (2000). *Ethnography*. Open University Press.

Butz, D., & Besio, K. (2004). The value of autoethnography for field research in transcultural settings. *The Professional Geographer, 56*(3), 350–360.

Castillo-Montoya, M., Hunter, T., Moore, W., & Sulé, T. (2022). Why the caged bird sings in the academy: A decolonial collaborative autoethnography of African American and Puerto Rican faculty and staff in higher education. *Journal of Diversity in Higher Education, 15*(5), 668–680.

Chang, H., Longman, K., & Franco, M. (2014). Leadership development through mentoring in higher education: A collaborative autoethnography of leaders of color. *Mentoring & Tutoring, 22*(4), 373–389.

Chang, H., Ngunjiri, F., & Hernandez, K.-A. (2013/2016). *Collaborative autoethnography*. Routledge.

Chapman-Clarke, M. (2016). 'Discovering' autoethnography as a research genre, methodology and method. 'The ying and yang of life'. *Transpersonal Psychology Review, 18*(2), 10–18.

Costley, C., Elliott, G., & Gibbs, P. (2010). *Doing work-based research: Approaches to enquiry for insider-researchers*. Sage.

Cruz, J., Macdonald, J., Broadfoot, K., Chuang, A., & Ganesh, S. (2020). "Aliens" in the United States: A collaborative autoethnography of foreign-born faculty. *Journal of Management Inquiry, 29*(3), 272–285.

Davids, N. (2022). *Out of place: An autoethnography of postcolonial citizenship*. African Minds.

Delamont, S. (2009). The only honest thing: Autoethnography, reflexivity and small crises in fieldwork. *Ethnography and Education, 4*(1), 51–63.

Denzin, N. (2003). Performing [auto] ethnography politically. *The Review of Education, Pedagogy & Cultural Studies, 25*(3), 257–278.

Deschner, C., Dorion, L., & Salvatori, L. (2020). Prefiguring a feminist academia: A multi-vocal autoethnography on the creation of a feminist space in a neoliberal university. *Society and Business Review, 15*(4), 325–347.

DeWalt, K., & DeWalt, B. (2011). *Participant observation: A guide for fieldworkers*. Altimira Press.

Doloriert, C., & Sambrook, S. (2012). Organisational autoethnography. *Journal of Organisational Ethnography, 1*(1), 83–95.

Dreistadt, J. (2022). A journey toward connection and belonging: Autoethnography of a Jewish student in Christian higher education. *Religions, 13*, 356.

Duncan, M. (2004). Autoethnography: Critical appreciation of an emerging art. *International Journal of Qualitative Methods, 3*(4), 28–39.

Edwards, J. (2017). Narrating experiences of sexism in higher education: A critical feminist autoethnography to make meaning of the past, challenge the status quo and consider the future. *International Journal of Qualitative Studies in Education, 30*(7), 621–634.

Egeli, C. (2017). Autoethnography: A methodological chat with self. *Counselling Psychology Review, 32*(1), 5–15.

Elbelazi, S., & Alharbi, L. (2020). The "exotic other": A poetic autoethnography of two Muslim teachers in higher education. *Qualitative Inquiry*, *26*(6), 661–666.

Ellis, C. (2009). Fighting back or moving on: An autoethnographic response to critics. *International Review of Qualitative Research*, *2*(3), 371–378.

Ellis, C., Adams, A., & Bochner, A. (2011). Autoethnography: An overview. *Forum for Qualitative Social Research*, *12*(1), 10.

Estes, J., Guthu, A., Flesey-Assad, D., Ringwelski, F., Jinks, K., Legat, V., Rice, E., & Whitlow, G. (2018). Reflective perspectives: Student autoethnography on Portland State's University Studies Program. *The Journal of General Education*, *67*(1–2), 14–32.

Forber-Pratt, A. (2015). "You're going to do what?" Challenges to autoethnography in the academy. *Qualitative Inquiry*, *21*(9), 821–835.

Gaitanidis, I., & Shao-Kobayashi, S. (2022). Polarized agents of internationalization: An autoethnography of migrant faculty at a Japanese university. *Higher Education*, *83*(1), 19–33.

Gander, M. (2024). Antagonistic identity discourses in career transitions: An autoethnographic study in higher education. *Studies in Higher Education*. https://doi.org/10.1080/03075079.2024.2319875

Godber, K., & Atkins, D. (2021). Covid-19 impacts on teaching and learning: A collaborative autoethnography by two higher education lecturers. *Frontiers in Education*, *6*, 647524.

Grenier, R. (2015). Autoethnography as a legitimate approach to HRD research: A methodological conversation at 30,000 feet. *Human Resource Development Review*, *14*(3), 332–350.

Hayano, D. (1979). Auto-ethnography: Paradigms, problems and prospects. *Human Organization*, *38*(1), 99–104.

Haynes, K. (2017). Autoethnography in accounting research. In Z. Hoque, L. Parker, M. Covaleski, & K. Haynes (Eds.), *The Routledge companion to qualitative accounting research methods* (pp. 215–230). Routledge.

Hernandez, K.-A., Ngunjiri, F., & Chang, H. (2015). Exploring the margins in higher education: A collaborative autoethnography of three foreign-born female faculty of color. *International Journal of Qualitative Studies in Education*, *28*(5), 533–551.

Higgins, P. (2023). "I don't even recognize myself anymore": An autoethnography of workplace bullying in higher education. *Power and Education*. https://doi.org/10.1177/17577438231163041

Hobbs, J., & Whitsett, L. (2023). Severed connections and timely reflections: A collaborative autoethnography navigating uncertainty amid Covid-19 in higher education. *Journal of Curriculum and Pedagogy*. https://doi.org/10.1080/15505170.2023.2187900

Holman Jones, S. (2016). Living bodies of thought: The "critical" in critical autoethnography. *Qualitative Inquiry*, *22*(4), 228–237.

Howard, L. (2019). Casting the 'net' in autonetnography: Exploring the potential for analytic autonetnography as an emerging e-research methodology. In J. Huisman & M. Tight (Eds.), *Theory and method in higher education research* (Vol. 4, pp. 163–187). Emerald Publishing Limited.

Humphreys, M. (2005). Getting personal: Reflexivity and autoethnographic vignettes. *Qualitative Inquiry*, *11*(6), 840–860.

Jackson, A., & Mazzei, L. (2008). Experience and "I" in autoethnography: A deconstruction. *International Review of Qualitative Research*, *1*(3), 299–318.

Jago, B. (2002). Chronicling an academic depression. *Journal of Contemporary Ethnography*, *31*(6), 729–757.

Jesson, J., Matheson, L., & Lacey, F. (2011). *Doing your literature review: Traditional and systematic techniques*. Sage.

Karra, N., & Phillips, N. (2008). Researching "back home": International management research as autoethnography. *Organizational Research Methods*, *11*(3), 541–561.

Keleş, U. (2022). Autoethnography as a recent methodology in applied linguistics: A methodological review. *Qualitative Report*, *27*(2), 448–474.

Kidd, J., & Finlayson, M. (2015). She pushed me, and I flew: A duoethnographical story from supervisors in flight. *Forum for Qualitative Social Research*, *16*(1), 15.

Kim, H. (2020). 'Where are you from? Your english is so good': A Korean female scholar's autoethnography of academic imperialism in US higher education. *International Journal of Qualitative Studies in Education*, *33*(5), 491–507.

Lapadat, J. (2017). Ethics in autoethnography and collaborative autoethnography. *Qualitative Inquiry*, 23(8), 589–603.
Le Roux, C. (2017). Exploring rigour in autoethnographic research. *International Journal of Social Research Methodology*, 20(2), 195–207.
Learmonth, M., & Humphreys, M. (2011). Autoethnography and academic identity: Glimpsing business school doppelgängers. *Organization*, 19(1), 99–117.
Lumsden, K. (2021). *Becoming* and *unbecoming* an academic: A performative autoethnography of struggles against imposter syndrome and masculinist culture from early to mid-career in the neo-liberal university. In M. Addison, M. Breeze, & Y. Taylor (Eds.), *The Palgrave handbook of imposter syndrome* (pp. 577–592). Palgrave Macmillan.
Matas, R. de (2019). Sensory autoethnography: Engaging the senses, emotions and autobiographical narrative towards a transformative pedagogical practice in higher education. *Journal of Writing in Creative Practice*, 12(1–2), 167–180.
Maydell, E. (2010). Methodological and analytical dilemmas in autoethnographic research. *Journal of Research Practice*, 6(1), M5.
Mertova, P., & Webster, L. (2020). *Using narrative inquiry as a research method: An introduction to critical event narrative analysis in research, teaching and professional practice* (2nd ed.). Routledge.
Montiel, G., Torres-Hernandez, G., Vasquez, R., Tiburcio, A., & Zavala, F. (2022). "It wasn't only the pandemic": A collaborative autoethnography of Latinx women in higher education navigating the Covid-19 pandemic in rapidly shifting immigration contexts. *Journal of Latinos and Education*, 21(3), 266–276.
Moosavi, L. (2022). 'But you're white': An autoethnography of whiteness and white privilege in east Asian universities. *Research in Comparative and International Education*, 17(1), 107–123.
Morikawa, T. (2023). EMI, EAP and pedagogy: An autoethnographic account of a case study at a university in Japan. *Asian Englishes*. https://doi.org/10.1080/13488678.2023.2243382
Ngunjiri, F., & Hernandez, K.-A. (2017). Problematizing authentic leadership: A collaborative autoethnography of immigrant women of color leaders in higher education. *Advances in Developing Human Resources*, 19(4), 393–406.
Ngunjiri, F., Hernandez, K.-A., & Chang, H. (2010). Living autoethnography: Connecting life and research. *Journal of Research Practice*, 6(1), E1.
Nordbäck, E., Hakonen, M., & Tienari, J. (2022). Academic identities and sense of place: A collaborative autoethnography in the neoliberal university. *Management Learning*, 53(2), 331–349.
O'Byrne, P. (2007). The advantages and disadvantages of mixing methods: An analysis of combining traditional and autoethnographic approaches. *Qualitative Health Research*, 17(10), 1381–1391.
Odriozola, M. (2023). Autoethnography as a tool for the achievement of deep learning of university students in service-learning experiences. *Social Sciences*, 12(7), 395.
Oleksiyenko, A. (2021). Global higher education and Covid-19: A virtual autoethnography of a faculty. In R. Chan, K. Bista, & R. Allen (Eds.), *Online teaching and learning in higher education during Covid-19* (pp. 167–180). Routledge.
Pahom, O., Box, C., Ellis, A., & Rains, S. (2023). Women, writing and the pandemic: An autoethnographic study on factors constraining or supporting women's research writing at a small Christian university. *Christian Higher Education*. https://doi.org/10.1080/15363759.2023.2181240
Paukova, A., Khachaturova, M., & Safronov, P. (2019). Autoethnography of tutoring in the Russian university: From theoretical knowledge to practical implementation. *Mentoring & Tutoring*, 27(2), 213–230.
Pearce, R. (2020). A methodology for the marginalised: Surviving oppression and traumatic fieldwork in the neoliberal academy. *Sociology*, 54(4), 806–824.
Peters, M., Wang, H., Ogunniran, N., Huang, Y., Green, B., Chunga, J., Quainoo, E., Ren, Z., Hollings, S., Mou, C., Khomera, S., Zhang, M., Zhou, S., Laimeche, A., Zheng, W., Xu, R., Jackson, L., & Hayes, S. (2020). China's internationalized higher education during Covid-19: Collective student autoethnography. *Postdigital Science and Education*, 2, 968–998.
Pheko, M. (2018). Autoethnography and cognitive adaptation: Two powerful buffers against the negative consequences of workplace bullying and academic mobbing. *International Journal of Qualitative Studies on Health and Well-Being*, 13, 1. https://doi.org/10.1080/17482631.2018.1459134

Pindi, G. (2018). Hybridity and identity performance in diasporic context: An autoethnographic journey of the self across cultures. *Cultural Studies ↔ Critical Methodologies, 18*(1), 23–31.

Qin, B., Zhu, G., Cheng, C., Shen, L., & Zhang, A. (2023). Bane or boon? An autoethnographic narrative of the English-medium instruction contradictions in a Chinese University. *Asia-Pacific Education Researcher, 32*(2), 251–262.

Richards, R. (2008). Writing the othered self: Autoethnography and the problem of objectification in writing about illness and disability. *Qualitative Health Research, 18*(12), 1717–1728.

Ruth, D., Wilson, S., Alakavuklar, O., & Dickson, A. (2018). Anxious academics: Talking back to the audit culture through collegial, critical and creative autoethnography. *Culture and Organization, 24*(2), 154–170.

Santiago, I., Karimi, N., & Alicea, A. (2017). Neoliberalism and higher education: A collective autoethnography of brown women teaching assistants. *Gender and Education, 29*(1), 48–65.

Snipes, J., & LePeau, L. (2017). Becoming a scholar: A duoethnography of transformative learning spaces. *International Journal of Qualitative Studies in Education, 30*(6), 576–595.

Sobre-Denton, M. (2012). Stories from the cage: Autoethnographic sensemaking of workplace bullying, gender discrimination and white privilege. *Journal of Contemporary Ethnography, 41*(2), 220–250.

Sparkes, A. (2000). Autoethnography and narratives of self: Reflections on criteria in action. *Sociology of Sport Journal, 17*, 21–43.

Sparkes, A. (2022). When judgment calls: Making sense of criteria for evaluating different forms of autoethnography. In T. Adams, S. Holman Jones, & C. Ellis (Eds.), *Handbook of autoethnography* (2nd ed., pp. 263–276). Routledge.

Spry, T. (2001). Performing autoethnography: An embodied methodological praxis. *Qualitative Inquiry, 7*(6), 706–732.

Struthers, J. (2014). Analytic autoethnography: One story of the method. In J. Huisman, & M. Tight (Eds.) *Theory and method in higher education research II. International perspectives on higher education research* (Vol. 10, pp. 183–202). Emerald Publishing Limited.

Syed, H. (2022). "I make my students' assignments bleed with red circles": An autoethnography of translanguaging in higher education in Pakistan. *Annual Review of Applied Linguistics, 42*, 119–126.

Szwabowski, O., & Wężniejewska, P. (2017). An (co)autoethnographic story about going against the neoliberal didactic machine. *Journal for Critical Education, 15*(3), 105–144.

Tienari, J. (2019). One flew over the duck pond: Autoethnography, academic identity and language. *Management Learning, 50*(5), 576–590.

Tight, M. (2021). *Syntheses of higher education research: What we know*. Bloomsbury.

Tolich, M. (2010). A critique of current practice: Ten foundational guidelines for autoethnographers. *Qualitative Health Research, 20*(12), 1599–1610.

Torgerson, C. (2003). *Systematic reviews*. Continuum.

Toyosaki, S. (2018). Towards de/postcolonial autoethnography: Critical relationality with the academic second persona. *Cultural Studies ↔ Critical Methodologies, 18*(1), 32–42.

Trahar, S. (2013). Autoethnographic journeys in learning and teaching in higher education. *European Educational Research Journal, 12*(3), 367–375.

Tsalach, C. (2022). Lost wants? An autoethnography of class and ethnicity on the long path to higher education. *Race, Ethnicity and Education, 25*(5), 722–737.

Vaishnav, S., Basma, D., Chen, S.-Y., & Farrell, I. (2023). An autoethnographic inquiry of the experiences of foreign-born women of color in higher education. *International Journal of Qualitative Studies in Education*. https://doi.org/10.1080/09518398.2023.2181458

Valentim, I. (2018). Between academic pimping and moral harassment in higher education: An autoethnography in a Brazilian public university. *Journal of Academic Ethics, 16*, 151–171.

Vickers, M. (2007). Autoethnography as sensemaking: A story of bullying. *Culture and Organization, 13*(3), 223–237.

Walford, G. (2004). Finding the limits: Autoethnography and being an Oxford University proctor. *Qualitative Research, 4*(3), 403–417.

Walford, G. (2021). What is worthwhile auto-ethnography? Research in the age of the selfie. *Ethnography and Education, 16*(1), 31–43.

Wall, S. (2006). An autoethnography on learning about autoethnography. *International Journal of Qualitative Methods, 5*(2), 146–160.

Wall, S. (2008). Easier said than done: Writing an autoethnography. *International Journal of Qualitative Methods, 7*(1), 38–53.

Wall, S. (2016). Toward a moderate autoethnography. *International Journal of Qualitative Methods, 15*, 1. https://doi.org/10.1177/1609406916674966

Warren-Gordon, K., & Jackson-Brown, A. (2022). Critical co-constructed autoethnography: Reflections of a collaborative teaching experience of two black women in higher education. *Journal of Black Studies, 53*(2), 115–132.

Winkler, I. (2018). Doing autoethnography: Facing challenges, taking choices, accepting responsibilities. *Qualitative Inquiry, 24*(4), 236–247.

Yoshida, R. (2024). Autoethnography of a Japanese academic in an Australian university: The development and changes of professional identity. *Higher Education.* https://doi.org/10.1007/s10734-023-01175-w

Zawadzki, M., & Jensen, T. (2020). Bullying and the neoliberal university: A co-authored autoethnography. *Management Learning, 51*(4), 398–413.

UBIQUITY WITHOUT CLARITY? WHAT DO WE MEAN BY THE 'HIGHER EDUCATION LANDSCAPE'? A SYSTEMATIC REVIEW

Richard Budd

Lancaster University, UK

ABSTRACT

The combination of previously unassociated terms in a metaphor can helpfully illustrate particular characteristics of a person, phenomenon or practice. However, it can also obfuscate because the focus on some elements may come at the expense of others. The metaphor of the landscape is somewhat ubiquitous in academic literature, and this paper is specifically interested in the 'higher education landscape', which is widely used in scholarly – as well as media and policy – writing. By applying thematic analysis to a sample of publications which invoke the term, this paper comprises what Haslanger calls a descriptive and ameliorative approach to investigate both how and why this metaphor is used. By considering these publications cumulatively, we can identify that the higher education landscape enables scholars to simultaneously acknowledge higher education's temporal, social and political positioning, its state of what can feel like permanent and wide-ranging flux, and its diverse cast of interrelated actors. In this way, it serves as a useful and evocative container metaphor for higher education's activities and constituents and the interrelationships and tensions between them. At the same time, its somewhat indiscriminate and indeterminate use can conflate and mask the detail and nature of these dynamics, and it is possible to discern in its application a collective sense of nervousness and uncertainty about higher education more generally.

Keywords: Higher education research; higher education landscapes; systematic review; metaphors; ameliorative inquiry

INTRODUCTION

> The essence of metaphor is the understanding and experiencing of one kind of thing in terms of another. Lakoff & Johnson (1980, p. 5)

Metaphors are 'woven into the fabric' of our language and frame our social understanding (Lakoff & Johnson, 1980). What 'happens' in a metaphor is that two usually separate conceptual domains are placed together, with words or phrases taken from their literal use and applied figuratively, such as the term 'emotional baggage' to reflect the cumulative mental impact of past, often negative, experiences (Cameron & Deignan, 2006). Lakoff and Johnson (1980) further distinguish between different types of metaphor, such as orientational (e.g. peak performance), ontological (e.g. economic inflation), container (e.g. territory) and anthropomorphic (e.g. organizational vision). There is a voluminous body of scholarship on the use of metaphor, and Cameron and Deignan (2006) highlight how they can range from the short-lived and locally contextual, such as 'in-jokes', to the widespread and durable, but that they rarely transfer between languages. Metaphors can serve a useful purpose in allowing us to think about phenomena in different ways – to see them from alternative perspectives – but while their use can sharpen our understanding, it may alternatively blur it (Lumby & Foskett, 2011).

Higher education is no stranger to metaphor, the 'ivory tower', which has seen shifts in its uses and interpretations over time (Shapin, 2012) being a well-worn example. The widely used concept of a 'university system' ontologically implies that higher education consists of tightly and directly controlled organizations with closely aligned purposes and functions (Bessant, 2002). Scholars often use metaphors to juxtapose different and competing, underlying orientations such as that of the university as monastery or economic enterprise (Ritchie, 2002). This can allow us to unpick and analyze the positions and protagonists in the purported 'battle' over the 'soul' of the university (Deering & Sá, 2018; Fabricant & Brier, 2016), where tensions between these orientations potentially engender an anthropomorphized 'schizophrenic university' (Shore, 2010). Metaphors are applied to our activities and constituents too, such as considering whether teaching is akin to an art or gardening (McEwan, 2007) or how/whether students can be seen as customers, clients or pawns (Tight, 2013). As Tight identifies, though, while higher education metaphors can offer useful ways of exploring varied and potentially competing facets or characteristics, they rarely capture a full understanding of the object of enquiry.

Some scholars have discerned a geographically metaphorical turn in higher education literature, and we can see examples in references to the shifting 'tectonic plates' of higher education (Hey & Morley, 2011) or the exclusionary 'climates' of university campus cultures (Jackson & Sundaram, 2018). We see disciplinary fields (another metaphor) being described as a space, terrain, domain, kingdom (Chen & Hu, 2012) or archipelago (Macfarlane, 2012) or university groups considered as a collection of 'atolls, islands and archipelagos' (Hanley & Bonilla, 2016). Higher education scholars often draw conceptual ideas from different disciplines (Huisman, 2023) and perhaps there is a transition into everyday language of established theorizations such as Becher and Trowler's (2001) tribes and territories, Bourdieusan intellectual fields or Bernsteinian professional knowledge regions (Clegg, 2012; Musselin, 2021). It is also not limited to academic use, with Hayes (2015) discerning a parallel tendency in university or government policy documents to employ terms such as pathway or roadmap – or landscape – in an attempt to lend a veneer of substance to largely abstract plans.

Landscapes in particular have become something of a buzzword in the social sciences (Lowenthal, 2007) and educational literature more generally (Terepyshchyi, 2017). Google Scholar returns nearly 80,000 items for the term educational or education landscape, with widespread use in academic publications (Sabol, 2013; White et al., 2010), government reports (Bourn et al., 2017), op-eds (Francke, 2021) and so on. The landscape of higher education or higher education landscape features over 30,000 times, alongside research landscape (37,000) and academic landscape (13,000). The genealogy (Haslanger, 2005) of the metaphor is not being explored here, but it does have a longer history: some uses can be found in literature from the 1970s (Counelis, 1971; Grupe, 1974) and 1980s (Bienayme, 1984; Weiner, 1986), while the magazine of what is now the US Council for Higher Education Accreditation (CHEA) ran a thematically wide-ranging editorial titled 'The Landscape' from 1993 to 2006. Higher education landscapes feature regularly in policy papers from organizations such as the United States Agency for International Development (USAID) (Lebrón et al., 2018) and the European Commission (Haywood et al., 2014), as well as in hybrid academic or mainstream media such as The Conversation (King, 2016) and The Atlantic (Fallows & Ganeshanthan, 2004).

Landscapes' application could thus be claimed to be ubiquitous, but we must be careful to distinguish between the metaphorical, such as the policy landscape (Burford et al., 2019), the literal as in university landscape planning (Li et al., 2011) and the theorized, such as learning landscapes (Tosh et al., 2006) or landscapes of practice (Wenger-Traynor et al., 2015). If metaphors serve a purpose, what purpose/s does the metaphor of the higher education landscape serve, and does it sharpen or blur our understandings of life in and around universities? This paper first outlines the methodology for a systematic review of peer-reviewed literature employing the higher education landscape/landscape of higher education as a metaphor, after which a description of the sample's thematic analysis and a subsequent discussion follow. For clarity, the guiding research question in this paper is as follows:

'What and who constitute the metaphor of the higher education landscape in academic scholarship, and to what end?'

METHODOLOGY

While it has been claimed that systematic reviews originated in educational research (Davies, 2000), there was a brief debate in the early 2000s as to their appropriateness outside medical fields (where they had become commonplace), which largely related to attempts to determine the effectiveness of educational interventions to influence policy (Evans & Benefield, 2001; MacLure, 2005). More recent work (Tight, 2019a), though, shows that review type studies – including meta-analysis – have become increasingly popular in higher education research, which Tight attributes to a maturation of the field. They take varied forms, often with less emphasis on capturing impact per se, but rather as an attempted 'mapping of the territory' (de Rijcke et al., 2016) of scholarship on higher education, such as through tracking co-citation (Tight, 2014) or the analysis of text across large bodies of literature (Kuzhabekova et al., 2015). Other work, with which this paper aligns, has sought to understand variations and potential gaps in scholarly debates around growing themes or topics such as decolonization (Shahjahan et al., 2021), transnational higher education (Kosmützky & Putty, 2016) or pedagogy with international students (Lomer & Mittelmeier, 2021).

While the forms of systematic review vary, literature highlights that transparency is key; with this in mind, the PRISMA-S guidance (Rethlefsen et al., 2021) has been suggested as a model. More specifically, this requires decision-making to be explicit, including the eligibility (inclusion and exclusion) criteria, information sources, search strategy and selection process. Seeking publications which used the term 'higher education landscape' or 'landscape of higher education' in the title, the Web of Science (WoS) was used as the primary source – while not exhaustive and being biased towards English, it is the largest database (see Kuzhabekova et al., 2015). This was supplemented by searches with OneSearch and Google Scholar. This approach gleaned 280 items which were reviewed and filtered according to the following in/exclusion criteria:

(1) original scholarly contributions (i.e. not book reviews),
(2) employing higher education landscape as a metaphor (i.e. not literal or theoretical),
(3) published in English,
(4) digitally accessible, and
(5) peer reviewed.

This reduced the overall body of items to 55 publications, which were imported into NVivo and reviewed with a thematic analysis (Braun & Clarke, 2006, 2019) approach. Thematic analysis is suitable for this type of study as the focus is on identifying themes – 'patterns of shared meaning' (Braun & Clarke, 2019, p. 593) – across a dataset by iteratively and reflexively reading, labelling and reviewing first level codes (i.e. instances) to develop second level, meta categories (Elliott, 2018). These second level categories constitute themes within which sub-themes of shared meaning could be identified.

As Table 1 details, the sample comprised 3 books, 12 book chapters and 40 journal articles, consisting of 41 different titles/journals, with 128 contributing authors in total. There was a notable presence of dynamism in the titles, with 25 – almost half – referring to higher education landscapes which were changing or

Table 1. Sample Overview.

	Count
Overview	
Items	55
Book/Chapter/Journal	3/12/40
Publication Titles	41
Authors	128
Landscape Mentions Frequency/Mean	0–27/4.85
Changing Landscapes	25 (45%)
Scale	
Global	15 (27%)
National	30 (55%)
Regional	7 (13%)
Local	3 (3%)
First Author Location	
Africa	7 (13%)
Asia	8 (15%)
Oceania	4 (7%)
Europe	16 (29%)
North America	20 (36%)
Latin America	0

changed, shifting or new, transforming/ed or transitioning. The most prevalent scale was at the national – over half – followed by global, regional and local in descending order. Reflective of the national scale described in the sample, literature reviews – in some cases supplemented with other data such as interviews and documentary analysis – were the most prevalent (32) methodological approach. Within this group, there was a slight tendency in some US-based papers (e.g. Floyd, 2007; Woodard et al., 2000) towards what Dale (2005) describes as methodological nationalism, where claims around broader higher education developments were solely supported by single country – i.e. US – statistics and literature.

Scholars have noted how the dominance of Global North, and English-speaking countries (in English language literature), signifies an imbalance – related to ongoing colonial legacies – in the geopolitics of knowledge (Shahjahan et al., 2021). This observation extends here; while first authors were located in 41 countries, those based North America, Europe and Oceania were most heavily represented, together comprising 85% of the total. From another angle, authors based in six countries contributed 73% of all publications, in descending order the USA, UK, Australia, South Africa, Canada and Ireland, with the USA presenting almost half of those. This dominance, including the presence of South Africa as a regionally prolific producer of higher education work, as well as an absence of Latin American scholarship, has been observed elsewhere (Ashwin, 2022; Tight, 2012).

This is problematic because it reflects the continuation of a Eurocentric bias across knowledge domains, philosophically, conceptually, and empirically, and risks marginalizing or erasing alternative viewpoints (Connell, 2014). Suffice to say, this bias in the sample and the limits it imposes on any corresponding knowledge claims are recognized here.

Also notable was the prevalence and diversity of landscapes within and beyond that of higher education. Landscapes were mentioned in the text (i.e. not including the title) on average almost five times per publication; the highest number (27) was a book, but a number of journal pieces also included it between 10 and 23 times while a fifth did not include it at all. The metaphor was also paired with 27 different terms, and 19 publications included three or more combinations. These pairings have been grouped for simplicity into five categories (see Table 2); in two instances, it was not possible to identify what a landscape was associated with while two used it metaphorically as well as literally (urban and environmental) in the same publication. This diversity appears not to be an anomaly – an earlier exploratory search of higher education-related scholarly publications employing landscape as a metaphor returned 202 different types from 287 items.

ANALYSIS – CORE THEMES: EXTERNAL, INTERNAL AND ACTORS

This section of the chapter relates to the thematic analysis of the sample. As per the process of iterative reading, coding and review (Braun & Clarke, 2006), and in relation to the research question around what and who constitutes a higher education landscape, themes were identified and grouped within the following core categories.

- external forces – phenomena which impact higher education landscapes,
- internal factors – processes and activities within higher education landscapes and

Table 2. Types of Landscapes Cited in the Sample.

Landscape Category	Landscape Type
Broad	Education, higher education, institutional, university and academic
Knowledge-oriented	Humanities, research, intellectual, disciplinary, knowledge, teaching and learning
Policy or practice	Academic library, app creation, MOOC, public policy, grandes écoles preparation and veteran enrolments
Scalar or material	Global, international, regional, national, local, environmental and urban
Other	Challenges and solutions, competitive, diverse, fractured and unclear

- actors – organizations, collectives, and individuals who operate within higher education landscapes.

Now, each of these features will be outlined in turn.

External Forces – Social, Economic, Political and Technological
Marked within the sample was a regular acknowledgement of the influence of 'social, political, economic and cultural forces that shaped the structures and processes of higher education' (Pescosolido, 2008, p. 96) and featured in the sample – in order of prominence – as social, economic, political and technological. These categories are distinct but overlapping, as we will see. It is notable that environmental issues did feature through sustainability but rarely and only in passing.

Social themes were the most often cited – 33 items included them. These related to inequality and demographic change, labour market developments and the impact of conflict. Inequality was referenced on a number of dimensions, both around general issues of social injustice (Crosbie, 2005) and deficiencies in public education provision (Storey & Schiavo, 2013). Other problems were identified such as the legacies of racial segregation in South Africa (Nukunah et al., 2019), how societal racism and media representations could lead to the poor treatment of international students (Ritter, 2016) and the ongoing effects of patriarchal norms on subject choices, particularly in relation to STEM disciplines (Nguyen et al., 2020).

Also prevalent was an awareness of how, in many countries, nations' social composition was changing. This was described in terms of population growth and rising numbers of school leavers (Levy, 2006; Samokhvalova, 2021), alongside increasing social diversity (Knight, 2013; Page, 2013) and middle class expansion (Hollands & Tirthali, 2015; Jayawardena, 2017) all having knock-on effects on the scale and nature of higher education provision. Changes in labour markets featured prominently as a concern for higher education's role in preparing future graduates for work that potentially involved international mobility (Fitzgerald et al., 2012), new technological and other skills (Mandernach et al., 2015; Orr et al., 2020), and faster working environments (Lloyd, 2009) over longer working lives (Edwards & Robinson, 2020). Ebbs and flows in the demand for workers in particular areas was acknowledged as influencing degree demand and provision (Small et al., 2021). Conflict featured in two ways – its catastrophic impact on life and learning in countries affected by it such as in Ethiopia (Yizengaw, 2007), as well as for returning military veterans who subsequently entered higher education (Hitt et al., 2015).

Economic conditions featured in just under half of publications. Economic growth and its associated rising demand for (higher) education were noted (Samokhvalova, 2021), but the prevalent focus was on the pressure that recessions placed on higher education. These included the difficulties faced by countries with low GDP and poor tax collection capacity (Yizengaw, 2007) or the collapse of control economies in former Soviet states (Ahn et al., 2018) impeding the development or maintenance of infrastructure and social provision. Unsurprisingly, the economic and political overlapped. Several items described how the emergence of new political arrangements following the dissolution of old orders in the USSR (Kalashnikova et al., 2016; Platonova, 2019) and South Africa (Bunting, 2006; Nukunah et al., 2019) had far reaching consequences on their waxing and waning economies and thus how higher education was funded and governed. Most prominent was the 2008 global financial crisis and ensuing recessions that led to curtailed public expenditure across regions and within nations (Birtwistle & McKiernan, 2008; Hong & Songan, 2011). Some highlighted how state commitment to liberalization as part of the neoliberal knowledge economy agenda had in part caused the crisis and continued to underpin policy decisions before and after 2008 (Birtwistle & McKiernan, 2008; Jayawardena, 2017). Several authors drew on arguments which recognized the ideological nature of marketisation and associated policies and the alignment of national economies towards global markets (Jayawardena, 2017; Jin & Horta, 2018; Samokhvalova, 2021), as well as the ensuing austerity politics (Pilkington, 2017). The indirect impact of these on higher education was noted, largely through the social implications of unemployment and parsimonious budgetary choices around public services (David & Fenton, 2015).

The final core theme of external factors influencing higher education related to technological change and was featured in a quarter of publications. Part of this was connected to the political and social in how technology enables the rapid interconnectedness of ideas, worldwide markets and knowledge flows that characterize globalization (Fitzgerald, 2012; Knight, 2013). This presented on the one hand a greater accessibility but variable quality of knowledge on the Internet (Edwards & Robinson, 2020; El-Hussein & Cronje, 2010), and on the other hand, an increased demand for – but potential lack of – digital and related transferrable skills (Mandernach et al., 2015; Orr et al., 2020).

Internal Factors – the 'League of -Ations'

Striking throughout the publications was the perception and realization of higher education in a state of wide-ranging flux. This was acknowledged in relation to its position within a changing world, but was particularly manifested in how a plethora of processes and activities in and around universities were being simultaneously and often significantly altered. These changes can be collectively described as a 'League of -Ations', in which they refer to a profusion of trends that characterize an ongoing and seemingly relentless rearrangement of the constituents, activities, and orientations, of higher education. These could be grouped into those which relate to social change and those associated with neoliberalism and new public management.

Higher Education Population Change

Half of the publications described major changes in relation to the student body, and these took two coinciding forms. The first was that of major growth in enrolments – usually to the point of *massification* or even *universalization* – across all of the regions featured, from North and Latin America (Birtwistle & McKiernan, 2008; Knight, 2013; Levy, 2006), to Southern Africa (Buckner & Zapp, 2021; Mwale & Simuchimba, 2019), Europe (Pilkington, 2017; Platonova, 2019; Purcell et al., 2016), Asia (Adi Badiozaman, 2017; Hong & Songan, 2011; Jin & Horta, 2018) and Australasia (Fitzgerald et al., 2012; Small et al., 2021). This was seen to be driven by the combination of greater numbers of school leavers (Flecknoe et al., 2017) cited alongside state-sponsored attempts to increase the graduate population for economic reasons (David & Fenton, 2015). As a corollary of this, but also as part of concerted attempts to address equity concerns around access and participation (Bunting, 2006; Small et al., 2021), there has been a *diversification* of higher education's learner population in terms of social class (Purcell et al., 2016), as well as age, race (Edwards & Robinson, 2020) and gender (Knight, 2013). This has, in many countries, been accompanied by an increase in international students which – alongside greater international staff mobility – represents part of an *internationalization* of higher education (Hong & Songan, 2011; Ritter, 2016).

The implications of this, recognized across this literature, are multiple. It has necessitated, first of all, a major growth in the number of places for students through an expansion of public higher education (Birtwistle & McKiernan, 2008; Kalashnikova et al., 2016), as well as through a greater presence of private domestic (Buckner & Zapp, 2021; Levy, 2006) and transnational provision (Adi Badiozaman, 2017; Samokhvalova, 2021). For state-funded higher education, this places burdens on public finances which are often alleviated through the problematic imposition of student fees (Buckner & Zapp, 2021; Platonova, 2019). For higher education institutions themselves, a larger student body stretches resources and creates workload issues for staff (David & Fenton, 2015) – including a *precaritisation* of roles (Adi Badiozaman, 2017; Erickson, 2012) – as well as concerns around appropriate support for learners who may not fit the stereotype of young, high achievers unencumbered with additional responsibilities (Hitt et al., 2015).

The Business Model
The pervasive presence across the sample of the 'spectre' of neoliberalism will surprise few scholars given that its 'popularity [...] as a diagnostic or explanatory term in the social sciences has grown exponentially' (Bacevic, 2019, p. 383). As Bacevic (2019) and Tight (2019b) both highlight, there is an ongoing debate over the definitions of neoliberalism but it serves as a useful, interdisciplinary (if overapplied) umbrella term for largely unwelcome developments in and around policy. What is important for higher education is how it both promotes state created or curated markets as the optimum means of resource allocation and valorizes knowledge according to its economic merits.

Prevalent in over half of the publications were references to a *marketisation* of higher education through the aggressive promotion of competition for students and research funding, reinforced by the presence of comparative league tables to better inform – or misinform – potential learners and sponsors (Fitzgerald et al., 2012; Purcell et al., 2016). This often featured as an element of a *globalization* of higher education due to its positioning as a component of national development plans in a competitive global knowledge economy (Chaka & Mashige, 2016; Ritter, 2016). This also speaks to a parallel element of *internationalization* where some institutions, supported by global rankings, market themselves internationally and/or establish overseas campuses (Birtwistle & McKiernan, 2008; Jin & Horta, 2018; Samokhvalova, 2021). Overall, it was recognized that this contest for students and funding engendered a heightened strategic responsiveness within higher education institutions (Woodard et al., 2000) driven by the rewards for winning – or the fear of losing, i.e. insolvency – that underpins the market. This requires the *responsibilization* of public (or quasi-public) higher education institutions, who are afforded more autonomy in return for having to optimize quality and balance their own books (Small et al., 2021; Yizengaw, 2007).

In combination, having to satisfy the 'needs' of policy, league tables and students induces something of a *standardization* of higher education profiles and services counterbalanced by a degree of *differentiation* as institutions still need to appear distinctively attractive (Chaka & Mashige, 2016; Kalashnikova et al., 2016; Mhichíl, 2013). This competition, though, favours those who already have – or are disproportionately awarded – greater shares of funding and status, leading to a heightened national and international *stratification* of institutions (Platonova, 2019; Purcell et al., 2016).

Having to be strategically active was in turn reported to have provoked widespread changes to how higher education institutions are structured and run (Woodard et al., 2000). This in many cases has taken the form of a *corporatization* though the mimicking of private enterprises (Adi Badiozaman, 2017; Whitford, 2014), with stronger central leadership and administrative control (Fitzgerald et al., 2012; Platonova, 2019). To some extent, this was reported as a form of *privatization* in that many former state institutions are no longer (or less) public in their decision-making or income streams, often outsourcing selected services to businesses (Chaka & Mashige, 2016; Mandernach et al., 2015). Another form of privatization is in the greater – and in some countries entirely new – presence of philanthropic and for-profit private providers, encouraged by governments seeking to increase competition and/or meet the swelling demand for a university education (Buckner & Zapp, 2021; Mwale & Simuchimba, 2019). Some see these as more agile, responsive to students and leaner in their administration, but there are concomitant concerns around a potential orientation towards profit at the expense of quality (Levy, 2006; Nukunah et al., 2019).

Further related changes in administrative practices can be seen in new modes of management and governance through the increased prevalence of accountability mechanisms and a greater *scrutinization* of higher education (Fitzgerald et al., 2012; Hong & Songan, 2011). Some of this relates to benchmarking and the establishment of shared national or international quality assurance standards (Mhichíl, 2013; Woodard et al., 2000). It was, though, more often reported to take the form of metrics for a state monitoring of higher education institutions

(David & Fenton, 2015; Erickson, 2012; Nguyen et al., 2020) and the imposition of measures for management to understand and drive organizational and staff performance (Adi Badiozaman, 2017; Woodard et al., 2000). This represents in part a logical extension of the need to be mindful of cost controls while acting strategically to thrive and/or survive in the higher education market (Chaka & Mashige, 2016; Yizengaw, 2007). At the same time, though, it was widely seen as an incursion into academic autonomy and a loss of democracy within institutions (Pilkington, 2017), forming part of an invasive 'managerialist' audit culture that reduces the richness of higher education to data points (Adi Badiozaman, 2017; Hayes, 2015).

Connected with this, it was regularly noted that we are witnessing a *commodification* of higher education in that neoliberalism champions financial outcomes as the primary or even sole indicator of merit (Ahn et al., 2018; Small et al., 2021). Alongside the policy changes mentioned earlier – competitively allocated and/or reduced state funding – it was widely seen that this encouraged a *commercialization* of university activities through a more entrepreneurial alignment towards income and profit/surplus generation in research and teaching (Buckner & Zapp, 2021; Penceliah et al., 2016). This in itself promotes an *instrumentalization* of knowledge in favour of applied/STEM disciplines – to the detriment of the arts and humanities – due to their more lucrative nature and more direct contribution to international competitiveness (Buckner & Zapp, 2021; Crosbie, 2005; Hayes, 2015). Alongside this, it places an excessive emphasis on graduate employment and salaries as the chief purpose of a university education (Erickson, 2012; Fitzgerald et al., 2012). This employability focus, justified by the framing of a degree as a personal career investment, in turn supports the widespread imposition of student fees that 'solves' the fiscal issues created by rising enrolments (Mhichíl, 2013; Purcell et al., 2016; Yizengaw, 2007), in many countries supplemented by even higher fees for international students (Ritter, 2016; Small et al., 2021).

A More Digital University
A proportion of authors described and analyzed wider technological changes visible in various ways within higher education providers. As Erickson (2012, p. 14) states, while campuses may appear materially unchanged at first glance:

beneath the surface[...] fiber and wireless networks permeate campus spaces permitting the near ubiquity of iPhones, iPads and other mobile devices. Information technology has changed the way we teach, the way we conduct research and the way we transfer knowledge.

Erickson and others (Hollands & Tirthali, 2015; Hong & Songan, 2011; Popa Strainu & Georgescu, 2017) describe a process of steady *digitization* across higher education administration and teaching, with an omnipresence of virtual learning environments, systems, and so on (Tan & Soo, 2017). This opens up opportunities for improved distance, mobile, lifelong and e-learning, and the potential for more student-centred forms of teaching (El-Hussein & Cronje, 2010; Orr et al., 2020; Sharma et al., 2017). It also potentially supports the development of digital skills that future employers are demanding but has engendered major changes in other services such as university libraries and student support (Lloyd, 2009; Mandernach et al., 2015). Staff and students therefore need to learn how to utilize these tools, learning and teaching in new ways, and this can be challenging for both groups (Edwards & Robinson, 2020; Erickson, 2012). At the same time, the *technologization* of services (Chaka & Mashige, 2016) offers financial opportunities for the providers of software and apps but cedes some control over higher education activities to them, while enabling new avenues for state surveillance.

Interrelated Actors

Notable in the literature was the profusion of diverse and interrelated actors engaged within the higher education landscape. There are a number of ways of classifying these actors, such as organizational and social, public and private, or profit and philanthropic, but one potentially useful distinction relates to whether their primary activity or interest is 'inside' or towards higher education, or if they are somewhat 'outside' it in terms of higher education being a secondary focus. Table 3 provides an overview of the actors who featured in the literature grouped in this way. This is not to suggest that this 'division' should be considered binary, fixed or absolute – governments and professional associations among others maintain a sustained interest in higher education, while for those such as mainstream media or financial institutions, the focus may be intermittent or cursory.

Table 3. Actors in the HE Landscape.

Predominant Location	Organization Type	Example
'Inside' HE	Higher education/Higher education institutions	The 'sector', universities, and colleges
	Higher education organizations	Disciplinary bodies, mission groups, leadership associations, funders, accreditation agencies, rankers, scholarly publishers, higher education media, and student unions
	Staff	Leaders, academics, managers, administrators, professional services, librarians, counsellors, and other support staff
	Students	Undergraduates, postgraduates
'Outside' HE	Public	Voters, taxpayers, educators, parents, potential students, and graduates/alumni
	Government	Ministries, ministers, politicians, state bodies, and regional/national/local legislatures
	Non-higher education organisations	Supranational/national non-governmental organisations, religious institutions, political parties, philanthropic bodies, lobbyists, professional associations, cultural institutions, and unions
	Private sector	Employers, corporations, businesses, industry groups, investors, media, suppliers, and financial institutions

This inside–outside grouping also suggests a potential distinction between higher education and the higher education landscape. It should be noted that there is no claim to comprehensiveness here; alumni, social media, and nonhuman actors were notably missing, but this does serve as a salutary reminder of the array of parties with complementary and contested interests in and around higher education.

Unsurprisingly given the focus of the literature selection, the most prevalently discussed actors were those inside higher education who were engaged in varying ways with its three intersecting missions of teaching, research and public service. Significant discussion space was dedicated to the nature and impact of sectoral competition (Buckner & Zapp, 2021; Fitzgerald et al., 2012; Mandernach et al., 2015) and its associated organizational changes (Fitzgerald et al., 2012; Jin & Horta, 2018) but also collaboration between institutions (David & Fenton, 2015), higher education and industry (Woodard et al., 2000) and between staff (Crosbie, 2005). Various public and private higher education organizations were seen through their roles in accreditation, benchmarking (Knight, 2013; Woodard et al., 2000) and professional standards (Mhichíl, 2013; Storey & Schiavo, 2013), funding (David & Fenton, 2015; Pescosolido, 2008), student admissions (Hayes, 2015) and rankings (Nguyen et al., 2020; Purcell et al., 2016).

Connecting to the internal trends noted earlier (Buckner & Zapp, 2021; Jin & Horta, 2018), authors noted how staff needed to be mindful of the growing and diversifying student body's pedagogical and other needs (Edwards & Robinson, 2020; Hitt et al., 2015; Holdsworth & Thomas, 2020), as well as incorporating technology into their practices (Woodard et al., 2000). These challenges were accompanied by the intensifying pressure of rising workloads and the balancing of research, teaching and other commitments (Ahn et al., 2018; Nguyen et al., 2020), set against a backdrop of reduced professional autonomy (Fitzgerald et al., 2012), intense competition for academic positions (Pilkington, 2017), and career precarity (Adi Badiozaman, 2017; Erickson, 2012; Hayes, 2015).

For students, their options could be limited by an insufficient supply of appropriate degree places (Page, 2013; Yizengaw, 2007) and financial concerns, particularly when having to pay to study (Jayawardena, 2017; Kalashnikova et al., 2016). For those overcoming these barriers, some faced discrimination at the point of admissions (Knight, 2013) or while at university (Ritter, 2016), and students could potentially encounter poor teaching (Agasisti & Pohl, 2012; Pilkington, 2017) and insufficient support (Penceliah et al., 2016), not least where staff were overstretched. In combination, these issues could contribute, particularly for marginalized students, to poorer academic outcomes and even dropout, all of which was bookended by the social inequalities that contributed to poorer preparation for study (Miron et al., 2021) and then challenging graduate labour market conditions (Bunting, 2006; Small et al., 2021).

In terms of those primarily 'outside' higher education, the state/government occupied the most prominent position, in terms of print space as well as influence over what higher education and higher education institutions were able to – or had to – do (Agasisti & Pohl, 2012; Flecknoe et al., 2017; Hollands & Tirthali, 2015; Purcell et al., 2016). As we might expect, this often related to policy making around neoliberal marketisation and actively positioning higher education within the knowledge economy (Ahn et al., 2018; Erickson, 2012; Fitzgerald et al., 2012; Jayawardena, 2017). Governments were not only seen as belligerent, with recognition of their largesse in supporting research and growth – sometimes enforcing legislation through litigation (Birtwistle & McKiernan, 2008) – as well as promoting equity (Penceliah et al., 2016; Ritter, 2016; van Vught, 2009) and teaching quality (Levy, 2006; Pescosolido, 2008). States were recognized as not being entirely autonomous, with their actions being tied by budgetary constraints (Hong & Songan, 2011; Jin & Horta, 2018; Yizengaw, 2007), the bounded jurisdictions of (somewhat) autonomous federal states or higher education institutions (Birtwistle & McKiernan, 2008), and the diverse demands of those who sought to influence or resist policy.

These other outside groups, as evident in Table 3, represented a number of different interests ranging from the religious or philanthropic to the corporate, some of whom funded research and/or even founded higher education institutions (Hong & Songan, 2011; Levy, 2006; Mwale & Simuchimba, 2019; Samokhvalova, 2021), while others provided outsourced services (Chaka & Mashige, 2016) or external certification and accreditation (Erickson, 2012). A procession of non-governmental organizations from the European Union and Council of Europe (Boland, 2011; Pilkington, 2017) to the World Bank and the United Nations (Birtwistle & McKiernan, 2008; Platonova, 2019) were oft-cited enactors and influencers of higher education-related policy. Some authors noted the additional presence and influence of cultural institutions such as the Confucius Institute (Chan, 2018) and British Council (Ahn et al., 2018) engaged in soft politics on behalf of their respective national governments.

Employers who recruited university leavers were dependent on – and thus invested in – the supply, quality and employability of graduates (Adi Badiozaman, 2017; Nukunah et al., 2019; Orr et al., 2020) and formed lobby groups to further their causes (Kalashnikova et al., 2016; Small et al., 2021). Unions were active in this space, too, often agitating for better working conditions and changes to employment law (Pilkington, 2017; Whitford, 2014; Woodard et al., 2000). The public's chief activity within this literature was in demanding access to higher education for future employment and social mobility (Edwards & Robinson, 2020; Hong & Songan, 2011), as well influencing academic practice through lay groups (van Vught, 2009). They could be hampered by an absence of knowledge about higher education (Hayes, 2015), but they nonetheless put pressure on governments (Jayawardena, 2017), protesting against some changes such as student fees (Fitzgerald et al., 2012) but supporting policies around equity and quality (Kalashnikova et al., 2016; Nukunah et al., 2019).

DISCUSSION

Outlining how scholars have used the metaphor of the higher education landscape constitutes what Haslanger (2005) considers a descriptive view. This is useful in that, through considering these publications collectively, we can see the higher education landscape as a dynamic space occupied by an array of actors whose interests pertain in varying ways to the multiple public and private purposes of teaching and research. This dynamism is connected to wider trends related to demographic change, evolving social norms and expectations, ongoing technological developments, fluctuating economic conditions, and political priorities and decision-making. It is also internally characterized by a significant growth and diversification of higher education alongside the greater presence and use of technology and a heightened set of developments related to neoliberalism, most notably competition, privatization, and financial instrumentalism. Furthermore, we can see that the actors – individual, organizational and collective – are differently oriented and hierarchically positioned, and their involvement with higher education ranges from the focused and sustained to the peripheral and passing.

A conspicuous observation within the publications reviewed is that the higher education landscape metaphor was almost never explained or even noted, and in a proportion of cases, was only used in the title. In a sense, this is to be expected where a term has entered common parlance and is widely understood – there is no need to say what we mean because everybody knows. Given its prevalence, we could argue that it has indeed entered everyday use, but there were still implied differences in what or who constituted the higher education landscape. For some, it appears to incorporate only what happens within and between higher education institutions (Agasisti & Pohl, 2012), while for others it seems to encompass higher education and the state (Bunting, 2006) and/or the church (Mwale & Simuchimba, 2019) and/or industry (Sharma et al., 2017). By and large, though, it was used interchangeably with the earlier noted metaphors of the higher education system or sector (Bessant, 2002), or more simply, with higher education. We might then ask why 'landscape' is used at all, while being mindful that, as Haslanger (2005, p. 16) observes in her analysis of the social use of expressions, 'some speakers may not be very thoughtful about their use of terms, and others may be simply confused'. However, through incorporating what Haslanger describes an as 'ameliorative approach', we can discern the rationale for an expression's employment by looking at the work it does.

In the round, we can see that the 'higher education landscape' serves as a synonym and can thus be exchanged for 'higher education more broadly', as the following extract illustrates:

> profound changes have occurred to higher education more broadly that have impacted significantly on what academics do and how they position themselves and their intellectual work [which are] acutely visible in the intensified scrutiny of research outputs, performance and publishing, the rating of universities through ranking exercises, and the flows of knowledge through a mobile academic labour market. Fitzgerald et al. (2012, p. 137), my amendment, underlined

The 'more broadly' here is key, in that it incorporates the recognition of activity being positioned in relation to a multiplicity of actors and phenomena, in this case scholarly endeavour being influenced by state/internal scrutiny, scholarly publishing, league tables and employment conditions. The authors here have taken care to identify and justify the connections to other elements of the landscape, but this was not widespread across the sample. From an uncharitable angle, in many cases one could replace the higher education landscape with 'higher education stuff', given the indeterminate and indiscriminate nature with which the metaphor was sometimes deployed. For some, the higher education landscape may represent little more than a linguistic flourish, while for others – for reasons of space or an unwillingness or inability (perhaps even laziness) to explain and evidence the interrelations – the metaphor offers a convenient and already widely used shorthand that authors hope can amorphously fill in all of the conceptual or empirical gaps (Hayes, 2015; Lowenthal, 2007).

However, as Lavrenova (2019, p. 161) asserts, metaphors have an ontological purpose in that they represent a 'process of construction of reality'. In this way, it may be that the higher education landscape's real value lies in how it insinuates an acknowledgement of the wider interconnectedness between a great many simultaneously moving parts but without having to name and substantiate them. In this way, while lacking the cohesiveness and determinacy of a theory, we can see that the higher education landscape serves as a social structural explanation (Haslanger, 2016) for understanding activity in and around higher education as agency determined by the relations between actors within a wider set of social and material conditions. There is an ongoing and related discussion about the comparatively atheoretical nature of higher education research compared with other fields (Hamann & Kosmützky, 2021; Huisman, 2023) and even recognizing the predominance of literature-based rather than empirical publications in this sample, less than half incorporated a theoretical framework. As Huisman indicates, there may be a connection between fields and the 'popularity' and use of different higher education-related metaphors that warrants further investigation.

It has been noted that academic writing not only says something about the object of enquiry but also about the writers themselves (Belluigi et al., 2019); as Bacevic (2019) identifies, critical opposition to neoliberalism represents both an analysis of neoliberalism's impact as well as an expression of progressive socio-political allegiance. Belluigi et al. (2019) illustrate how metaphors are often evocative, providing a means of expressing feelings about whatever the metaphor is being associated with, often as a way of conveying uncertainty. Despite the recognition of agency and activity, across the sample there is a palpable undercurrent of scholarly anxiety and stoic resignation, of being somewhat passively located within this collectively designated 'shifting landscape'. There is perhaps a correspondence here with the overapplication of the term 'crisis' to all manner of change in higher education, regardless of whether it is wide-ranging and/or negative (Tight, 2024), and it is interesting to observe that both crisis and landscape work equally well at different scales.

As a final point, in a rare but clear attempt to highlight the metaphor's meaning, Platonova (2019, p. 414) states that 'the higher education landscape is the result of various impacts from stakeholders, governance regimes, the political economy, social structures, and trends, internal to the higher education sphere'. Their focus is on the twin role of the state and public demand in influencing institutional diversity, but (setting their mixed metaphors of landscape and sphere aside) this statement does reflect some of the broader, interconnected dynamics described in this paper. It also suggests a potential distinction – elided by most authors in this sample – between higher education and the higher education landscape. If we accept that higher education is nested within a wider configuration of particularly national but also broader political, economic, and social dynamics (Hüther & Krücken, 2016), we might suggest that higher education consists of those actors whose activity is entirely or at least primarily oriented towards tertiary-level, scholarly teaching, research, and social missions. While the boundaries are likely to be somewhat porous and indistinct, the wider higher education landscape could then incorporate those whose interest or involvement with higher education is secondary or passing because they are primary actors in other landscapes, such as policy, or specific professions or industries. At times, this distinction may not be necessary, but equating higher education and the higher education landscape potentially implies that higher education 'is' everyone and everything which has a connection – however tenuous or indirect – with it.

CONCLUSION

At one level, this systematic review provides an unintentional and incomplete but perhaps unusually broad and concise 'Higher Education 101', in which it includes many if not most of the core issues, trends and actors in and around higher education. It recognizes the external social, economic, political, and technological developments such as changing demographics, waxing and waning financial conditions, issues of governance, and technological progress, all of which impact higher education. Within higher education itself we can see – among other things – a growth and diversification of populations and university types, an enforced prevalence of often unequal competition between institutions for funding, students, and status, alongside attempts to more closely monitor and manage them, as well as a more pronounced presence and need for digital tools and capabilities. Those chiefly oriented towards and involved in higher education include staff, students, leaders, funders, rankers, scholarly publishers and funders, alongside those whose interest in higher education is secondary or fleeting, including governments, nongovernmental organizations, professional bodies, religious institutions, corporations, employers, and the public. Some elements were missing, notably alumni and post-human actors, and climate/environmental concerns barely featured. Despite these omissions, it serves as a useful reminder of the 'peculiar location of higher education as the intersection of multiple institutions' (Stevens et al., 2008), and how this places it within complex policy and other networks operating at different levels and in relation to many different and potentially competing 'domains of interest' (Chou et al., 2017).

More importantly, though, we can see that in its usage by scholars, the metaphor of the 'higher education landscape' (or landscape of higher education) implies a social structural explanation (Haslanger, 2016) for the interrelationships and activities of an extensive diversity of groups, organizations and individuals who are engaged with higher education in either concerted or peripheral ways. It thus operates as a useful container metaphor (Lakoff & Johnson, 1980) for the constituent elements of higher education that even works across scales from the local to the global; although it seems to be applied most commonly to the national, an observation was also made by Huisman (2023). The term landscapes culturally – linguistically and through art – suggests a representation, a breadth of view (Olwig, 2004), and this appears to be its attraction, in which the higher education landscape allows for a wider acknowledgement of the compound and multitudinous links of higher education-related issues, practices and actors. It is unsurprising, given the size, nature and scope of these, that the higher education landscape is depicted as in a state of constant and multifarious flux so that it feels – to extend the landscape metaphor – that the ground is moving beneath our feet. In combination, this engenders an uncertainty and anxiety, a form of motion sickness, particularly when many changes undermine established norms or practices. It may be for this reason that the landscape is invoked because the changes are considered so widespread, simultaneous, and sometimes undesirable, that they are difficult to fathom and capture in their entirety. At the same time, a vague and indiscriminate invocation of changing landscapes runs the risk of conflating and collapsing what is changing and how, insinuating that nothing at all in higher education is stable when this is not the case (Tight, 2024).

The same may hold true of how other landscapes are portrayed, be they academic, disciplinary, curricular, professional, policy and so on, and we would thus argue that the value of the metaphor would be enhanced if we maintained its breadth and inclusiveness while being clearer about what and who it consisted of.

REFERENCES

Adi Badiozaman, I. F. (2017). Understanding academic identity development in a changing landscape: The case of university English teachers in Malaysia. *The Journal of AsiaTEFL, 14*(2), 307–319.

Agasisti, T., & Pohl, C. (2012). Comparing German and Italian public universities: Convergence or divergence in the higher education landscape?. *Managerial and Decision Economics, 33*(2), 71–85.

Ahn, E. S., Dixon, J., & Chekmareva, L. (2018). Looking at Kazakhstan's higher education landscape: From transition to transformation between 1920 and 2015. In J. Huisman, A. Smolentseva, & I. Froumin (Eds.), *25 Years of transformations of higher education systems in post-Soviet countries* (pp. 199–227). Springer.

Ashwin, P. (2022). The educational purposes of higher education: Changing discussions of the societal outcomes of educating students. *Higher Education, 84*, 227–1244.

Bacevic, J. (2019). Knowing neoliberalism. *Social Epistemology, 33*(4), 380–392.

Becher, T., & Trowler, P. (2001). *Academic tribes and territories: Intellectual enquiry and the culture of disciplines* (2nd ed.). Open University Press.

Belluigi, D. Z., Alcock, A., Farrell, V., & Idahosa, G. E.-O. (2019). Mixed metaphors, mixed messages and mixed blessings: How figurative imagery opens up the complexities of transforming higher education. *Scholarship of Teaching and Learning in the South, 3*(2), 110–120.

Bessant, J. (2002). Dawkins' higher education reforms and how metaphors work in policy making. *Journal of Higher Education Policy and Management, 24*(1), 87–99.

Bienayme, A. (1984). The new reform in French higher education. *European Journal of Education, 19*(2), 151.

Birtwistle, T., & McKiernan, H. H. (2008). The changing landscape of higher education: An analysis of how national change might be brought about in American higher education compared with the Bologna signatory states. *Education and the Law*, *20*(4), 317–336.

Boland, J. A. (2011). Positioning civic engagement on the higher education landscape: Insights from a civically engaged pedagogy. *Tertiary Education and Management*, *17*(2), 101–115.

Bourn, D., Blum, N., Ndaruhutse, S., & Mattingly, J. (2017). *Overview of UK development education landscape with a focus on partnerships between UK schools and those overseas*. Institute of Development Studies.

Braun, V., & Clarke, V. (2006). Using thematic analysis in psychology. *Qualitative Research in Psychology*, *3*(2), 77–101.

Braun, V., & Clarke, V. (2019). Reflecting on reflexive thematic analysis. *Qualitative Research in Sport, Exercise and Health*, *11*(4), 589–597.

Buckner, E., & Zapp, M. (2021). Institutional logics in the global higher education landscape: Differences in organizational characteristics by sector and founding era. *Minerva*, *59*(1), 27–51.

Bunting, I. (2006). The higher education landscape under apartheid. In N. Cloete, P. Maassen, R. Fehnel, T. Moja, T. Gibbon, & H. Perold (Eds.), *Transformation in higher education*. Springer.

Burford, J., Uerpairojkit, T., Eppolite, M., & Vachananda, T. (2019). Analysing the national and institutional policy landscape for foreign academics in Thailand: Opportunity, ambivalence and threat. *Journal of Higher Education Policy and Management*, *41*(4), 416–429.

Cameron, L., & Deignan, A. (2006). The emergence of metaphor in discourse. *Applied Linguistics*, *27*(4), 671–690.

Chaka, C., & Mashige, M. C. (2016). Revisiting the postmodern condition of a higher education landscape. *Journal of Higher Education in Africa/Revue de l'enseignement supérieur en Afrique*, *14*(1), 19–42.

Chan, S.-J. (2018). Changing landscapes of Asian higher education. *Asian Education and Development Studies*, *7*(2), 122–126.

Chen, S.-Y., & Hu, L.-F. (2012). Higher education research as a field in China: Its formation and current landscape. *Higher Education Research and Development*, *31*(5), 655–666.

Chou, M.-H., Jungblut, J., Ravinet, P., & Vukasovic, M. (2017). Higher education governance and policy: An introduction to multi-issue, multi-level and multi-actor dynamics. *Policy and Society*, *36*(1), 1–15.

Clegg, S. (2012). Conceptualising higher education research and/or academic development as 'fields': A critical analysis. *Higher Education Research and Development*, *31*(5), 667–678.

Connell, R. (2014). Using southern theory: Decolonizing social thought in theory, research and application. *Planning Theory*, *13*(2), 210–223.

Counelis, J. S. (1971). The open systems university and organizational intelligence. In *Association for Institutional Research Forum, May 17–20* (pp. 1–31). San Francisco University Department of Education.

Crosbie, V. (2005). Future directions for modern languages in the higher education landscape: An interview with Alison Phipps and Mike Gonzalez. *Language and Intercultural Communication*, *5*(3–4), 294–303.

Dale, R. (2005). Globalisation, knowledge economy and comparative education. *Comparative Education*, *41*(2), 117–149.

David, R., & Fenton, M. (2015). Partnership and collaboration in the new higher education landscape: The 3U Partnership experience. *All Ireland Journal of Teaching and Learning in Higher Education*, *1*(1), 1–24.

Davies, P. (2000). The relevance of systematic reviews to educational policy and practice. *Oxford Review of Education*, *26*(3), 365–378.

de Rijcke, S., Wouters, P. F., Rushforth, A. D., & Franssen, T. P. (2016). Evaluation practices and effects of indicator use—A literature review. *Research Evaluation*, *25*(2), 9.

Deering, D., & Sá, C. (2018). Do corporate management tools inevitably corrupt the soul of the university? Evidence from the implementation of responsibility center budgeting. *Tertiary Education and Management*, *24*, 115–127.

Edwards, M. T., & Robinson, P. A. (2020). Baby boomers and online learning: Exploring experiences in the higher education landscape. In I. R. Management Association (Ed.), *Five generations and only one workforce* (pp. 48–74). IGI Global.

El-Hussein, M. O. M., & Cronje, J. C. (2010). Defining mobile learning in the higher education landscape. *Journal of Educational Technology & Society, 13*(3), 12–21.

Elliott, V. (2018). Thinking about the coding process in qualitative data analysis. *The Qualitative Report, 23*(11), 2850–2861.

Erickson, R. A. (2012). Geography and the changing landscape of higher education. *Journal of Geography in Higher Education, 36*(1), 9–24.

Evans, J., & Benefield, P. (2001). Systematic reviews of educational research: Does the medical model fit?. *British Educational Research Journal, 27*(5), 527–541.

Fabricant, M., & Brier, S. (2016). *Austerity blues: Fighting for the soul of public higher education*. Johns Hopking University Press.

Fallows, J., & Ganeshanthan, V. V. (2004, October). The big picture. *The Atlantic*. https://www.theatlantic.com/magazine/archive/2004/10/the-big-picture/303520/

Fitzgerald, T. (2012). Chapter 8. Continuing challenges. In T. Fitzgerald, J. White, & H. M. Gunter (Eds.), *Hard labour? Academic work and the changing landscape of higher education* (pp. 163–176). Emerald Group Publishing Limited.

Fitzgerald, T., White, J., & Gunter, H. M. (2012). *Hard labour? Academic work and the changing landscape of higher education*. Emerald Group Publishing Limited.

Flecknoe, S. J., Choate, J. K., Davis, E. A., Hodgson, Y. M., Johanesen, P. A., Macaulay, J. O., Murphy, K., Sturrock, W. J., & Rayner, G. M. (2017). Redefining academic identity in an evolving higher education landscape. *Journal of University Teaching and Learning Practice, 14*(2), 16–34.

Floyd, C. E. (2007). Know your competitor: Impact of for-profit colleges on the higher education landscape. *New Directions for Higher Education, 2007*(140), 121–129.

Francke, A. (2021). *The changing landscape of education, before and after Covid-19 [online]*. Chartered Management Institute. https://www.managers.org.uk/knowledge-and-insights/article/the-changing-landscape-of-education-before-and-after-covid-19/. Accessed on February 1, 2022.

Grupe, F. H. (1974). Consortia and institutional change. In C. Dwyer & L. D. Patterson (Eds.), *Institutional interface: Making the right connection* (pp. 12–21). American Association of Higher Education.

Hamann, J., & Kosmützky, A. (2021). Does higher education research have a theory deficit? Explorations on theory work. *European Journal of Higher Education*, 1–21.

Hanley, L. F., & Bonilla, D. (2016). Atolls, islands, and archipelagos: The California OER Council and the new landscape for open education in California. *Open Praxis, 8*(2), 131–142.

Haslanger, S. (2005). What are we talking about? The semantics and politics of social kinds. *Hypatia, 20*(4), 113–130.

Haslanger, S. (2016). What is a (social) structural explanation?. *Philosophical Studies, 173*(1), 113–130.

Hayes, R. (2015).The beast in the jungle: The humanities in the future higher education landscape. In *Higher education in transformation symposium – Proceedings: Book of papers, Dublin, 31st of May 1–April 1, 2015* (pp. 87–96). https://arrow.tudublin.ie/st1/3/

Haywood, J., Connelly, L., Henderikx, P., Weller, M., & Williams, K. (2014). *The changing pedagogical landscape: New ways of teaching and learning and their implications for higher education policy*. European Commission.

Hey, V., & Morley, L. (2011). Imagining the university of the future: Eyes wide open? Expanding the imaginary through critical and feminist ruminations in and on the university. *Contemporary Social Science, 6*(2), 165–174.

Hitt, S., Sternberg, M., Wadsworth, S. M., Vaughan, J., Carlson, R., Dansie, E., & Mohrbacher, M. (2015). The higher education landscape for US student service members and veterans in Indiana. *Higher Education, 70*(3), 535–550.

Holdsworth, S., & Thomas, I. (2020). Competencies or capabilities in the Australian higher education landscape and its implications for the development and delivery of sustainability education. *Higher Education Research and Development*, 1–16.

Hollands, F. M., & Tirthali, D. (2015). *MOOCs in higher education: Institutional goals and paths forward*. Palgrave Macmillan.
Hong, K.-S., & Songan, P. (2011). ICT in the changing landscape of higher education in Southeast Asia. *Australasian Journal of Educational Technology, 27*(8), 1278–1290.
Huisman, J. (2023). Higher education and organizational theory. In P. Mattei, X. Dumay, E. Mangez, & J. Behrend (Eds.), *The Oxford handbook of education and globalization* (pp. 191–210). Oxford University Press.
Hüther, O., & Krücken, G. (2016). Nested organizational fields: Isomorphism and differentiation among European universities. *Research on the Sociology of Organisations, 46*, 53–83.
Jackson, C., & Sundaram, V. (2018). 'I have a sense that it's probably quite bad … but because I don't see it, I don't know': Staff perspectives on 'lad culture' in higher education. *Gender and Education*, 1–16.
Jayawardena, D. (2017). The "MacBurger". Non-state universities and the changing landscape of higher education in Sri Lanka. *Journal for Critical Education Policy Studies, 15*(3), 213–240.
Jin, J., & Horta, H. (2018). Same university, same challenges? Development strategies of two schools at a prestigious Chinese university in a changing higher education landscape. *Tertiary Education and Management, 24*(2), 95–114.
Kuzhabekova, A., Hendel, D. D., & Chapman, D. W. (2015). Mapping global research on international higher education. *Research in Higher Education, 56*(8), 861–882.
Kalashnikova, S., Kovtunets, V., Luhovyy, V., Prokhor, I., Satsyk, V., & Talanova, Z. (2016). Transformations of higher education landscape in Ukraine. *International Scientific Journal of Universities and Leadership, 2*, 1–19.
King, R. (2016, May 17). New competitive landscape for higher education confirmed in white paper. *The Conversation*. https://theconversation.com/new-competitive-landscape-for-higher-education-confirmed-in-whitepaper-59494
Knight, J. (2013). The changing landscape of higher education internationalisation – For better or worse?. *Perspectives: Policy and Practice in Higher Education, 17*(3), 84–90.
Kosmützky, A., & Putty, R. (2016). Transcending borders and traversing boundaries: A systematic review of the literature on transnational, offshore, cross-border, and borderless higher education. *Journal of Studies in International Education, 20*(1), 8–33.
Lakoff, G., & Johnson, M. (1980). *Metaphors we live by*. University of Chicago Press.
Lavrenova, O. (2019). *Spaces and meanings: Semantics of the cultural landscape*. Springer.
Lebrón, J. L., Griffin, A., & DePietro-Durand, R. (2018). *USAID higher education landscape analysis 2014-2018*. United States Agency for International Development.
Levy, D. C. (2006). The private fit in the higher education landscape. In J. J. F. Forest & P. G. Altbach (Eds.), *International handbook of higher education* (pp. 281–291). Springer Netherlands.
Li, G., Huang, Y., & Chaen, C. (2011). Characteristics of university landscape planning and design. *Advanced Materials Research, 250–253*(May), 3401–3404.
Lloyd, A. (2009). *Information literacy landscapes: Information literacy in education, workplace and everyday contexts*. Chandos Publishing.
Lomer, S., & Mittelmeier, J. (2021). Mapping the research on pedagogies with international students in the UK: A systematic literature review. *Teaching in Higher Education*, 1–21.
Lowenthal, D. (2007). Living with and looking at landscape. *Landscape Research, 32*(5), 635–656.
Lumby, J., & Foskett, N. (2011). Power, risk, and utility: Interpreting the landscape of culture in educational leadership. *Educational Administration Quarterly, 47*(3), 446–461.
Macfarlane, B. (2012). The higher education research archipelago. *Higher Education Research and Development, 31*(1), 129–131.
MacLure, M. (2005). 'Clarity bordering on stupidity': Where's the quality in systematic review? *Journal of Education Policy, 20*(4), 393–416. https://doi.org/10.1080/02680930500131801
Mandernach, B. J., Radda, H., Greenberger, S., & Forrest, K. (2015). Challenging the status quo: The influence of proprietary learning institutions on the shifting landscape of higher education. In A. Dailey-Hebert & K. S. Dennis (Eds.), *Transformative perspectives and processes in higher education* (pp. 31–48). Springer International Publishing.
McEwan, A. E. (2007). Do metaphors matter in higher education?. *Journal of College and Character, 8*(2), 4.

Mhichíl, M. N. G. (2013). The changing landscape of higher education: An analysis of Bologna policy and Ireland's engagement with the process. *Irish Studies in International Affairs, 24*(1), 331–345.

Miron, J., Eaton, S. E., McBreairty, L., & Baig, H. (2021). Academic integrity education across the Canadian higher education landscape. *Journal of Academic Ethics*, 1–13.

Musselin, C. (2021). University governance in meso and macro perspectives. *Annual Review of Sociology, 47*(1), 305–325.

Mwale, N., & Simuchimba, M. (2019). Religion in public life: Rethinking the visibility and role of religion as an ethical resource in the transformation of the higher education landscape in post-1990 Zambia. *Changing Societies & Personalities, 3*(3), 207–224.

Nguyen, T.-H.-T., Tran, T., Dau, T.-T., Nguyen, T.-S.-H., Nguyen, T.-H., & Ho, M.-T. (2020). How scientific research changes the Vietnamese higher education landscape: Evidence from social sciences and humanities between 2008 and 2019. *F1000 Research, 9*, 152–166.

Nukunah, C. N. T., Bezuidenhout, A., & Furtak, A. (2019). The contribution of a private higher education institution to the South African higher education landscape. *South African Journal of Higher Education, 33*(1), 283–300.

Olwig, K. R. (2004). "This is not a Landscape": Circulating reference and land shaping. In H. Palang, H. Sooväli, M. Antrop, & G. Setten (Eds.), *European rural landscapes: Persistence and change in a globalising environment* (pp. 41–65). Springer Netherlands.

Orr, D., Luebcke, M., Schmidt, J. P., Ebner, M., Wannemacher, K., Ebner, M., & Dohmen, D. (2020). *Higher education landscape 2030: A trend analysis based on the AHEAD international horizon scanning*. Springer International Publishing.

Page, J. (2013). Hispanics: A diverse population of students to influence the landscape of higher education. *Journal of Hispanic Higher Education, 12*(1), 37–48.

Pescosolido, B. A. (2008). The converging landscape of higher education: Perspectives, challenges, and a call to the discipline of sociology. *Teaching Sociology, 36*(2), 95–107.

Pilkington, M. (2017). *Indo-French educational partnerships: Institutions, technologies and higher education*. Palgrave Pivot.

Platonova, D. (2019). The differential effect of state and market on the higher education landscape in Belarus and Russia: Soviet-type division and bifurcation. *European Journal of Higher Education, 9*(4), 412–432.

Popa Strainu, R. M., & Georgescu, M. (2017). SOA – The link between modern educational technologies and mobile learning in the higher education landscape. *Timisoara Journal of Economics and Business, 10*(1), 120–133.

Purcell, W. M., Beer, J., & Southern, R. (2016). Differentiation of English universities: The impact of policy reforms in driving a more diverse higher education landscape. *Perspectives: Policy and Practice in Higher Education, 20*(1), 24–33.

Rethlefsen, M. L., Kirtley, S., Waffenschmidt, S., Ayala, A. P., Moher, D., Page, M. J., & Koffel, J. B. (2021). PRISMA-S: An extension to the PRISMA statement for reporting literature searches in systematic reviews. *Systematic Reviews, 10*(1), 39.

Ritchie, D. (2002). Monastery or economic enterprise: Opposing or complementary metaphors of higher education?. *Metaphor and Symbol, 17*(1), 45–55.

Ritter, Z. S. (2016). International students' perceptions of race and socio-economic status in an American higher education landscape. *Journal of International Students, 6*(2), 367–393.

Sabol, F. R. (2013). Seismic shifts in the education landscape: What do they mean for arts education and arts education policy?. *Arts Education Policy Review, 114*(1), 33–45.

Samokhvalova, A. (2021). New actors in Africa's higher education landscape: Malaysia's branch campuses and their motivation to enter the African market. In M. Kaag, G. Khan-Mohammad, & S. Schmid (Eds.), *Destination Africa: Contemporary Africa as a centre of global encounter* (pp. 80–105). Brill.

Shahjahan, R. A., Estera, A. L., Surla, K. L., & Edwards, K. T. (2021)."Decolonizing" curriculum and pedagogy: A comparative review across disciplines and global higher education contexts. *Review of Educational Research*. https://doi.org/10.3102/00346543211042423

Shapin, S. (2012). The ivory tower: The history of a figure of speech and its cultural uses. *The British Journal for the History of Science, 45*(1), 1–27.

Sharma, S. K., Palvia, S. C. J., & Kumar, K. (2017). Changing the landscape of higher education: From standardized learning to customized learning. *Journal of Information Technology Case and Application Research*, *19*(2), 75–80.

Shore, C. (2010). Beyond the multiversity: Neoliberalism and the rise of the schizophrenic university. *Social Anthropology*, *1*, 15–29.

Small, L., McPhail, R., & Shaw, A. (2021). Graduate employability: The higher education landscape in Australia. *Higher Education Research and Development*, 1–15.

Penceliah, S., Konyana, S. V. M., & Maharaj, M. (2016). The choice of public universities in a restructured and transforming higher education landscape: A student perspective. *Problems and Perspectives in Management*, *14*(3), 276–282.

Stevens, M. L., Armstrong, E. A., & Arum, R. (2008). Sieve, incubator, temple, hub: Empirical and theoretical advances in the sociology of higher education. *Annual Review of Sociology*, *34*(1), 127–151.

Storey, V. A., & Schiavo, M. A. (2013). Redefining the higher education landscape through problem-based learning. In V. Wang (Ed.), *Handbook of research on teaching and learning in K-20 education* (pp. 517–534). IGI Global.

Tan, E. S. Q., & Soo, Y. J. (2017). Creating apps: A non-IT educator's journey within a higher education landscape. In A. Murphy, H. Farley, L. E. Dyson, & H. Jones (Eds.), *Mobile learning in higher education in the Asia-Pacific region* (pp. 213–238). Springer Singapore.

Terepyshchyi, S. (2017). Educational landscape as a concept of philosophy of education. *Studia Warmińskie*, *54*, 373–383.

Tight, M. (2012). Higher education research 2000 – 2010: Changing journal publication patterns. *Higher Education Research and Development*, *31*(5), 723–740.

Tight, M. (2013). Students: Customers, clients or pawns?. *Higher Education Policy*, *26*, 291–307.

Tight, M. (2014). Working in separate silos? What citation patterns reveal about higher education research internationally. *Higher Education*, *68*(3), 379–395.

Tight, M. (2019a). Systematic reviews and meta-analyses of higher education research. *European Journal of Higher Education*, *9*(2), 133–152.

Tight, M. (2019b). The neoliberal turn in higher education. *Higher Education Quarterly*, *73*, 273–284.

Tight, M. (2024). The crisis literature in higher education. *Higher Education Quarterly*, e12504. Advance online publication. https://doi.org/10.1111/hequ.12504

Tosh, D., Werdmuller, B., Chen, H. L., Light, T. P., & Haywood, J. (2006). Chapter III: The learning landscape – A conceptual framework for ePortfolios. In A. Jafari & C. Kaufman (Eds.), *Handbook of research on ePortfolios* (pp. 24–32). IGI GLobal.

van Vught, F. (2009). *Mapping the higher education landscape towards a European classification of higher education*. Springer.

Weiner, S. S. (1986). Shipyards in the desert. *The Review of Higher Education*, *10*(2), 159–164.

Wenger-Traynor, E., Fenton-O'Creevy, M., Hutchingon, S., Kubiak, C., & Wenger-Traynor, B. (2015). *Learning in landscapes of practice: Boundaries, identity, and knowledgeability in practice-based learning*. Routledge.

White, S., Bloomfield, D., & Cornu, R. L. (2010). Professional experience in new times: Issues and responses to a changing education landscape. *Asia-Pacific Journal of Teacher Education*, *38*(3), 181–193.

Whitford, H. (2014). The role of graduate student unions in the higher education landscape. *New Directions for Higher Education*, *2014*(167), 17–29.

Woodard, D. B., Jr., Love, P., & Komives, S. R. (2000). The changing landscape of higher education. *New Directions for Student Services*, *2000*(92), 5–16.

Yizengaw, T. (2007). Implementation of cost sharing in the Ethiopian higher education landscape: Critical assessment and the way forward. *Higher Education Quarterly*, *61*(2), 171–196.